THE STEAM LOCOMOTIVE

THE STEAM LOCOMOTIVE

AN ENGINEERING HISTORY

KEN GIBBS

AMBERLEY

To all those railway pioneers mentioned in the book.
They certainly started something!
And the world became a smaller place.

First published 2012

Amberley Publishing
The Hill, Stroud
Gloucestershire, GL5 4EP

www.amberley-books.com

British Library Cataloguing in Publication Data.
A catalogue record for this book is available from the British Library.

ISBN 978 1 4456 0918 8

Typeset in 9.5pt on 13pt Sabon.
Typesetting and Origination by Amberley Publishing.
Printed in the UK.

CONTENTS

Author's Note

This book has been compiled from a number of magazine articles written by me over a number of years, making a miscellany of steam locomotive construction notes, tied together by additional relevant information, with reference to sights and operations from the workshops experienced in my apprentice years and subsequent practical knowledge gained in the works from 1944 to the end of official 'steam', and really beyond, as I am still working for several heritage railway groups. The photographs are from all sources acquired over many years, and selected for the book. Most modern photographs by the author.

As for the apprenticeship; I would do it all again!

Ken Gibbs
LCGI (M.Eng.)

INTRODUCTION

Let's have a quick look at the first real steam pioneers.

The first recorded person fascinated by Steam was Hero of Alexandria in 200 BC, who devised what could be called an embryonic steam turbine. This consisted of a hollow ball supported with two horizontal bearings, with two opposed bent spouts, looking like two arms of a swastika. Filled with water and heated, the steam generated exited through the spouts and rotated the ball. Really a curio and not exploited!

So while the world developed and settled down somewhat, hundreds of years went by while technology developed beyond the physical strength of man and horse. The extraction of minerals of various sorts from the earth had, by the seventeenth century, considerably developed. Mining techniques were among the technologies developed, and it was found that the deeper man dug into the earth, the more he was hampered by the essential to life itself, water.

The old saying 'Necessity is the mother of invention' is still as true today as it has always been. Lifting water a short distance without pumping it or carrying it in buckets was assisted by the experiments of one Thomas Savery, who devised a system of forming a vacuum which sucked up water through a pipe, then having delivered it to a higher level chamber, delivered it to another higher level chamber by the pressure of steam on the water surface, forcing it up a delivery pipe. Savery also set up the world's first steam engine (stationary) manufactory in London in 1702. His pump is described and illustrated in his work of the same date, titled *The Miner's Friend*. While his pump was suitable for big houses, it would not work in mines. The Steam Age was opening up, continual improvement was inevitable, and 1705 saw the next important step.

The improvements applied by Thomas Newcomen represented a great step forward. The illustration shows the beam, pump rods one end, steam cylinder the other. Steam entered the cylinder, a jet of cold water condensed the steam which had entered as the weight of the pump rod pulled the piston up to the cylinder top, and the atmospheric pressure forced the piston down, thus raising the pump rod. This system operated in mines for about sixty years, when a young James Watt started his model-making and experimenting. He noted the jet of cold water cooled the cylinder and left the walls of the cylinder wet. He considered this a waste of heat and thus the power of the steam.

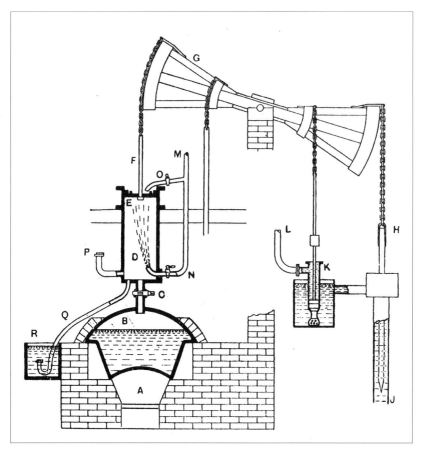

Newcomen's 'Atmospheric' Engine. A: Boiler furnace; B: Steam boiler; C: Steam valve; D: Engine cylinder; E: Piston; F: Piston rod; G: Main beam; H: Heavy pump-rod; J: Mine pump; K: Pump for condensing water; L: Pipe leading to condensing water-tank; M: Condensing water pipe; N: Injection cock to cylinder; O: Water tap to top of piston; P: Relief or snifting valve; Q: Eduction pipe with no-return valve at end; R: Feed-water tank.

How the railway story began: the *Pennydarren* locomotive of Richard Trevithick, 1804.

He devised a separate chamber where the steam could be condensed with the cold water, keeping the heat in the cylinder, making the operation more effective. Development continued.

So, steam, cylinders, rocking beams, static engines spreading over the countryside. But James Watt, double-acting steam, and no cold water spray changed all that!

It was inevitable that such a power source would find another application. So while theories were discussed, and models made, it was a Cornish man who decided on a mobile application in full size. Richard Trevithick decided to replace the limited power of man and horse with a mobile application of the principles of the static steam engine; thus 1804 saw the introduction of the steam locomotive to the mining and quarrying tram roads and plate ways. The power of man and horse had been overtaken!

1
EARLY LOCOMOTIVE DESIGN AND MANUFACTURE

Books on railway history, and the steam locomotive in particular, appear to always begin in one of two ways. They either start with the father-and-son combination of the Stephensons and their winning locomotive *Rocket*, or they begin with the 'Father of Railways', Richard Trevithick and his locomotive of 1804 for the Pennydarren tram road. In both cases, it was not the first venture of either of them into the world of steam power. Several others of the period soon followed on the heels of the 1804 Trevithick venture. Blenkinsop patented and Murray completed a two-cylinder (vertical) engine to run on a rack rail system in 1812. Blacket of Wylam Colliery followed with a smooth-wheel version made by Hedley in 1813. This was not successful but was rebuilt, emerging as *Puffing Billy* in 1813, reverting to two cylinders vertically operating a beam system. George Stephenson began building his first locomotive in 1814, made at the West Moor Workshops of Killingworth Colliery. This locomotive also had vertical cylinders and crossbeams, vertical rods working cranks and gear wheels to the smooth-wheel drivers. Steam was discharged as exhaust into the chimney, thus assisting the blast and keeping the fire glowing. In 1816, Stephenson produced a chain-driven locomotive for Killingworth. Up to about 1820, the emerging and developing steam locomotives had been employed solely for the purpose of achieving a replacement for the horse in moving around the product of the collieries, but thoughts of passenger traffic as well as goods were beginning to emerge.

A Bill submitted to Parliament was rejected three times but eventually was passed in 1821 and 27 September 1825 saw the first public railway in the world opened for traffic, with the *Locomotive No. 1* pulling wagons and passengers.

In the years prior to 1804 and the introduction of the steam locomotive, engineering skills were being honed in the workshops of mine and quarry, building and installing the Boulton & Watt power sources for improved designs of machine tools and for improved versions of the stationary steam plants.

The budding locomotive engineers were already thus partway up the 'learning curve', developing skills 'from scratch' as they ran into problems which could not be allowed to hold up progress.

To return to the 1804 *Pennydarren* locomotive, there do not appear to be any contemporary engineering drawings in existence and the drawings that do exist appear to be based on interpretations of what the locomotive looked like. There have been replicas made based on these drawings. There are numerous drawings from various sources which lead to some confusion. One has the fire hole door for the return flue of the design at the chimney end of the boiler, the cylinder on the other end. (This version is at the National Waterfront Museum at Swansea as an actual replica locomotive.) There is also a replica steaming at the Beamish Museum. Seemingly based on interpretation of descriptions without any backup drawings, many models have been made, and drawings prepared after the event have been published over the years. So there is bound to be a conflict of opinion. Another drawing has the cylinder at the front, adjacent to the chimney as well as the fire hole door (this appears to be completely impractical). Another appears to have the chimney and cylinder in the front and, more sensibly, the fire hole door at the other end of the boiler. So, they probably resembled the original in parts! Therefore how did they make it?

The materials would be cast iron, wrought iron, brass and bronze. (Brass is an alloy of copper and zinc, and bronze an alloy of copper and tin.) 'Machine tools' such as they were would have improved, machine beds would in many cases be no longer of wood but would be cast iron, giving more rigidity and accuracy.

The *Pennydarren* wheels from the drawings look very thin and narrow, while the Swansea replica at least looks as though the gear wheels and the running wheels are separate, but secured together. Would it not have been simpler to have the gear wheels and running wheels cast in iron complete? This would certainly have been more simple than wrought or cast iron running wheels and gear wheels separate. Certainly, the gear wheels would have been in cast iron, the boiler in comparatively thin ⅜ in. or 5/16 in. small wrought

Section of locomotive, 1837.

iron sheets; there were no 'rolling mills' to produce large iron sheets. Construction would have been by riveting sheets together. Always preferred to period hole-drilling attempts, the holes would be hot-punched as much as possible by the smith.

However, we do know about a couple of locomotives (illustrated below). *Puffing Billy*, a wooden frame example of early design mentioned later in the chapter on Frames, was gear driven from a crankshaft and the usual vertical cylinders and 'beam' action. Driven from the rear and stoked from the front adjacent the chimney, the 20 in. return flue had a return bend back to the front.

The *Stourbridge Lion* is again beam operated from vertical cylinders and was an American purchase for the Delaware & Hudson Railroad in 1829. The Americans were soon designing their own, and in the early years some were quite weird! But they soon got into the swing of things with some most effective and distinctive designs, illustrated in the following pages.

During this early period, a number of manufacturers came into being, in effect basically copying what had been shown to work, spreading out from Britain to the main continents. We have here introduced a massive subject.

EARLY LOCOMOTIVE DESIGN

Stourbridge Lion. Sold to the Delaware & Hudson Railroad in 1829, it was made by Messrs Foster & Rastrick.

Puffing Billy. Built by William Hedley for Wylam Colliery in 1813 (and rebuilt several times), it is sometimes shown with a barrel not a rectangular tank on the tender.

The mechanism of a tram engine. Note the two brass scales of the Salter spring-balance safety valves, and the two modern-looking water gauges with box shatter guards over the gauge glasses (later additions).

Steam Loco Development into the 1840s.

Right and above, overleaf: Two contenders in the Rainhill Trials of 1829.

Note the bar-framed *Bury* locomotive and the emerging 'sandwich'-framed four-wheel *Planet* type and the six-wheel development.

Note the substantial brackets attaching the sandwich frame to the boiler.

Right: R. Stephenson's locomotive the *Rocket*, 1829.

Below: Bury's locomotive, originally introduced 1830.

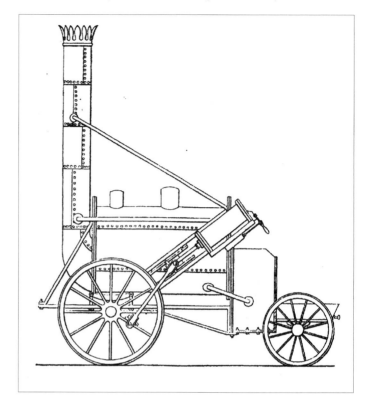

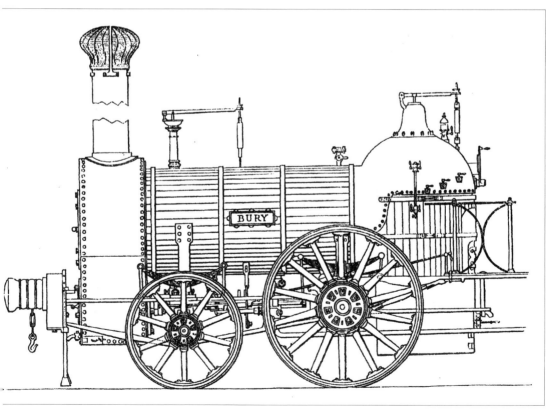

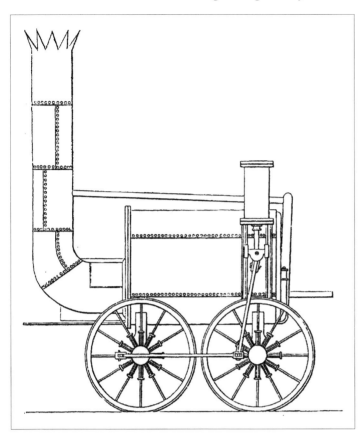

Left: Hackworth's locomotive the *Sanspareil*, 1829.

Below: Four-wheeled locomotive, with inside cylinders, on the model of the *Planet*, 1830, by Fenton, Murray & Jackson. Cylinder 11 by 16 in., wheel 5 ft.

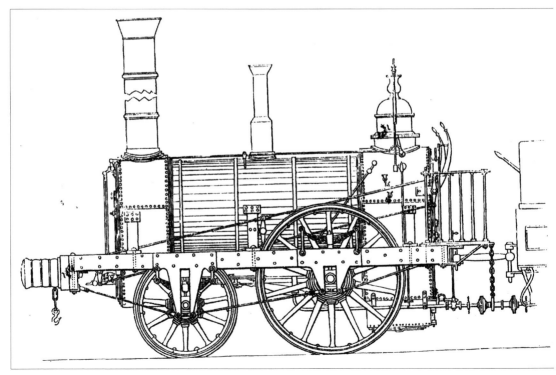

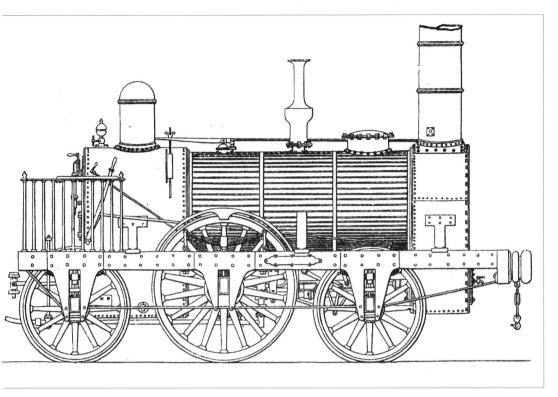

Stephenson's six-wheel locomotive, with inside cylinder, 1838. General type of the six-wheel class. Cylinder 12 by 18 in., wheel 5 ft.

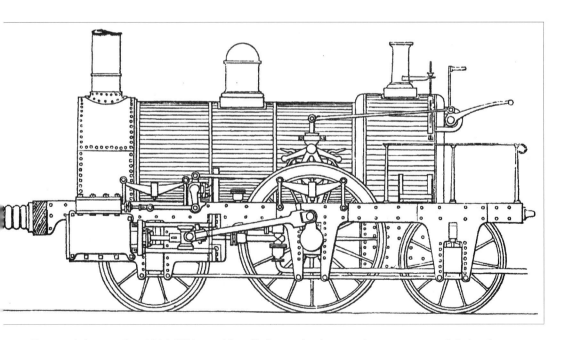

Forrester's locomotive, 1834. With outside cylinders and valve gear, it was an unusual design for the period.

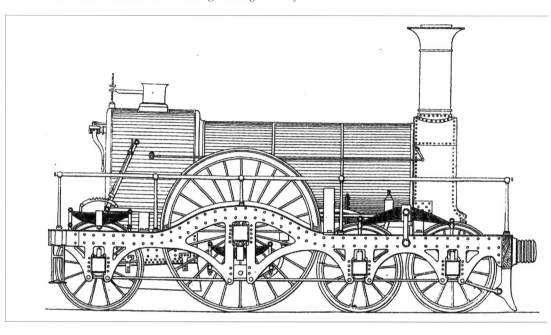

Gooch's locomotive, Great Western Railway, 1846. Cylinder, inside, 15 by 24 in., wheel 8 ft. Ultimatum for the 7 ft gauge. This design of GWR locomotive lasted until the demise of the 'Broad Gauge' itself in 1892. The only improvement was the concession of a cab! Travelling from Bristol to Exeter in a winter blizzard at 60 mph was certainly no picnic with just the protection of the firebox backhead.

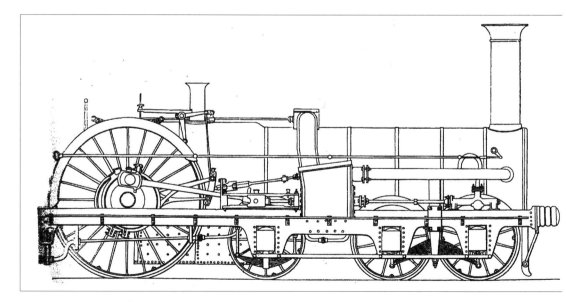

Crampton's locomotive, London & North Western Railway, 1849. Outside cylinders, 18 by 24 in., wheel 8 ft. Ultimatum for the 4 ft 8½ in. gauge. The *Crampton* design was not universally accepted in Britain but certainly found favour on the European railways. The design stemmed from a desire for more stability when running. This was before 'balancing' the reciprocating parts had fully developed and moving cylinders and drive wheels further back had a beneficial success.

STEAM LOCOMOTIVE DESIGN AND DEVELOPMENT

The early work of the Stephensons, father and son, and their first (and indeed the world's first) locomotive manufactory, set the principles of design of the steam locomotive, one could almost say, in tablets of stone. There have been many *improvements*, but very few radical *design changes* over the very long life of the steam locomotive. So set was the Stephensonian concept that redesign was generally an uphill struggle. Some of the early improvements were, of course, essential for safety. The 'spring balance' safety valve, which could be screwed down by the driver to increase steam pressure (often fatally) was eventually superseded by the set and locked valve which could only be readjusted in the workshop. The height of water in the boiler over the firebox crown and plate, essentially maintained at a certain level, could only be determined before 1829 by operating plug cocks (usually three) set one above the other on the firebox and spanning the correct water level position. Carefully operated, steam from the top one was 'OK', steam from the second meant 'keep an eye on the level', and steam from the bottom one usually warned 'watch out for the big bang'! Foster and Rastrick's introduction of the water gauge changed all that to what we recognise today, although often the cocks were incorporated into the water gauge as a secondary check.

Water feed to the boiler, initially by hand pump, changed to axle or crosshead-driven feed pumps as boiler pressures became higher. A major problem with the design was that there was no way of stopping the pumping action when running, except by a bypass valve that just circulated the water back to the tank from which it had been pumped. A fault with either valve or pump could introduce serious hydraulic damage. A second major problem was that, with the engine stationary, no water could be pumped into the boiler at all, leaving a static locomotive as a time bomb. A short length of track, not always to be had, was essential to allow the engine to move to top-up the water level. In situations where such a length of track was not available, a method which I have seen in print claimed that drivers often oiled or greased the rails under the driving wheels, opened the regulator, and the spinning wheels did the rest. This must have been a much frowned on practice as it certainly did not improve the wheel tyres, rails or motion! These problems ended in 1858 when Giffard introduced the 'injector', the device by means of which water is carried into the boiler by using the boiler's own steam. The required combination of steam jet and cold water to make the injector operate meant manipulating hand-wheels attached to threaded valve rods. Experience had to be gained by practice to obtain the correct adjustment of the steam and water valves to make the Giffard injector work at all. Often when the locomotive lurched or bounced over an uneven rail joint, the Giffard 'knocked off', and the hand-wheels had to be fiddled with again to get the water flowing.

The modern injector is a 'self-starter'. Once the steam is flowing, there are designs which lift hot water, and designs which operate using exhaust steam from the cylinders diverted for the purpose. It is probably not well known that the Swindon Railway Museum has an early sectioned Giffard injector mounted on a board; it is well worth a look next time you are in the museum.

Before the injector was to end problems, Joseph Beattie of the London & South Western Railway was experimenting with feed water heating apparatus and a separate 'donkey pump', steam operated, to supply the boiler feed water when standing. These mid-century attempts, while quite successful, also introduced yet another steam-using apparatus to the locomotive, along with additional maintenance. To digress for a moment, some of Beattie's engine designs were among the first to burn coal, which was generally becoming accepted practice in this mid-century period, while the engines of Gooch were still coke burners.

Although early locomotives on the Stockton & Darlington were coal burners because of its easy and cheap availability, the techniques of coal burning were not fully understood, and attempts to reduce the smoke problem continued to the extent that a clause in the Act for the Liverpool & Manchester Railway specifically forbade the emission of smoke. Hence the designs of many of the country's railways featured coke-burning fireboxes. Many and varied were the proposals, complicated by the differing natures of coal from the various sources, which had different properties and required careful handling for the best results. A further problem was the need to have a larger firebox for coal burning than for coke. Often conversions were not possible, and the use of coal in a coke firebox led to all sorts of operating and maintenance problems; there will be more on boiler design later in these jottings.

Within the safety context, brakes must be mentioned. Early locomotives, such as Gooch's Firefly class of around 1840, had brakes which operated on one side of the six-wheeled tender only, and these were applied by hand. Some of the earlier locomotives had no brakes at all, and were stopped, after reducing speed, by baulks of timber thrust under or through the wheel spokes! This may have been acceptable in the early application of the steam locomotive to the horse-drawn tram roads for mineral traffic, but the introduction of the human passenger called for something better.

Note that the tram engine brakes are wood blocks operating on the cast iron wheels.

From quite early on in the locomotive development story, attempts at effective braking are listed. The number of trains continued to grow, speeds generally were increasing (it took a number of years for other companies to match the Great Western broad gauge in this respect) and with these increases, so the number of accidents increased. From mid-century there were numerous attempts to devise a satisfactory brake system which could be applied to the complete train, not just selected brake-fitted vehicles, often only on one side of the tender, and a whistle-signalled application of a handbrake by the guard (see Chapter 19).

Locomotive development was introducing increasingly heavier trains, and among the many problems to be encountered was that of a heavily laden train breaking in two when a coupling failed. Thus, to be included in any design was the 'fail safe' requirement of brake application should the train separate. So, the field of experimentation was wide open. Theories were expounded, inventors burned the midnight oil, and their proposals started to roll in, all awaiting the chance to prove themselves.

Mention was made of the influence of the Stephensons in the development of the steam locomotive. While George Stephenson is often described as 'the father of the steam locomotive', this is really an error, as the locomotive was advancing on several fronts before George came on the scene. If we amend the reference by inserting the word 'modern' before 'steam locomotive', we are nearer the truth.

In the early years, it was not a question of 'consulting the experts' when a new railway company wanted to order its motive power, as there were virtually no other experts to consult, and there were several competing ideologies floating about at that time. The 'professional engineer' was emerging, as evidenced by the years nearly half a century before – the start of the canal boom. Then, internal transport was revolutionised by the pioneering engineers, who, when they came upon a problem which often contained both civil and mechanical engineering aspects, had to solve it themselves.

Thus was invented the Institution of Civil Engineers as we know it today, a pooling of knowledge of the few 'experts' of the period. Having improved the steam locomotive, and with the expectation of having one's name added to the professional ranks in acknowledgement of the new facets of engineering now rapidly coming to the fore, George Stephenson applied to the Civil Institution for membership as the only professional body extant at that time. Seemingly so trained were the civil engineers of the period that the bridge building and structural construction members debated at length on the desirability of having a mere locomotive engineer as a member. They insultingly (to modern eyes) requested that George submitted a paper in the usual way before membership could be considered. I would imagine that he told them in no uncertain terms at which warm station they should alight, and then waited until brother engineers formed a 'Mechanical' version of the Civil Institution. Incidentally, George became the first president, and his countenance still gazes from the certificates of membership of the Institution of Mechanical Engineers.

There have been many discussions and theories put forward over the years about the origins of the current 'standard' gauge of British track. The rather weird size of 4 ft 8½ in. – and it *is* a strange measurement – seems, like Topsy, to have 'just growed'! At the time of the introduction of the steam locomotive, the canals, which were mentioned earlier, only existed where the terrain was suitable. Many canals had sections which were completely unsuitable for excavation etc. due to the gradients and the often inaccessible places from which the mineral wealth of the country was being extracted.

Thus the forerunners of the railways, as we know them, were the strange and often ramshackle tram roads and plate ways, well known at mining, smelting and quarrying sites, where little wagons drawn by horses carried the products over roughly laid track to the nearest canal for the required transport to cities and ports. Each establishment had its own little trucks, horses and track, and each usually had its own unique 'gauge'.

Within the clauses of permission to construct a canal was often included the permission to build a connecting railway; thus with all the various sites anxious to get to the new canal transport system, the odd gauges of plate ways and tram roads proliferated. From tram roads and plate ways powered by the universally employed horse, the coming of steam posed many problems, quite possibly more than it actually solved. To take advantage of the new power now on offer, a known manufacturer had to be approached, one with the knowledge and experience to produce what was required.

From discussions with the manufacturers, the potential customer must have emerged with his head spinning when the new technology had been explained to him. Not only was the steam locomotive he desired going to be much heavier than his existing horses, he was probably told in no uncertain terms that a locomotive would not, and could not be made to fit his track gauge! Such gauges as 4 ft 5½ in., 4 ft 2 in., 3 ft 6 in., 4 ft 0 in., 3 ft 9 in., 2 ft 3½ in. and virtually anything in between and smaller, to 1 ft 8 in., were to be found.

It is more likely, with this very controversial subject, that many potential buyers were told: 'The locomotives I make are to 4 ft 8½ in., so reinforce your track, smooth out the bumps, relay it to that size and I have got just the loco for you!' Probably some of the first orders were for locomotives to fit track 'near enough' to 4 ft 8½ in. and axles could probably be altered to suit. However, without accurate measuring devices and large machine tools (there were no steam hammers, slotting machines, millers or large planers) a locomotive just grew as a 'one-off' as the smith-made components were fitted together. Perhaps this may account for the introduction of the 4 ft 8½ in. measurement. It could be that the potential customer ordered a locomotive, and then found when he got it that the gauge of its wheels was 4 ft 8½ in., thus controlling everything else he did; this had a knock-on effect. At home he expanded and wanted more locomotives, thus he had later to re-order and ensure he received a loco to fit his existing gauge! Hence the consolidation of 4 ft 8½ in.; the debate on the origins of 'standard' gauge will just go on and on.

Not all railways, of course, were to accept the 4 ft 8½ in. and there is a really funny but factual tale recorded in Williams' book *Our Iron Roads* (1884). My volume, incidentally, is a very prized possession, having been given to me by my grandfather when I was nine years old. Apparently, the line from Belfast to Dublin was started from both ends by two different companies. The Ulster company constructed for 25 miles to a gauge of 6 ft 2 in., while the Drogheda company, setting out from Dublin to meet the Ulster line, was working to a gauge of 5 ft 2 in.! When the directors of the Ulster line complained, the Irish Board of Works answered that, although both ends had been completed, and this would

Robert Stephenson.

leave an awkward situation, there was absolutely no need to worry, as it was more than likely that the two lines would never join up in any case! Eventually, 5 ft 3 in. was adopted as the national gauge for Ireland – a happy compromise but a historical comical episode.

There were companies in Britain that also disagreed with the Stephensonian 4 ft 8½ in. gauge. Mr Braithwaite, of the Eastern Counties & Blackwall Railway, built a gauge of 5 ft 6 in., while the Scottish Northern was constructed to 5 ft 0 in. The widest gauge of all was, of course, that proposed by Brunel for the Great Western Railway (GWR). There are several facets of his submissions that are not well known. While his technical reasoning for such large rolling stock is sound – one train could carry far more than was possible on the 'narrow' gauge – his environmental argument is flawed. Not appreciated nowadays is the fact that the GWR was intended to join London to Bristol – a fast route, with massive loads, from point A to B with nothing in between! Any connecting branches would have been to the same gauge, and it was Brunel's contention that, as it would not be necessary to connect with anywhere much further north, the whole system would be a self-contained southern monopoly enterprise.

This was rapidly proved to be a misconception, and the resulting problems stemming from the transfer points for goods inevitably going to all parts of the country are well known. Throughout the 'gauge wars' which resulted, most nineteenth-century parties agreed generally that, while the broad gauge concept throughout the period provided the most powerful, the fastest, safest, most comfortable rolling stock with the greatest potential, no one else actually wanted anything to do with it. In attempts to spread the introduction of broad gauge, some were actually physically opposed to it and meetings broke out in mini-riots. It was, in fact, the Victorians' 'Concorde' project. All agreed on how good it was, but no one else would touch it, put off generally by the initial costs of land, cuttings, tunnels and so on. They did not consider the potential for growth of the massive loads which could eventually have been transported using the existing clearances necessary for broad gauge track.

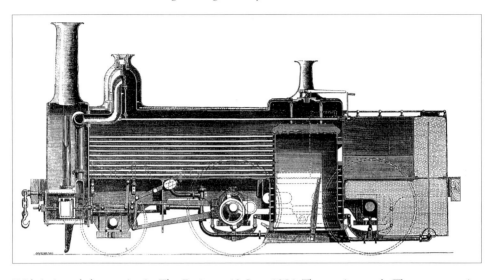

Fairbairn's tank locomotive in *The Engineer*, 13 June 1856. The caption read: 'The accompanying engraving represents the tank locomotive recently tried on the Oldham incline on the Lancashire & Yorkshire Railway. The Oldham incline is about 1½ miles in length, the gradient being 1 in 27. Up this incline, the engine took nine loaded passenger carriages at the rate of 15 mph. The carriages averaged 6½ to 7 tons each. The principal dimensions of the engine are, cylinders: 15 in. diameter; stroke: 22 in. diameter; driving wheels: 5 ft diameter; trailing wheels: 5 ft diameter. The weight of the engine in working trim was about 22 tons, and the heating surface in firebox plus tubes measured about 815 sq. ft.'

When one considers the development of American rail roads, with loading gauges often bigger than the broad gauge loading gauge yet still on 4 ft 8½ in. track, the potential lost to the railways of Britain by the restricted views of the broad gauge has been a great loss to us all.

However, having cleared the way for 7 ft ¼ in., the problems of the power source and rolling stock were only just beginning for the Great Western and its persuasive engineer.

However great the reputation of Brunel as a versatile Victorian engineer may be, dabbling successfully (and sometimes unsuccessfully) in many and varied engineering projects, one aspect of engineering which must come in the latter category is his attempt at a specification of a steam locomotive.

It is well known that the specification that Brunel distributed for his first locomotives was, in practical terms, virtually impossible to achieve. The unfortunate companies which tendered for the work and attempted to make something which would achieve the requirements of the specification landed themselves with all sorts of problems. The principles of the steam locomotive that we recognise today were already established when Brunel placed his orders. Steam locomotives of the period were already being subcontracted out by the Stephenson Father & Son firm, and a healthy export market already existed.

Brunel did not issue any drawings for his locomotives (the engineering drawing as we know it was in its infancy at this time); he just issued a specification setting out the criteria of his requirements. It was left to the builders to do the necessary designing to match the requirements of the specification, and it was here that the problems arose. The fact that history has condemned these first locomotives as useless, and hence implied that the builders, and thus the designers, were incompetent, must be viewed in the light of the provision of a totally impractical specification in the first place.

The 'tooling up' and provision of facilities at the works of those concerned with actually making the locomotives led to another quite major problem to be faced by all concerned. Workshops had been laid out to accommodate the locomotive as it had developed to that date, track gauges up to, say, 5 ft 6 in. already being accommodated. Not only were the makers up against the design problems, but, once actually designed, the requirements were for huge locomotives, far bigger, as it turned out, than anything made before. The specified piston speed for 30 mph required large driving wheels. Large driving wheels meant smaller boilers, thus introducing steaming problems. Such large locomotives could not possibly be contained within Brunel's specified weight limits and so the problems multiplied.

There was at this time no rail 'network', so locomotives ordered could only be delivered to the customer virtually as a DIY kit. Transport was usually to the coast, thence by ship to the nearest port, river or canal; the locomotive was probably then transferred to a road vehicle (the roads and horsed transport of the 1830s presented yet another set of problems) and dragged to the site for assembly. If the purchaser did not like what he had received, he was really lumbered with it, as he had no means of sending anything back except by the same way it had been delivered.

Each manufacturer of Brunel's order, while attempting to follow the principles and design features current at the period, produced totally different locomotives. Two of the differing designs caught in the faulty specification problem had driving wheels of 10 ft in diameter, far bigger than anything then made, and remember that one of the pairs of wheels was made up by blacksmithing techniques, built up and smith-welded in the coke forge spoke by spoke. The other large wheel pair (for *Ajax*) was constructed from plates, but still required a tyre, smith-made from metal over 33 ft long and smithed into a circle.

It is recorded that the 10 ft wheels could not be machined at first. Although the early lathe was big enough, it was positioned too close to the workshop wall and this necessitated a large groove being hand-chipped out of the stonework to accept the diameter. The speed of the lathe as it stood was also too fast. A separate length of shafting had to be erected and driven from the next machine, both geared down to revolve at the slowest possible speed.

As technology improved, and designs were effectively changed, the later Firefly class of around 1840 were still virtually the same format as all of the other locomotives of the period. Here follows the now well-known story of the Firefly class, virtually copies of really the only successful engine of the period on the Great Western – the Stephenson-built *North Star* (a replica is in the museum). This locomotive was acquired more by luck than judgement, and was certainly not to Brunel's weird specification. Originally built for the North American market, the 5 ft 6 in. gauge New Orleans Railway, the purchasers apparently could not pay for it when the crunch came, and it fell fortuitously into the lap of Daniel Gooch, who had it altered to suit Great Western metals. He had been appointed by Brunel, and his job of nominally checking on the progress of construction of the weird lot triggered by Brunel's specification was really, reading between the lines, not so much

Hurricane, built by R. & W. Hawthorn of Newcastle.

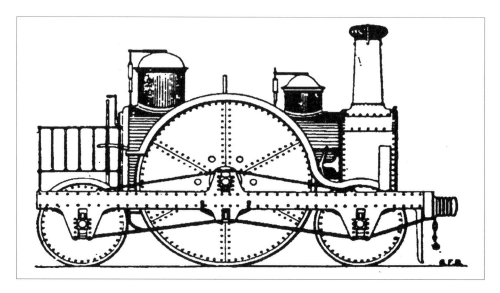

Ajax, built by Mather Dixon & Co. in 1838.

checking on progress but listing the problems which could be his lot to solve when the engines were eventually delivered.

If one follows the broad gauge passenger locomotive design to a conclusion, it will be noted that, as the 'gauge war' continued and the Firefly class *Ixion* carried all the honours at the first trials, something bigger and better was required to really punch home the advantage of broad gauge. Following the Firefly design (the design was very successful, so why change it?) *Great Western* was nominally designed and built in thirteen weeks! It is interesting to go into the pros and cons of the *Great Western*. How was it designed and built in such a short period of time? If one considers that *Firefly* had 7 ft diameter driving wheels, *Great Western* was to have 8 ft diameter wheels. Now 8 ft is an increase of about 14.3 per cent on 7 ft, so, by working within the parameters of the loading gauge, buffer beam height and track gauge, by increasing all else proportionally we come to a virtual 'overlay' of *Great Western* covering the outline of a Firefly which had been expanded by 14.3 per cent.

Again exceptionally successful in the continuing gauge war, a war really already lost, but still hammering home the superiority of the broad gauge, *Great Western* had problems which developed from uneven weight distribution. Front axles broke quite frequently and

Great Western, as built as a 2-2-2.

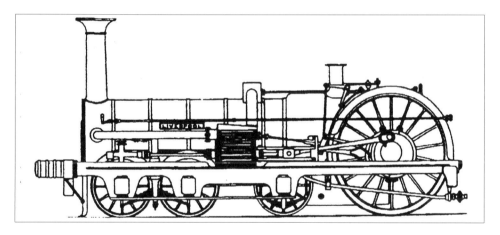

Crampton locomotive *Liverpool*, LNWR, 1848.

the answer was to add another pair of wheels in front! This gave the classic 2-2-2-2 (often mistakenly quoted as 4-2-2) of the GWR's broad gauge passenger locomotives right up to the fateful year of 1892 when the broad gauge finally died, and the engines, other than those designed for conversion to standard gauge, went to the scrap yard.

True, *Great Western* was 'developed', and the famous *Lord of the Isles* was in reality only a large Firefly with a cab! The latter was anathema to Gooch, who maintained that fumes would overcome the driver and fireman. Reluctantly, a weather board or 'spectacle' plate had been fitted to some engines, but a look at American locomotives of the period showed cabs that looked like country bungalows complete with double sliding windows! I have often wondered how much actual 'designing' Daniel Gooch really did for the locomotives the GWR produced. On his staff in the early days he had Archie Sturrock and Thomas Crampton. Both were to become outstanding designers in their own right, and they must have had ideas which were, even at that early stage, ahead of their time but which, following almost slavishly the Stephensonian format of *North Star*, they could not put into practice. (Maybe at the instance of Gooch: *North Star* works – so copy it!)

A problem which was inherent in early 'unbalanced' locomotives (covered later in these jottings) was the fact of instability due to relatively short wheelbases. Thomas Crampton was Gooch's chief draughtsman at this early period and he had a great interest in design. In later years, when he and the Great Western had parted company, he expanded his theories on stability and produced some quite outstanding designs which overcame to a great extent the problems of pitching and rocking. He moved his cylinders and consequently his driving wheels further and further back along the frame so that eventually his cylinders were positioned along the centre point of the boiler and his driving wheels were behind the firebox, with axles placed under the footplate. I have often speculated on what would have happened if a) Brunel's early specifications had been successful, and/or b) *North Star* had been unavailable and they had really had to design something from scratch.

The first British exports to the American continent were thus comprised of the constructors' most successful products, and so the general design of locomotives followed British practice to the letter. Thus the Americans started with designs based mainly on the very successful *Planet* format, but, as with everything else which takes time to develop effectively, once seen to work, adaptations, alterations and modifications flow thick and fast.

Copying a successful design is not usually a problem, and in 1832 the founder of the famous Baldwin Locomotive Works produced *Ironsides* for the Philadelphia, Germantown & Norristown Railway. *Ironsides* was a typical 2-2-0 with a very tall chimney, 4 ft 6 in. diameter driving wheels and 8½ in. diameter by 18 in. stroke cylinders. Such was the growth of the American locomotive industry that a very interesting episode occurred twelve years later.

There were intentions at the time, certainly with an eye to the future, to develop a great rail route to join the North with the West of England. The engineer, Captain Moorsom, made a stumbling block for both himself and his proposed (and accepted) route by accepting the necessity of having the famous (or infamous, depending how you view it) Lickey Bank, a 2-mile stretch between Bromsgrove and Blackwell, as part of the route. He compounded this error by assuming (I've not seen any proof to the contrary) that there was no British design capable of successfully traversing the 1-in-37 incline. From Norris & Co. of Philadelphia, he ordered eight American locomotives and the first four when they arrived were named *Columbia*, *Atlantic*, *England* and *Philadelphia*. These were unique for the period as they had a four-wheel bogie and outside inclined cylinders, 10½ in. diameter by 18 in. stroke. With wheels of 4 ft diameter and a weight, as working, of about 9½ tons, these really little locomotives could take about 33 tons at, say, 14 mph straight up the Lickey; at slower speeds 39 tons at 10½ mph; and as much as 53 tons at 8½ mph. This quite impressed the punters, and on loaning one of his locomotives to the Grand Junction Railway, she took a load of 110 tons up an incline of 1 in 330 at about 20 mph.

All this was too much for Edward Bury, he of the export market, who wrote to the Birmingham & Gloucester directors in terms of the recent musical song 'Anything you can do, I can do better!' So there! Transporting his loco, self-named *Bury*, from the London & Birmingham Railway, he invited Mr Gwynn, who had arrived as engineer to the American locomotives, to join him. 'No thanks!' was the reply. 'You won't make it, so I prefer to wait here!'

Starting off with a run in grand style, the little *Bury* started to wheeze, and came to a stop halfway up the incline. Red faces all round, and the American newspapers took up the embarrassment by headlining: 'Britain makes excellent inclines, but has to come to America for engines to work them!' This was too much for the locomotive superintendent of the Birmingham & Gloucester Railway, so, chasing up the directors, he got the OK to ease the humiliation by designing and building a very powerful tank loco. Built at the Bromsgrove Works during 1843/44, it began work in 1845. This loco was a completely different concept to both the American designs and the *Bury* types, which were as miniatures compared to the six-coupled-wheel tank which had 3 ft 9 in. diameter wheels, cylinders of 18 in. diameter by 26 in. stroke and which weighed in, complete for the road, at 30 tons. There was now 'no contest', and the Lickey was conquered by a British locomotive at last.

There were, of course, still American experimenters who realised from illustrations and reports that with the locomotive there was immense potential to supersede the traditional horse. Thomas Cooper of the Baltimore & Ohio Railroad was such a character and while he didn't have the facilities to produce a 'locomotive' in the accepted mould, he was convinced, and so attempted to convince others, that here was the future staring them in the face. So was produced *Tom Thumb*, really looking like an open four-wheel flat-top rail wagon with a handrail all round, and carrying a small vertical boiler and an engine which drove a pair of wheels from a large gear wheel on a separate crankshaft. The boiler flue tubes were reputedly old musket barrels! The whole arrangement must have been a rather Heath Robinson concoction, but, having said that, it worked.

The South Carolina Railroad lays claim (which is controversial) to being the first successful steam railway in the South, its first locomotive being the *Best Friend of Charleston*, another vertical boiler Heath Robinson lookalike. A rear-mounted vertical boiler on the rear end of a flat-bed, four-wheel truck was fired by logs of wood stored in a box mounted in the centre of the truck. The driver sat at his controls at the front, in the manner of a seated tram driver, and fronted by a handrail, there being no protection for either driver or fireman in the form of a 'cab'.

During the trials of the 'daddy of them all', the *Rocket*, and its opposition, there had attended two American gentlemen – Horatio Allen, the chief engineer of the Delaware & Hudson Canal, and E. Miller, a resident of Charleston, South Carolina. On return, the latter ordered a locomotive from the West Point Foundry, from where it was delivered during 1830. After a derailment caused by a broken wheel, in December of that year during a further trial, towing trucks laden with 'volunteers' (very questionable!) from the company's labour force, it attained a speed of 20 mph. Although quite successful, it was completely destroyed six months later when the fireman, reputedly annoyed by the noise of steam from the safety valve, decided to stop it by screwing down the valve! He was scalded to death by the subsequent explosion. Mr Miller appears to have been influenced regarding design – and very strangely, bearing in mind the winner of the Rainhill trials

– by the design of *Novelty*, which of course had broken down and failed at Rainhill. *Tom Thumb*, mentioned earlier, also had similarities to *Novelty*.

Mr Allen, on the other hand, had come to Rainhill with the express purpose of ordering four locomotives 'of successful design', for which he had full authorisation, along with 'sufficient rails for a railway', although how many that entailed isn't recorded. Already ordered during 1828 and supplied by Stephenson's, the other three were to be made by Messrs Foster & Rastrick of Stourbridge. The Stephenson locomotive was named *America* and followed the design of the *Lancashire Witch*, itself the prototype of *Rocket*. Delivered in January 1829 and reputedly the first steam locomotive to be seen in America, a mystery surrounds its existence as apparently no record exists of its service life, performance or subsequent fate.

The *Stourbridge Lion* by Messrs Foster & Rastrick was reputedly the first locomotive to actually run on American track, having as its trial run, driven by Horatio Allen, the first section of the Delaware & Hudson Canal's lines along the banks of Lackawazen Creek. Sadly, all of the Foster & Rastrick locomotives, *Stourbridge Lion*, *Hudson* and *Delaware*, each at about 7 tons, were much too heavy for the completely inadequate track, and were rapidly removed from service into early retirement. The reduced *Lion* became a stationary engine at a foundry in Carbondale, but the fate of the other two is not known, though probably very similar to that of *Lion*. Incidentally, the *Lion* was rescued and rebuilt for exhibition at the Chicago Railway Exposition of 1884. Again incidentally, *Tom Thumb* of the Baltimore & Ohio Railroad resides in the massive 'Roundhouse' (reputedly the biggest in the world and actually built for carriages) at the Baltimore & Ohio Railway Museum in Baltimore. During 1988 I visited the museum while staying in Baltimore, and, while very interesting, it did not compare with our National Museum at York. The Roundhouse had a selection on the development of the American locomotive in the examples set on the radiating lines from the central turntable, with a giant *Mallet* on the outside tracks, with several other locomotives too big to be housed inside. There was also a (to me) surprisingly small 'components' section to the museum, along with a few models. It was all quite fascinating, giving a completely fresh viewpoint to locomotive design.

2

THE EARLY YEARS OF 'THE AMERICAN APPROACH'

We mentioned earlier the fate which had overtaken the *Best Friend of Charleston*, but not to be deterred, Mr Miller continued in confident mood, and a second locomotive from the same source soon appeared on the scene. Weighing in at about 4 tons, the same size and weight as its predecessor, *West Point* took to the tracks in 1831. In March of that year it pulled four coaches and 117 people, with, as a precaution against the same mishap as suffered by the *Best Friend*, a truck loaded with bales of cotton set between coaches and locomotive. It differed from *Best Friend* in a most significant way. The boiler of the former, a vertical design, was replaced by the now conventional horizontal type, reputedly the first in America actually made in America. Although now with a horizontal boiler and after the fashion of the Stephenson design, it apparently had only eight tubes of the very large size of 3 in. diameter, and generally followed Horatio Allen's design.

Even in the very early, not to say experimental years, thoughts on design were racing ahead. The fact that such designs reflected that designers were running before they could walk did not deter the far-seeing experimenters. While *West Point* carried out all of the company's traffic during the rebuilding of the *Best Friend* (which was to emerge very appropriately as the *Phoenix* later in the year), Horatio Allen was back at the drawing board, and his next effort was the *South Carolina*. This was a quite astonishing context; with a single off-set firebox in the centre, *South Carolina* appeared as two locomotives joined back to back (shades of the Fairlie). Both boilers rested on pivoted frames and each locomotive had only one cylinder. These became, in effect, the first articulated locomotives and appear to have been quite successful, lasting until 1838. We shall follow its later development in future jottings.

Early in 1831, advertisements were placed in leading newspapers announcing the trials and the competition, and setting out parameters as well as specifying the value of the prizes. A first prize of $4,000 and a $3,000 second prize was offered to the best of the designs capable of certain efforts. Locomotives of 3½ tons had to draw trains of 15 tons at a minimum speed of 6 mph. Design features included a boiler pressure below 100 lbs per square inch (a very high limit for this period), a boiler which would burn coal and coke (this must have caused some head-scratching among the designers), and an important stipulation: the boiler had to have two safety valves, one completely isolated and safe from tinkering by either driver or fireman. It had been recognised early that a higher boiler

York, 1831 – winner of the B&O contest.

pressure meant more power, and tinkering by screwing down the safety valve meant that not only was the actual pressure then not known (the pressure gauge as we know it had not been invented at that time), but the boiler could blow up before the safety valve blew off. The company would supply water, fuel and a suitable tender, and the locomotive had to run for a period of thirty days with no hiccups, otherwise it would be rejected.

Four locomotives were entered for the contest, and it seems very strange that three of the four, bearing in mind the success of *Rocket* several years earlier, should have been of the tiny vertical boiler format, almost like a platelayer's trolley powered by a steam engine. The only horizontal boiler version possessed two oscillating cylinders (like those on a child's stationary steam engine) and appears to have dropped out before the competition began. One of the others, actually named *Childs* after its designer and builder, one Ezekiel Childs, had a rotating steam engine and just did not work. Then *York* was the winner, vertical boiler and vertical cylinders acting downwards mounted on each side of the centrally placed boiler. Also in effect a steam-powered platelayer's trolley, its watchmaker designer, one Phineas Davis of Pennsylvania, not only received first prize but was also made 'Master Mechanic' or chief mechanical engineer of the Baltimore & Ohio! (As a watchmaker he followed our own I. K. Brunel in profession, but certainly not in loco design.)

There is no denying that the *York* was successful in that it entered service in July 1831; the cost of operating was about half that of the horses which had previously provided the motive power, easily pulling five light passenger cars. Both *York* and *James*, the runner-up in the contest, were later altered to angled cylinders operating behind the vertical boiler, driving through gears onto one axle. The apparent success of these strange little engines appears to have started a unique design feature peculiar to the Baltimore & Ohio (B&O). From Baltimore, by 1834 the B&O metals had reached Harper's Ferry (a place

South Carolina, 1831.

name to become one of the triggers that began the Civil War of the 1860s), and the little *York*, struggling valiantly, was no longer man enough for the job, and replacements were ordered.

In the meantime, watchmaker Davis had established the B&O workshops at Mount Clare and, now very much in charge and with two assistants, designed a similar but more powerful version of *York*. These designs became known as the 'Grasshoppers' or 'Crabs', due to the apparent reintroduction of cylinders working vertically upwards onto two swing beams, which in operation resembled the legs of a grasshopper. Davis seems to have been out of touch completely with the concepts of locomotive design of the period, which had for years had a different format and now in no way resembled the early mobile beam engines of the formative years.

The weird design was faulty also in that it made the 'platelayer's trolley' format completely top-heavy, and any sudden lurch tipped it over, which always happened in the event of a derailment. It was a fatal flaw, and coupled with the up-and-down motion caused by the rods and beams, made for not only an uncomfortable ride but also a dangerous one, Phineas Davis being killed in just such an accident. His assistant, Ross Winans, took over the design chair, and possibly in an attempt to update his predecessor's work, brought the cylinders down outside the frame to the horizontal so that the locomotive looked, at least from the level of the footplate down to rail level, like an ordinary locomotive, albeit still with the incongruous vertical boiler. Two locomotives, *Mazeppa* of 1837 and *Mckin*, followed this design, now being called 'Crabs' because they appeared to be running backwards. These designs proved to be quite successful, and Winan had built about thirty of them by 1842. Still four-wheeled, they were sold to the Reading Railroad, Philadelphia & Columbia Railroad and the Patterson & Hudson River Railroad. The remaining 'Grasshoppers' were relegated to slow freight or shunting in the Mount Clare Workshops. The success of the 'Crabs' led Winan to patent the design in 1842, and becoming known as a successful designer, he ordered two of a much more powerful design from the Baldwin Locomotive Works for the Western Railroad of Massachusetts.

The vertical boiler locomotives had very shallow grates of quite large diameter and were ideal for burning anthracite, which needs a large area as it burns in thin layers. These designs really formed the end of a unique design period of the American locomotive, as they soon became, as with many of the period, developed to their limit and were found wanting as loads became bigger and heavier. Winan's last design was for an 0-8-0 format with four wheels at each end of a frame with a 'well' in the centre to accommodate the boiler, which by now was of maximum possible diameter and was also set as low on the frame as was practical. Thus *Buffalo* of 1844 saw the end of the vertical boiler design which, although spread to several other rail roads, soon became obsolete. The vertical boiler did not disappear from the scene, and of course, was retained for special applications ranging from steam cranes (and returning to Britain for a moment) to our own steam rail-motor of 1903 by the GWR's G . J. Churchward.

As Britain was at the forefront of locomotive development in this period, a number of foreign railway companies sent representatives to look at the developments in Britain, and if possible, to place orders for locomotives and accessories. Following the lead of the Hudson & Delaware, the Camden & Amboy Railroad headed its chief engineer, Robert Stevens, in Britain's direction to purchase a locomotive and rails, again the number of the latter not specified. As we have seen from various examples, the nature of rails at this period formed such varied design formats that some form of standardisation was definitely required. The existing rails often comprised relics of the horse tramways, all sorts of gauges from cast iron mounted on stone blocks to wrought lengths in cast iron chairs bolted to wooden sleepers as suited the whim of the particular mine, foundry or canal company engineer. In America, simplicity and ease of laying were the main criteria, so Stevens reputedly conceived the idea on the way to Britain of a directly spiked rail, straight on to the 'crossties' as they call them. The latter were usually trees cut to length and sawn longitudinally; speed of laying was more important than uniform rectangular timber baulks, often tarred or creosoted for preservation, as in Britain. In the early years, speed was not so important as actually getting to a destination, and examination of old photographs of pioneering American railway track makes one wonder how locomotives actually stayed on it. However, with directly spiked track of flat-bottom format, the name of Charles Vignoles springs immediately to the European mind, so who actually developed what must remain slightly controversial.

Other rail roads in the States were following the Stephenson concept of locomotive design, and other typically American designs were evolving.

While the Baltimore & Ohio Railroad had pursued a very individual locomotive design theme, other companies (and they were proliferating just as they were in Britain) were developing locomotives with a decidedly different appearance to those evolving in Britain, although following the Stephenson concept.

We mentioned in our earlier jottings that Robert Stevens of the Camden & Amboy Railroad (later to become the Pennsylvania Railroad) had visited Britain with the object of purchasing a locomotive and suitable rails. The locomotive was to be obtained from Stephenson's, but with certain modifications to be specified by Stevens and based on the Stephenson Samson class. The four-wheeled locomotive which evolved from this visit was rather a hybrid, in that it had a Sampson-type frame and motion, but only a Stephenson-type boiler barrel. The firebox was a cross between a vertically oval *Bury* type and the haycock version flattened at the crown.

As with all locomotives of the period, the *John Bull*, as this one was named, was forwarded as a kit of parts. The evolving skills of the American engineer are highlighted by the fact that the Camden & Amboy's 'Master Mechanic', recorded as Isaac Dripps, assembled the loco on delivery of the parts, without assistance and with no drawings! Beginning in service in 1831 on a 21½ mile route, a major problem soon became apparent. This was probably caused not so much by the design of the locomotive itself (it was, after all, only a four-wheeler) as by finding that it could not negotiate the curves in the track, which to me, at least, points to the fact that they did not really know what they were doing!

I wonder if there was here the beginning of the antagonism always seeming to exist between the locomotive engineers and the permanent way people. This was (and probably still is) the bouncing of blame off one or other for problems arising. 'Your locos are too heavy for my track!' countered with: 'Rubbish – your track is not man enough to take my locos!' With the Camden & Amboy, 'Your wheelbases are too long for my curves!' was countered with 'You should have made your curves to suit my wheelbases!'

Who was in the right we shall not know, but it fell to Isaac Dripps to remove his connecting rods and give his leading axle some side play, so in this instance it appears that the permanent way boys came out on top. It must have been a very short-sighted policy, as future developments with even bigger locomotives must have caused an unholy row. To enable *John Bull* to have a better ride, and to protect both trains and local livestock from 'fatal attractions', Dripps devised a sort of pony truck complete with cow-catcher to be attached to the front of the locomotive, although what this did to the wheelbase controversy is not stated, but we do know it virtually doubles the wheelbase. Within their

John Bull, Camden & Amboy Railroad, 1832.

Experiment, 1832.

idea, of course, is the embryo of the swivelling pony truck and bogie which were to have such an influence on stability and guidance around corners.

The benefits to be gained from a swivelling pair of guiding front wheels were soon recognised, but as with all new ideas, it is often the case that 'someone has done it before'. In the case of the truck swivelling around a central pin, the suggestion by Robert Stephenson in 1828 to a group of visiting engineers from the Baltimore & Ohio had been pre-dated by a patent granted to William Chapman sixteen years earlier.

The radial axle box was, of course, not known at this period, although an amount of side play in axles was now recognised as beneficial in certain circumstances. The first swivelling bogie in the world to be applied to a locomotive was that devised by John Jervis and formed a feature of a locomotive delivered in August 1832 by the West Point Foundry to the expanding Mohawk & Hudson Railroad. This locomotive had some unique features, and while built around the concept of a Stephenson *Planet* – indeed, it had a *Planet* boiler and main frames – there was even a touch of Thomas Crampton, although he was not, of course, involved.

Originally named *Experiment* (it was re-christened *Brother Jonathan*, maybe after Jervis himself), its design included the driving wheels set behind the firebox (á la Crampton) and a wooden-framed, iron-plate-reinforced four-wheel pivoting bogie, with the wheels inside the framework. The firebox was found to be unsuitable for burning the readily available anthracite, but when modified, *Brother Jonathan* was reputedly the first American locomotive to achieve 60 mph.

Locomotives of this design were proved to be very successful and their design fame spread to other developing rail roads. The fame reflected back to manufacturers in Britain; Stephenson's received an order from John Jervis for a 4-2-0 to Jervis' design for the Saratoga & Schenectady Railroad (Jervis being the chief engineer), the locomotive being delivered in 1833. The orders continued to come in to Stephenson's and other companies until about 1841, and there was now a distinct 'American' feel to developing designs. The famous locomotive works of Baldwin, who in the first instance had faithfully copied a Stephenson *Planet*, was so taken with the 4-2-0s of Jervis' design that he immediately followed suit after seeing one in action.

A typical early Baldwin locomotive was the *Martin Van Buren* of 1839, which had a Baldwin individual feature in the crank axle (remember, mounted behind the firebox in the design) having only one crank web on either side, the other formed by the inner face of the wheel boss, the crankpin being pressed in from the inside. This gave greater flexibility to have as wide a firebox as was possible. The influence of Bury, in this respect, was still very powerful. Based on this design concept, William Norris (he of Lickey Bank-conquering fame), after a couple of false starts in the locomotive design business, changed partners and was almost immediately on the trail of success.

The wood-iron plate combination frame, with the complication of inside cylinders, crank axle-crank web combinations, and accessibility problems, led Norris to a re-think, and the embryo of the typical early American locomotive was the result. In 1836 this first locomotive, about which little is known regarding its design detail, was incidentally put through its paces on a stretch of the Philadelphia & Columbia Railroad which actually had a rope-hauled section with a gradient of 1 in 14! A couple of tests proved its effectiveness, on the first occasion successfully pulling a load of 8.7 tons uphill and on the second, a load of 14 tons. A second locomotive to the same or very similar design rapidly followed, and this one is documented, including general arrangement drawings. Here, then, we have the beginnings of the typical early American-style locomotive so easily recognised from the film world (particularly Westerns). Still retaining its wooden lagging strips and boiler barrel bands of the period, the tall chimney with the bell mouth (to become the familiar diamond shape of the spark arrester) and its *Bury*-style firebox, there were now other significant differences from the Baldwin and Jervis locomotive designs.

The neatness and openness of the *Bury* bar frame, and the positioning of outside cylinders, valve gear and the connecting rod working on an outside crankpin in the driving wheel gave that 'see-through' look below the boiler level, thus giving excellent accessibility to the moving parts. Another arrangement which made for very easy access was the location of the steam chest and its slide valve on top of the cylinders, and of course the complications of a crank axle were avoided. All of these problems were being built into the locomotives of Britain. The Great Western in particular had its huge broad gauge locomotives with everything inside and the plate-sandwich frame which were, although very powerful, still complicated to maintain. This trend, as we shall see later, was continued on the Great Western in Britain for the next half-century.

Worldwide in this period, as rail travel caught on, there was a growing need to transport larger and larger loads, both freight and passengers; this meant that inevitably

Campbell, 1837.

the locomotives were becoming bigger and more powerful, or at the very least indicated that developments were required. Having done so much to influence American design, Edward Bury in Britain refused to acknowledge, or just plainly ignored, the trends which were becoming obvious to the world's engineers, and so continued to churn out his little locomotives. Thus, those with Bury engines as the staple type for their particular railway found that they were having to double-head, triple-head, or even add a 'banker' to their trains to cope with the additional loads.

As in Britain, so in America, where having established a workable format, it now became a case of larger and larger variations on the same theme. A patent granted on 5 February 1836 to Henry Campbell of the Philadelphia, Germanstown & Norriston Railroad covered the next logical move of adding another pair of wheels to the established 4-2-0 wheel arrangement of the very successful Norris locomotives. Thus arrived the classic 4-4-0 wheel format; although the first locomotive, named *Campbell* after its designer, was found to be very powerful, at higher speeds it derailed itself very easily.

This was attributable in some measure to the very poor quality of the 'platelaying' or track construction. The track seems to have been considered a necessary evil in the attempt to get an engine and its train from point A to point B; 'the quicker it's laid the sooner we can run on it' seemed to be the idea. The Campbell locomotives were capable now of hauling 140 tons up gradients of 1 in 100, and this adhesion from the increased locomotive weight, coupled with crude or non-existent balancing and uneven weight distribution, all combined to really hammer the track and its bed.

Many engineering minds were now focussing on the same problem, and as with many generally realised problems, it often happens that several engineers working quite independently carefully analyse the problems and inevitably come up with the same answer. The classic locomotive format had now evolved for the 4-4-0 of a swivelling bogie or guide truck in front, and the four coupled driving wheels, one pair in front of the firebox and one pair behind. An American patent granted in 1838 provided one effective solution to the equalisation of weight on the wheels.

The question of the importance of equal weight distribution on the wheels of a steam locomotive had for some time concerned the foreman of the locomotive construction company of Garrett & Eastwick, a comparatively new firm which had taken advantage of the locomotive boom and established itself in Philadelphia.

Following the new 4-4-0 concept, Joseph Harrison's 1838 patent was applied to a locomotive designed for the delightfully named Beaver Meadow Railroad. (I have a mental picture of Roland Emmett's *Far Twittering & Oyster Creek Railway* and his other drawings so beloved of railway enthusiasts, but I digress!) Delivered in 1838, *Hercules* had an arrangement of leaf springs and compensating levers; thus an ideal 'three point suspension' was achieved. Further improvements came with the decision of the Philadelphia & Reading Railroad to use the readily available anthracite, so the makers, now named Eastwick & Harrison, introduced the wide firebox, which was above and not

Hercules, 1837.

between the frames. (We discussed in an earlier jotting that anthracite burns in shallow layers and is not a long flame, so a wide, shallow firebox is the ideal.)

This new locomotive (strangely enough, named after the English bank of Gowan & Marx, who may have loaned or underwritten the project) had a very carefully worked out suspension of leaf springs and compensating beams and performed excellently. The ten years since 1830 had seen great improvements in the power of the steam locomotive, and *Gowan & Marx*, during 1840, hauled 280 tons on a track with a section of gradient of 1 in 67 at a speed of about 11 mph. The locomotive had an active life of about twenty years, and was still in a condition to be accepted by the Baldwin company in a part-exchange deal for a new locomotive.

The effectiveness of the 4-4-0 wheel arrangement was now spreading to rail roads and manufacturers alike. Norris was granted a patent in 1843 for a leaf spring combination on the 4-4-0s that he had enthusiastically begun to build during 1839, experience developing his ideas. There are no details of the earlier designs, but from 1842, one named *Virginia* is the first of these early engines to survive in illustration. The weight equalisation is obtained by a leaf spring mounted between the driving wheels on each side, the ends secured to the outside frame and the buckle onto a separate frame containing the pair of drivers.

Virginia, 1842.

Mathias Baldwin also realised quickly that he had to hop aboard the 4-4-0 concept, which both Campbell and the Eastwick Harrison firm had well 'tied up' in patent rights, the former for the 4-4-0 and the latter for the weight compensating designs. Payment of fees enabled Baldwin to commence designing. His idea was, although in principle like the Norris method, to mount a really massive leaf spring upside down over the drivers on each side, the leaf ends over the relative axle boxes and the central buckle secured to the frame. This locomotive still had a 'half-crank' arrangement, with the other 'crank' being the inside face of the wheel boss. The outside frame was now of solid iron bar form, the design now consolidating within the American locomotive design sphere.

This 'American' concept also included the use of the bar frame to support the cylinders which were not now solely attached to the smoke box. This new approach came in 1849 with the Baldwin design for the Pennsylvania Railroad, this positioning of the cylinders also ensuring that the connecting rods now acted outside the wheels on external crank pins in the wheel boss. At one stroke, therefore, the 'curse of the crank axle' had been eliminated, and the vast majority of future American locomotives would have bar frames and outside cylinders. With this locomotive, an unnamed freight type, the introduction of two more innovations set the pattern for the next half-century.

The equalisation of weight problem was now finalised by the use of individual springs over each driving axle box, the inner top leaves between a pair of wheels on the same side now joined by a link. A classic addition to locomotives of the late 1830s and into the 1840s had been some form of protection against the weather for the driver and fireman. Even in 1831, *Tom Thumb* of the Camden & Amboy Railroad had an extended roof over the footplate, built into the almost freight wagon-like tender. While in Britain the crew on the locomotives of the Great Western Railway got soaked, cooked by the sun or frozen by driving snow and sleet, among the pioneers of the American rail roads, protection for the crew had been a first consideration.

Daniel Gooch's theory or statement (real or imaginary, it certainly appeared to have been an influence) that fumes would overcome those on the footplate if they were encased in any form of shelter led to the major passenger locomotives of the GWR having no provision at all to protect the footplate crew from inclement weather. An example could be the Firefly class, in direct use for thirty years into the 1870s, with an open footplate and only a haycock firebox in front, providing virtually no shelter at all. A seemingly reluctant application later of a 'spectacle plate', just a flat plate with two circular windows, gave at least some slight protection. With just the firebox affording what protection could be gained, conditions of driving and firing at 50 mph into the face of snow or sleet storms must have been particularly grim. It would be interesting to know if any – or how many – suffered from exposure or frostbite while driving under such conditions.

The American cab, a development from the freight locomotive of 1849, really indicated a care for footplate crew. In the early years they became quite highly decorated, appearing almost bungalow-like, with half-doors and sliding windows. A further unique feature was the retention for virtually half a century of an all-wood construction. Introduced in the early years, primarily in the north where the weather really bites in the winter, the general design soon spread throughout the railway systems of the country, and by about 1850 it was virtually a standard fitting.

The Gowan & Marx, 1939.

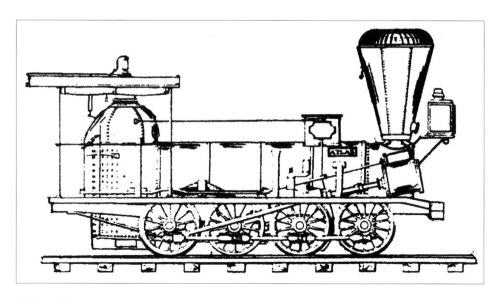

Atlas, 1846.

4-4-0 freight locomotive, 1849.

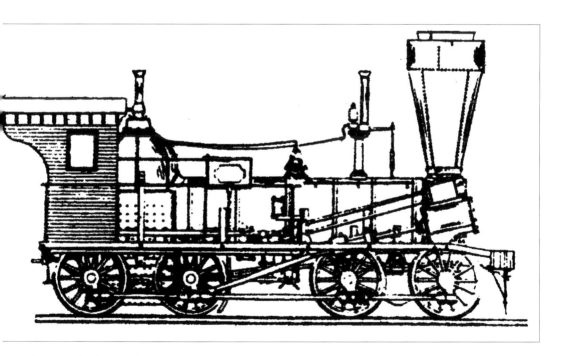

Eight-coupled locomotive, 1850.

Seminole – a wood-burning locomotive, built in 1868 for the Union Pacific Railroad. Overall length 50 ft, weight 115,000 lbs, fuel capacity 2 chords, tender capacity 2,000 gallons, tractive power 11,000 lbs. The cab of the old *Seminole* was of varnished walnut and the engineer's seat was made of ash; the pilot was made of wood.

A COMPARISON OF CABS

A second most distinctive American feature is, of course, the shape of the chimney. We have recently experienced in Britain much adverse publicity and strong objections from our currently weird subcontractors of railway operating companies on the fire risk occurring inevitably from the use of steam on mainline steam-hauled specials. How they would have coped under the old conditions when we had an efficiently run railway system which was *all* steam, I just cannot imagine. I have not heard anything about the American railways having problems with the 'wrong sort of snow' or 'leaves on the line'! Although they did have problems with herds of buffalo wandering about and attacks by hostile Native Americans.

However, to return to the American-style chimney; when solid fuel is burned, problems arise with associated sparks, and of course, in many areas of America the locomotive fuel was wood. Similar spark problems also occurred in those European countries where peat was used, and also from the notorious European brown coal. So, to avoid really massive fires from chimney sparks and a 'scorched earth' situation adjacent to the quickly spreading rail roads, chimney designs were given critical examination. Very early in the American rail road story, the problem of sparks was fully realised, and early in 1833 the Camden & Amboy Railroad had developed a double chimney with an internally curved ring at the top which itself hid an inverted cast iron cone. Sparks and minute ignited residues would strike the cone and drop into the outer casing, being extinguished as they

The British: the Gooch (very reluctant) 'Weather board' or 'spectacle plate'. (Could they see through windows on *Nemesis*?) Picture is the old broad gauge engine *Nemesis*, constructed in January 1855, condemned in December 1877.

The American: the 'bungalow'-like US cab. This is *Locomotive 119*, built by Rogers. The loco pulled the train to the Ceremony of Driving the Golden Spike at Promontory Point on the Union Pacific Railroad, 10 May 1868.

did so. The American use of fine anthracite residue, nominally waste coal, was effective as a cheap fuel on rail roads with ready access to the mines and waste dumps. However, this also gave off an unacceptable amount of sparks. This double shell arrangement, which gave the early American locomotives such a distinctive appearance with seemingly out-of-proportion chimneys, solved a very critical and dangerous problem.

Innovations were flowing thick and fast in the American locomotive world of the mid-nineteenth century. The problem was the ever recurring one of conflict between the permanent way people and loco designers. As the locomotives inevitably got bigger, more powerful and heavier, so light track and sharp curves frustrated the locomotive design men. The curve problem was overcome to a great extent by the Baldwin patent of 1834, used for the first time, for a Georgia Railroad loco, in 1842. It also got around Campbell's truck patent by using independent beams with parallel axles. In operation then, the beams were parallel and formed a rectangle on straight track, but on encountering a curve, the beams formed an oblique parallelogram as the axles went in opposite directions. Quite a number of such locomotives were built and operated very successfully in general use for about twelve years. A loco of the Philadelphia & Reading Railroad recorded the first pulled weight of over 1,000 tons, with the 1,130 tons of a train taken over the 94 miles of the journey between the named towns of the rail road. This was about twice the normal working load, and the speed of 7 mph reflected this, but it did show what an 18-ton locomotive could achieve.

In 1846 the 'flexible beam truck' principle was applied to the first eight-coupled design, which was patented in 1842, and while probably quite acceptable and indeed once again very successful, the very flexibility of bearings etc. gave, in the long run, heavy wear and tear, particularly as higher speeds were attempted. This is one of those cases where Baldwin's refusal to allow use of the patent under licence to his main competitors (who could, of course, have been clients) led some clients to experiment on two fronts. Firstly, in some way to get around those same patents, and secondly to simplify and improve on them. Such competition led William Norris to introduce in 1847 what is claimed as a world first in design – the 4-6-0. American locomotive design was certainly leaping ahead.

3
DEVELOPMENT OF MATERIAL – THE METALS

For thousands of years man has exploited the earth's minerals, and over those years has developed the ability to work those minerals to his own ends, from the silver and gold ornaments of the ancients, through the bronze and iron ages to the current use of minerals for many purposes, particularly the use of the metallic elements now worked in many combinations and by many methods.

So, very early on, the materials were known and the ability to work them seemed to accelerate with the invention or discovery of gunpowder. The foundry men making bells now turned their attention to gun barrels. The blacksmith, from horse shoes and agricultural instruments, turned his attention to gun barrels, made of staves and hoops like a wooden container.

When Savery and Newcomen came on the scene around 1700, the elements of work experience were already in the background to further exploit and develop technology. The available metals were thus iron, which could be cast; bronze, which could be cast; and a different condition of iron which could be 'wrought' or worked to shape by the blacksmith. Another condition of iron was steel, available in very small quantities and requiring difficult preparation. The bulk preparation of steel had to wait another 150 years or so.

Early fuel for small furnaces was charcoal, until coke was introduced, a derivative of coal. Wrought iron is produced in a 'puddling' furnace, the operator working the pig iron into a large, soft treacly lump, hammered to remove – but also to incorporate – some slag. It has a property to withstand shock loads, is easily forged and bent cold, and is used for crane hooks, railway couplings, etc. A further process produces malleable cast iron. Steel is produced by altering the carbon content up to about 1.5 per cent, the range producing dead mild steel, medium-carbon steel and high-carbon steel. Adding a number of other elements changes the structure of the steel, controlled by the addition, to serve many special purposes. There is also a range of cast irons, developed as technology and metallurgy improved, as well as a considerable range of 'yellow' metals, all developing to those listed below, as experience developed along with requirements, and all uses depending on selected small percentage additions to the melt. Many of the small percentage elements are also added to iron and steel castings.

Engineering materials have gone through a complete change in the years since the demise of official steam. Plastics, carbon fibre and adhesives are used in place of welding etc., and one of the biggest changes has been with foundry work. Automatic furnaces and moulding pump molten metal into such machines from 'holding' furnaces, which retain the metal at the correct temperature. Moulding sands, which are self-hardening and supporting, are rammed up with the pattern, the moulding box is removed and used again, the molten metal poured into a completely unsupported block of sand. The block often contains a polypropylene pattern (the pattern made from a master pattern) which is left in the mould and evaporates when the metal is poured. All would amaze the old railway workers. Furnaces are now fired by gas or electricity. Machine tools are computer-controlled. Design is by CAD (Computer Aided Design). Gone are the tee square and drawing board. Progress?! (See Chapter 23 – Foundry Work.)

The yellow metals, iron, steel and aluminium are available in bar or sheet form.

Outline of Metals Available at the Height of the Steam Years

METAL	USE – The 'Yellow' Range
ALUMINIUM BRONZE (additions vary for selected use)	Alloy for high grade sand and die-castings, i.e. worm and gear wheels, will stand superheated steam. Hot rolling, forging, stamping and extrusion production of bars.
BRASS (additions vary for selected use)	Hot rolling, forging, stamping and extrusion. Used for water fittings, valves, plaques, and ornaments. High speed machining, screw cutting, heavy cold rolling. High grade castings.
NAVAL BRASS	Hot and cold stamping, rolling, die-casting. Good anti corrosion properties.
GILDING METAL	Two alloys is this use. Can be bronzed and enamelled. For decorative items.
GUN METAL (leaded) LG1, LG2, LG3	Superior to brass where strength, bearing and high temperatures are to be faced. LG2 – excellent casting alloy, pressure resisting castings, superior machining qualities. LG3 – high bearing anti corrosion properties. Not suited for stresses such as unbacked bearings and steam equipment.
ADMIRALTY GUN METAL	Standard alloy for marine castings. Pressure resisting up to 4,000lbs per square inch.
LEADED BRONZE	For bearings where lubrication is not reliable.
MANGANESE BRONZE	High tensile brass ingots for special castings e.g. ship propellers
PHOSPHOR BRONZE (additions vary for selective use)	A range of 3 high quality finish – gear blanks, worms, slide valves. Will stand heavy loading. Bearings.
SILICON BRONZE	For withstanding corrosion from mineral, vegetable and organic acids.
ALUMINIUM	For sand and for chill casting (i.e. metal mould) – 20 variations of casting alloys with varying additions to suit purpose.

CAST IRON (additions vary for selective use)	There are many variations of cast iron for a vast range of products. Alloying elements include: aluminium, titanium, vanadium, and zirconium. All affect the structure for the required purpose of the resulting casting.
SPHEROIDAL GRAPHITE IRON (a 'cast iron')	This is a late addition to the cast iron range. It has a number of the properties of steel. Easier to cast than steel, and can be welded.
STEEL	Steel now comes in a number of alloys, all for specific purposes containing a range of the elements listed above.

4

HOW WERE MEASUREMENTS DETERMINED?

Something we don't usually think about!

A major factor in making anything is being able to specify a correct range of measurements. A half is something divided or cut into two pieces, a quarter divides into four, etc., etc. A decimal system divides into ten pieces or sections, etc., but in the early years a half, quarter or a tenth of *what* was a linear measure?

Up until the reign of Elizabeth I, measurement was a very hit-or-miss affair and was based on such gems as 'three barley corns round and smooth equal 1 inch'. A positive move in 1588 was the making of a brass bar, its length over the ends being classified as 'one yard', which was subdivided as written into 'three feet' (replacing the actual average 'foot' length) and into 36 in. A variable used for many years was the 'pace', and artillery range tables of this and the following centuries follow some weird examples. Like the proverbial piece of string, how long is a pace?

It is to this Elizabethan 'standard' that the early steam pioneers were working, even Stephenson in his early years. There was no way of knowing if his 'foot rule' was actually a true foot based on the standard yard or some other official or unofficial 'secondary standard'. Anyway, it was more than likely that it was not exactly the same length as that used in the workshop of the nearest mine complex. The next version of the 'standard yard' did not appear until 1824 and in this case consisted of lines scribed on gold plugs set in a bronze bar. This was destroyed by a severe fire in 1834 and was replaced by a similar bar. The standard yard had by now thus changed from an 'end standard' to a 'line standard'. There was no such thing as an atmosphere- or temperature-controlled room or environment for the bar, so its length must have fluctuated between the height of summer and the depths of winter.

At the time of Newcomen and his predecessor Savery, the mathematician had outstripped the progress of the budding engineers. While a circle may be split into 360 degrees, there was no accurate way of measuring a diameter. The Greek letter Pi had been established as 3.14157 times the diameter for determining its circumference from its nominal diameter measurement, but there was no way those decimal places could be physically measured. (Incidentally, the value of Pi had been determined to sixteen decimal places.)

Up until the 1820s, the engineering drawing as we know it did not exist, so no one in the early years could sit down with drawing instruments and draw a proposal, calculate stresses and strains, internal loading, etc. and then build it. True, there are today beautifully drawn examples of 'technical illustrations' of Newcomen and Boulton & Watt engines. These were drawn by artists not engineers, and what they did not understand, they guessed. These drawings were made from the finished article, not as a guide to its construction, and are more 'illustrations' as opposed to 'engineering drawings'.

The early engineers, self-taught, were practical men with a skill that it is difficult to explain to those without such skill. They could translate an idea and a few 'measurements' into a practical model, and from the model build a full-size version. Certain components of the Boulton & Watt engines were made for sale but were erected on site by the 'millwright' using local timber and brickwork. It was for such work that the first instruction manuals were issued to enable the millwright to assemble the engines, using sketches of which piece fitted where. It was the first approach to 'engineering drawing', but still relating to components already made. Possibly one of the first 'construction manuals' was the 1797 publication of *The Canal Viewer and Engine Builders' Practical Companion*, a book of 'technical' drawings of components, without any measurements it must be noted, for the construction of tramway rails (in cast iron) and tramway trucks and other items showing the wood and iron work required for two designs of truck and winding drum. The rails, incidentally, showed straight, curved and crossover designs. The outlines of the components were shown. It was left to the builder to decide on the sizes.

The heaviest items made in the sixteenth and seventeenth centuries were the cannon barrels for the Navy and Army, the cylinders and other components of the Newcomen and Watt engines and associated pumps. Even here no two items were strictly identical, although of the same design for the same purpose; technology was not up to it. There were no measuring instruments to use the mathematicians' decimal places, and until the Ironmaster, Wilkinson, developed the boring machine in 1775 they could not get a parallel bore in the cylinder of a Newcomen Atmospheric engine. They had to put up with it and the engines still worked! With James Watt's improvements to the engine something had to be done to improve machining, as they had difficulty working to the nearest quarter of an inch, let alone three decimal places, hence the Wilkinson design. Other makers followed rapidly on his heels.

In the course of construction without measuring instruments, often designing as building progressed, the first locomotives, or mobile steam used just for road transport, started out as models. The first thoughts were for a better power source than the horse, to pull stone and coal wagons on tracks in collieries and quarries to transport to the nearest canal. None of the early engineers was a mathematician, but all were brilliant at translating ideas into practicalities. When you have decided to build a locomotive, a frame is required, a boiler follows, then an engine mechanism and all must be assembled.

In the course of construction of the early locomotives, machine tools developed as the necessity arose for special requirements. The pioneers started with only primitive drilling equipment, drills made by the blacksmith, and it was the blacksmith who formed as many holes as possible by hot-punching to avoid drilling. Indeed, a great deal was actually done by the blacksmiths, who were often the sole occupiers of the workshops tackling the first locomotive building attempts at the collieries and quarries. Watchmakers' small screw-cutting lathes appeared in the 1600s; the first steam hammer was still in the future, awaiting Nasmyth in 1850; and bulk steel production waited for Bessemer in 1854. Shaping machines and slotters waited for the 1830s, and the Americans sorted out the milling machine in the 1860s. Measurement also improved with Maudslay's 'bench micrometer' and the 'comparator' of Whitworth in 1835, thus solving the use of the decimal place figures! Inevitably as technology improved, machine tools improved and got bigger, along with requirements. Wooden lathe beds changed to cast iron and the drilling machine improved, but the drills they used were still the blacksmith-made 'D' bits and diamond points; the 'twist' drill we know today waited for the development of the 1860s milling machine.

In the early years of design, nuts and bolts caused a problem. All manufacturers of any mechanical device used their own design of screw thread, therefore the maintenance man had to be especially careful! You lost a nut at your peril, as matching a replacement thread could be impossible. Whitworth solved the problem by specifying certain pitches and form for the usual imperial diameters of bolts. The difficult part was getting it generally accepted, but everyone could see the logic of the argument for such a move and so development progressed.

Richard Trevithick started the locomotive era with his idea of utilising the power of the now well-developed principle of the Boulton & Watt beam engines, now in view over the whole country, to drive a cart, and disposing of the usual horse.

Having proved that steam power worked, it now became 'open season' on principle, as always happens, everyone trying to improve on it. Measurement had slowly improved until, as with many things, we nowadays rely on electronics!

The British standard yard bar is maintained at 62 degrees F and resides in the Standards Office of the Board of Trade.

The French or metric system (with which we are now lumbered) comprises a Platinum/Iridium bar. The measure is derived from a quadrant of the Earth's meridian, divided into 10,000,000 equal parts. The metre is thus a subdivision. The bar is maintained at 0 degrees C.

This now causes some confusion in the steam locomotive preservation world, as all measurements on drawings are in the Imperial (yard) measure, as are the existing locomotives being preserved, while virtually all material, length, thickness, weight, etc. is in metric, even to nuts and bolts and associated screw threads.

Even more confusing is the American standard inch, as it is derived from a conversion from metric, stemming from French influence following the War of Independence in 1776.

TWO OTHER CRITICAL MEASUREMENTS FOR STEAM LOCOMOTIVE DESIGNERS

On the subject of 'measurements', there are two groups which are critical for locomotive design. One is the obvious gauge of the railway track. This varies worldwide, some countries using Imperial feet and inches and others using the Metric system, each with its own variations, coming down from the old Great Western 7 ft ¼ in. to about 2 ft, all with passenger-carrying use; in Britain 4 ft 8½ in. is the standard.

The second critical measurement is the 'loading gauge'. We have all seen pictures of double-decker buses with the tops ripped off through trying to get under a low bridge, and there have been recent cases where a heritage railway steam locomotive has its safety valve cover damaged in the same way after the rail track had been re-ballasted and re-laid! This would not have happened in the official steam days!

Every railway had its own 'loading gauge', which conditioned not only the maximum sizes to which a locomotive could be designed but also the positioning and clearances of all station platforms, tunnels, cuttings, line-side equipment, buildings and bridges. With the Great Western some of the existing clearances may appear excessive, but this is due to the original broad gauge which was in use until 1892.

In America, with its wide open countryside and long distances, several railways have clearances in excess of the old Great Western broad gauge, still on the standard 4 ft 8½ in. track! In Britain, having converted to 4 ft 8½ in., did we lose out on the Great Western not also having bigger locomotives and rolling stock to take advantage of the wide loading gauge? We shall never know.

These are some loading gauge examples. Usually all goods yards, etc. had a chain-supported curved beam suspended from a gibbet-like structure, under which all loads had to fit on stacking goods in the wagons.

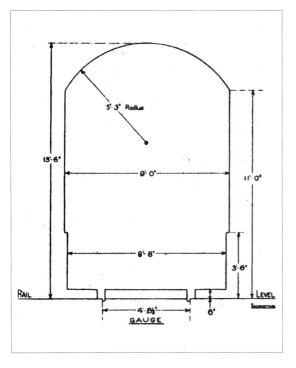
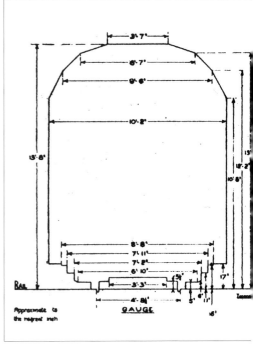

Above left: England (Average). Gauge 4 ft 8½ in.

Above right: Europe (Passe-Partout). Gauge 4 ft 8½ in.

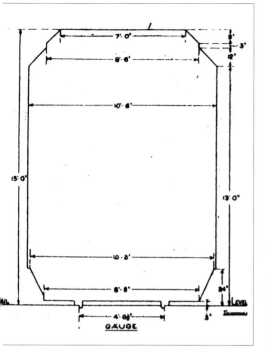

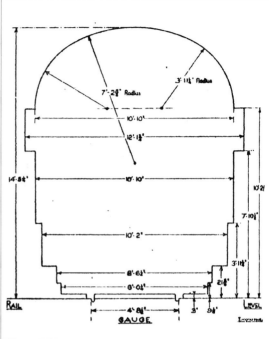

This page: United States (New York & Pennsylvania Railroads). Gauge 4 ft 8½ in.

Argentina (Government Requirements). Gauge 4 ft 8½ in.

South Africa (Government Lines). Gauge 3 ft 6 in.

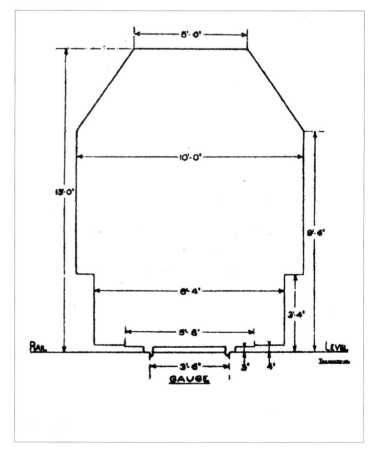

RAILWAY GAUGES

The length of line of the gauge specified is indicated as follows:

Full print (thus India) more than 1,000 miles

Italics (thus *India*) more than 100 miles and less than 1,000 miles

* More than 10 miles and less than 100 miles

‡ Less than 10 miles

Except in special circumstances, only countries with more than 10 miles of the specified gauge are mentioned

Metres	Ft	In	COUNTRIES
1.676	5	6	Argentine, Chile, India, Portugal, Spain. *Ceylon.*
1.600	5	8	Australia, Ireland, Brazil.
1.524	5	0	Finland, Latvia, Manchukuo, Russia. *Estonia, Panama, Turkey**
1.500	4	11$^1/_{16}$	France (*measured between centres of rails*)
1.450	4	9$^1/_{16}$	*Algeria, France*, Spain**
1.445	4	8$^7/_8$	Italy, *France*
1.485	4	8½	Argentina, Australia, Austria, Belgium, Bulgaria, Canada, China, Cuba, Czechoslovakia, Denmark, Egypt, France, Germany, Great Britain, Holland, Hungary, Korea, Manchukuo, Mexico, Norway, Peru, Poland, Rumania, Sweden, Switzerland, Turkey, United States, Uruguay, Yugoslavia *Algeria, Chile, Bermuda*, British Guiana*, Greece, Hawaii*, Honduras*, Hong Kong*, Iraq, Ireland, Italy*, Jamaica, Japan*, Java, Latvia, Lithuania, Luxembourg, Mauritius, Morocco, Paraguay, Persia, Porto Rico*, Spain, Syria, Trinidad, Tunis*
1.219	4	0	*Great Britain ‡*
1.2	8	11¼	*Switzerland ‡*
1.188	8	10¾	*Java**
1.16	3	9$^{11}/_{16}$	*Spain**
1.098	3	7	*Sweden**
1.067	3	6	Australia, Belgian Congo, Japan, Java, New Zealand, Nigeria, Rhodesia, South Africa, Sudan *British Guiana*, Chile, Colombia*, Costa Rica, Ecuador, Formosa, Gold Coast, Great Britain‡, Honduras, Newfoundland, Nicaragua, Norway, Nyasaland, Peru*, Portuguese East Africa, Portuguese West Africa, Saghalien, Santo Domingo, Sweden, Sumatra, Philippine Islands, Tasmania, Venezuela*
1.055	3	5$^9/_{16}$	*Algeria*
1.05	3	5$^5/_{16}$	*Hedjaz, Syria*, Turkey**
1.00	3	3$^3/_8$	Argentine, Belgium, Brazil, Burma, Chile, France, French West Africa, India, Indo-China, Kenya and Uganda, Malay States, Siam, Tanganyika *Abyssinia, Algeria, Belgian Congo, Bolivia, China, Colombia, Czechoslovakia*, Dutch Guiana, Egypt, Germany, Greed, Iraq, Luxemburg, Madagascar, New Caledonia*, North Borneo, Norway*, Peru*, Porto Rico, Portugal, Portuguese West Africa, Reunion* Russia, Spain, Switzerland*, Tunis, Venezuela*, Yugoslavia*
0.955	3	1$^3/_8$	*Italy*
0.914	8	0	Colombia, Mexico, United States *British Honduras*, Cuba*, Great Britain*, Guatemala, Hawaii, Honduras, Ireland, Panama*, Paraguay, Peru, Salvador, Venezuela*
0.891	2	11$^1/_{16}$	Sweden
0.825	2	8½	*Great Britain‡*
0.802	2	7$^9/_{16}$	*Sweden**
0.800	2	7½	*Great Britain‡, Switzerland (rack)**
0,785	2	6$^7/_8$	*Germany**
0.762	2	6	India *Australia, Barbados*, Belgian Congo, Brazil, Bulgaria, Ceylon, Chile, Cyprus*, Cuba*, Czechoslovakia, Ecuador, Egypt, Formosa, Gold Coast*, Korea, Mexico* Nigeria, Portuguese East Africa*, Santo Domingo, Sierra Leone, South African Yugoslavia*
0.750	2	5½	Germany, South America *Argentine, Egypt, Estonia, Finland*, Latvia, Lithuania, Norway*, Poland, Russia, Spain*, Sumatra, Turkey, Uruguay**
0.724	2	4½	*Great Britain‡*
0.711	2	4	*Great Britain‡*
0.686	2	3	*Great Britain‡*
0.700	2	8$^9/_{16}$	*Czechoslovakia*, Luxembourg*
0.610	1	11$^5/_8$	*Algeria*, Argentine, Brazil, Bulgaria, Chile, France, French West Africa, Germany*, Greece*, Java*, Latvia, Lithuania, Morocco, Peru*, Poland, Portuguese West Africa*, Sweden, Yugoslavia*
0.597	1	11½	*Great Britain**
0.891	1	8	*Great Britain**

5

BUILDING A LOCOMOTIVE — FRAMES: 'SANDWICH', 'PLATE' AND BAR

For the final 100 years of building, official steam locomotives started out built-up on and around a 'frame'. It was not always thus.

Two types of frame emerged, one of plate and one of wrought iron (or eventually cast steel) known as a 'bar frame', but the early years were the experimental years before the two methods evolved.

Trevithick's locomotive of 1803 had no 'frame' as such, and a number of designs by various early builders followed the idea of using the boiler as the base on which to hang every fitting. George Stephenson's 1816 Killingworth Colliery locomotive had four tubular 'legs' attached to the boiler to support the two axles of this four-wheel chain coupled example. His famous Stockton & Darlington 1825 opener, *Locomotive No. 1* (like the former, a beam-operated vertical cylinder example), was another without a frame as such.

Several locomotives evolved with not so much a frame as a solidly built timber platform to which the wheels were attached and on which the boiler rested. George Stephenson's first engine of 1814, still following the 'beam' tradition of an overhead small beam operated by vertical cylinders, was a gear-driven example, all attached to a hefty wood 'platform'. Several of the early locomotives were copied, having been successfully run, and thus were re-ordered.

A couple of famous locomotives that caused problems due to their weight (they kept breaking the tram plates, which were of cast iron) were gear-driven four-wheelers, boiler and mechanisms mounted on a substantial wood base. The base was altered in 1815, two years after manufacture, and an attempt was made to spread the load by adding another four wheels, thus forming a gear-driven eight-wheeler. When a more substantial track had been re-laid, the locos were returned to original design in 1830. (The two were *Puffing Billy*, now preserved, and *Wylam Dilly*.)

By the late 1820s new designs of frame were making an appearance. The *Stockton & Darlington No. 6 'Experiment'* of 1826 had a fabricated girder-style iron frame with 'buffer beams' and was 'six-coupled', six-wheel versions now becoming the vogue.

The interest in the steam locomotive was spreading world-wide and the American Delaware & Hudson Canal sent a representative to England to order four locomotives; Stephenson's received orders for one and three went to Foster & Rastrick. The locomotive from Stephenson's, named *America*, was the first locomotive to introduce mobile steam

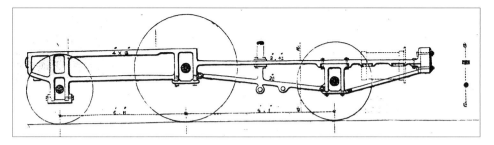

Bury's Frame, *c.* 1830s. Part of the blacksmith's learning curve, the example was probably made in sections for ease of handling and then scarf-joined in the fire or with other sections made and bolted and riveted. The only machining was probably holes drilled and the 'horns' where the axle boxes slide in, machined to fit the boxes.

to the continent, but not the first to run. That was Foster & Rastrick's *Stourbridge Lion*. Direct cylinder drive to a crankpin was now increasingly being introduced, and the overhead vertical cylinder drive to a beam arrangement was being phased out.

1829 was a momentous year in locomotive history, but we must never forget the earlier experiments and designs which set the early scene. The Rainhill trials showed the superiority of the Stephenson *Rocket*, a locomotive that introduced the basics of locomotive design that would last until the end of official steam.

A further set of major developments came with the 1830 introduction of the *Planet* design for the Liverpool & Manchester Railway. Gone was the 'bar' or girder frame, replaced by a distinctive plate and sandwiched wood example which set the trend toward the later complete plate version. Incidentally, it is claimed that the 'bar' frame version of the *America* set the trend for the almost sole use of the bar frame on that continent. The firm of Edward Bury was an exponent of the bar frame, and some of his locomotives exported to America may have influenced the adoption of the type. The design certainly leaves any internal mechanisms between the frames more accessible and visible, but the American builders seemed to have an aversion to inside cylinders and valve gear after the first flush of imports had been evaluated.

BAR FRAME DEVELOPMENT – C. 1930S

At the other end of the lifespan of official steam, or at least approaching an end which no one appreciated at the time, the example below says it all as regards development of the bar frame, and the progress of the American locomotive manufacturers. The illustrations sadly point to the swansong of commercial use of the steam locomotive.

The Second World War probably halted the trend for a decade or so, but the writing was on the wall, pointing to a phasing-out and a takeover by the diesel, the design of which did not call for such often massive patterns or components.

From the beginning of steam, and we have looked at examples up to 1840 and the building of early examples, the locomotives got bigger, allied to developing technology and metallurgy. Costs also escalated, and technical developments meant that short-cuts to production could be applied. Machine tools had developed beyond the recognition of the early engineers, who had no steam hammers, milling machines, etc., and whose files were made by hand by the blacksmith, as well as drills.

Probably the zenith of steam locomotive design came with the gigantic *Mallet* loco, a design really combining two locomotives into one. Leaving aside the mighty *Triplex* loco (which was really three locos in one, a power unit under the tender), which wasn't a real success, although pulling a train a mile long with loads weighing 18,000 tons, the *Mallet* remains a good example.

The illustrations show the two complete *Mallet* locomotive frames, front and back, both cast in steel as complete units, and steel is a difficult material. The official description states: 'By the use of these cast steel frames ... 66 major parts as well as 634 minor parts are displaced. Two mechanical lubricators supply oil from 33 leads to 72 outlets for lubricant to the cylinders, steam chests, guides and other sliding surfaces.' What an engineering achievement!

The frames illustrated are for a 2-6-6-4 wheel arrangement. There were also 4-8-8-4s, much bigger versions weighing about 536 tons and 132 ft long. Known as the Big Boys, twenty-five were built for the Union Pacific Railroad. There would have been a considerable amount of machining on this example, but probably when analysed not needing so much space, manpower and machinery as if made in the conventional way, each workshop dealing with its own particular skill. The pattern-making for the casting was probably the most skilled requirement of the lot! (Any preservation group volunteers for DIY pattern-making for a replica!?)

Front frame casting with cylinders.

Rear-end cylinders and frame casting. Photograph taken from *The Locomotive*, 15 March 1937.

While America concentrated more on the bar-type frame, British builders were moving toward a frame design which still included wood but was the forerunner of the now almost traditional plate frame. The illustrations show clearly the look of the new frames: one large flat plate about ⅜ in. (10 mm) thick on the outside, a similar plate on the inside sandwiching an oak filling, making a 4 in. 'sandwich' frame plate. When first used, the sandwich frames, while they supported the wheels and axles, were only really a 'skirt' to the boiler, which held the frame with securely riveted brackets. The mechanism of the valve gear, and *Firefly* is a good example, had a pair of inner frames securely attached to the front of the firebox and back of the smoke box for support, so the boiler became part of the frame system.

The sandwich gave way to the standard form of steel plate during the 1860s; any plate prior to Bessemer bulk steel production after 1858 was of wrought iron. Production of plate was a difficult process and up to the end of the century, plates were machined in large planning machines to ensure flatness. Modern plate cut by laser or plasma cutting systems offers a very clean cut. Plates are drilled for all the various fittings, generally cleaned up and de-burred before use. The preservation groups building new locomotives have a much easier time than their predecessors!

THE FRAME (PLATE)

Frame-plate planing machine, 1893. There was difficulty in producing a flat plate, so it had to be planed.

Large combined slotter and driller, *c*. 1930.

Operators at work on the new universal frame-cutting machine in the No. 15 shop, Swindon Works, *c*. 1930. (Photo by Sims (Photographers) Ltd)

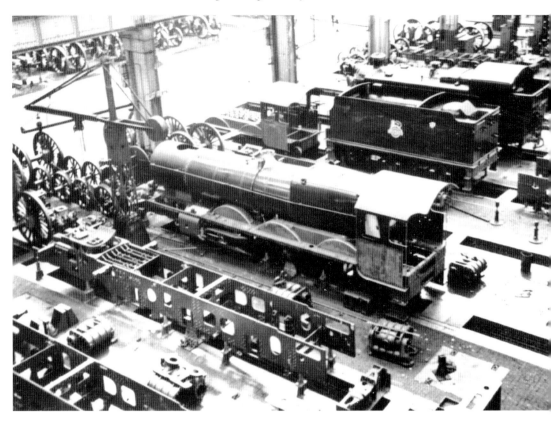

Above: Locomotive frame assembly, *c.* 1950. Frames are first assembled on stands that are adjustable to ensure diagonal and horizontal squareness.

Left: The 'new work' area. Drilling from both sides an inside Castle class cylinder block, on specially adapted pits in the shop complex, to be fitted into the nearest frame, shown previously. Note the 'bed' either side of the pit along which the drilling heads ran for repositioning, also transporting the operators.

6
MAKING A CRANK AXLE — METHOD AND PROBLEMS

Having reared its ugly head, and as a 'must' with inside cylinders, the 'crank axle' was among the heavy engineering components of the steam locomotive that were constructed, in the early years, entirely by hand. The construction of the built-up wheel and its associated handling difficulties were mentioned earlier, and the out-of-balance construction of a crank axle was equally as difficult. In the formative years, there was no counterbalance design of the crank webs with additional material to counterbalance the webs and crank bearing, so handling would have been very difficult.

John Nuttall's record (mentioned earlier in these notes) contains a sketch and notes (written in dialect by a very good hand, presumably by John Nuthall himself). The sketch shows a crank axle made in two distinct parts, each containing a complete crank; all bearing and wheel boss surfaces; and by means of shading or cross hatching on the sketch, a clearly defined joint in the centre section. The joint must have been welded by a smith, the two component crank end forgings heated to sparkling white, the joint faces cleaned off and the two pieces then brought together as a scarf joint and hammered to fuse. He states that this method was in use from 1831 to 1840, but does not say what a new method entailed.

Experiments with crank axles continued, along with fractures and other splitting faults inherent in scarfed joints and wrought iron and inefficient (but also very difficult) smith welds on such large and important items. By 1851 experiments had been concluded and both Sturrock and Hawthorn introduced the shrinking of a strap or band over crank axle webs. A couple of years later, the superintendent of the Oxford, Worcester & Wolverhampton Railway, the well-known David Joy, had added a further safety measure in the shape of a large bolt through the crank pin and web joint just in case the crank pin cracked in shear.

Around the end of the 1850s, experiments on the Eastern Railway of France had included the use of the 'built-up' crank axle from five separate pieces as opposed to the usual solid forged version. Who first attempted a built-up axle construction in Britain is open to debate, but F. W. Webb specified built up crank axles for his three cylinder compounds in 1890. 1895 saw the introduction of built up crank axles for his two cylinder goods engine designs, the assembly of the nine separate pieces requiring skilful handling.

The GWR at this time had developed a method of machining crank axles from massive forgings which literally had a cylindrical axle with two solid lumps, in place of the 'cranks', at 90 degrees angles to each other. A series of ingenious machine operations were required to form the crank pin and web from the solid blocks. Mounted in a 25 ft long lathe, six tools and two saddles turned the axle, wheel and bearing seats. A large-diameter wheel with inserted cutters then removed, in a separate machine and in the manner of a wide circular saw, the metal as far as the crank pin position. The axle was held stationary for this operation, the cutter revolving slowly and advancing as the cut progressed into the solid block of the crank web material. The cutters, having thus reduced the web to a rough square crankpin section, were again set in motion when the crank axle position had been changed to revolve around the centre line of the crankpin. The pin thus became roughly cylindrical when the corners of the square section had been removed. Transfer to another machine allowed a special cutter to revolve slowly around the crankpin to complete the cylindrical bearing surface. Finally, a reset into a form of 'shaper' allowed a reciprocating tool to profile the periphery of the crank web into an oval form, thus completing the crank axle.

Machining a crank web – turning the crankpins, 1893.

Lathe for turning crank axles, 1893. The bed is 25 ft long, the head stocks 2 ft 6½ in.

Right: A built-up 1950s crank axle with balanced webs and eccentrics fitted.

Below: Planing machine for finishing crank webs, 1893.

In the course of development of the crank axle made from the solid, machining was further complicated by the addition of integral eccentric sheaves, making even more machining, although I have found no reference that this design was attempted by the Great Western. The skill of marking out the axle prior to machining to include the sheaves called for very accurate measuring, particularly obtaining the 'angle of advance' for the sheaves to lead or follow the relative position of the crank (follow if the valve gear included a 'rocker' in its design). It was soon found easier to use separate eccentric sheaves than to have integral forgings, entailing two cranks and four eccentric sheaves (for Stephenson valve gear) positioned correctly to allow forward or backward motion with the correct valve lead.

By the end of steam, particularly with reference to Swindon, the manufacture of crank axles had developed into a smooth-flowing process. A small section in the 'A' machine shop was set up to assemble all of the components of the built-up crank axle. Bored crank webs were heated by specially positioned gas jets until they expanded to allow the machined cylindrical pins and axle sections to be dropped into the holes in the webs. I worked for about two years on the reversing gear gang in the 'A' Shop, to which the crank axle section was annexed, and in all that time I did not see a mistake made or an incorrectly machined component which failed to assemble as it should have done.

There was a further method of assembly, although I believe not tried at Swindon. This entailed really the opposite way of doing things in that cylindrical components were frozen in liquid carbon dioxide, dropped into position in the webs and there allowed to expand on thawing out. In either method, a screwed plug inserted in the joint between web and axle or crankpin section stopped any possibility of the crank web moving, should, for example, a hot bearing cause sufficient expansion for the web to move or reduce its grip on the axle.

The wheel shop. This is the crank axle section – crank axles await machining.

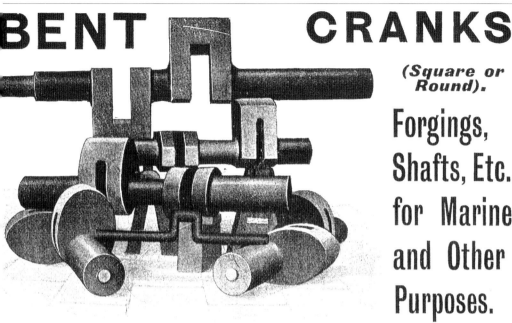

BENT CRANKS

(Square or Round).

Forgings, Shafts, Etc. for Marine and Other Purposes.

The above represents a group of Crank Axles bent by hydraulic pressure all throws bent in position, twisting being dispensed with.

A group of crank axles bent by hydraulic pressure, all throws bent in position, twisting being dispensed with. This is a Sheffield firm's advertisement from 1903. Note the unusual method of manufacture.

The gripping power of the assembled components was illustrated when I worked in the AE shop. A short walk into the wheel section, which adjoined the erecting pits, had on one occasion offered the interesting sight of a crank axle onto which the axle box had seized. Although the box had been removed by now, the relevant journal was a very deep blue and deeply scored; the wheel had actually been twisted off the axle, complete with the axle stub still inside the wheel centre. Fortunately, this was a very rare occurrence and I only ever saw the one example.

7

THE LOCOMOTIVE BOILER – DESIGN AND CONSTRUCTION

The locomotive boiler is the power source of the locomotive, and, no matter how developments in size have progressed, the basic principles are the same as those introduced by Stephenson with *Rocket* in 1829.

The fittings on the boiler that control all aspects of the steam produced have also developed as innovations were proposed and served the desired purpose. The use of the steam has improved with more control, making its production within the boiler more economical. Boilers have been designed to suit several kinds of fuel, the usual being coal, coke, wood, oil, even a design to burn old tyres, but the latter was a modern-day economy drive! There are even, in special applications, locomotives with a 'container' in place of, but at first glance resembling a boiler, but charged from a special point with compressed air or steam, running where no fire-carrying locomotive was allowed to venture.

On ordinary locomotives the fire was controlled by 'dampers' operated from the footplate, which regulated the amount of air allowed through the bed of the fire. Early dampers were in the smoke box and were in the form of a Venetian blind over the front tube plate, but development positioned them in front and rear of the base of the firebox, covering the open front and partial open rear of the ash pan. It is important to control the amount of air allowed into the bottom of the firebox under the fire bed through which it travels, assisted by the 'blast' effect in the smoke box when the cylinders exhaust steam, still with some pressure at the end of each piston stroke, hence the loud distinctive noise from the chimney.

In the early years, the first locomotives exhausted into the atmosphere, but the noise of the blast frightened farm horses and animals so local by-laws condemned the noise. It was found that by exhausting into and up the chimney, there were two benefits; first it did as instructed, deadening the noise, and secondly it had a drawing-up effect on the fire. This then entailed the strict control by dampers, as the fire without any control damaged the fire bars and firebox, acting like a blacksmith's blown forge, and eventually sucking unburnt or glowing fuel particles through the boiler tubes to the smoke box, which started to clog up and also suffered damage to its box, tube ends and plate with the excess heat. This problem was to spread to other period loco designs.

A further problem to which local authorities took exception was the wreaths of smoke and grit spreading over the countryside, due to steam locomotives becoming common sights as the railways developed. The recommendation to solve the problem was the use of coke, and this meant a redesign somewhat of the firebox as the burning properties of coke, almost smokeless, are different to that of coal, so the instruction was to burn your own smoke! Easier said than done, with inadequate combustion of the fuel if you continued to burn coal. To complicate matters, there were different grades of coal! This also had an effect on the design of the firebox. A firebox for hard coal – 'WDS' or Welsh Dry Steam – differed from that of soft or 'long-flame coal', the firebox end of the latter's boiler having a built-in combustion chamber. With coke, taking as an example the Firefly class of Gooch's Great Western Railway, the firebox had a 'feather' or extra passage across it and a very high-placed fire hole door. Coke left an ash when burned but coal left a clinker, and to try coal in a coke firebox would be difficult because with the 'feather' you would have difficulty wielding the 'pricker' bar to break it up for removal.

Once the fire is going, as soon as coal starts to ignite it starts to smoke, while air forced through it speeds up combustion and it smokes quite badly until fully ignited. The air solution was not possible in the early days, so a boiler fitting was developed, known as the 'blower'. This used the developing steam pressure to produce a draught, or a forced draught when stoking was done on a running locomotive. The arrangement was a fitting on top of the exhaust steam blast nozzle in the smoke box and was controlled from the footplate. It can often be heard operating, for example, when a steam loco is waiting at a station platform. With no exhaust from the cylinders it keeps the fire glowing.

For a waiting engine, say, at the same platform, it was always essential to keep the water level over what was called the 'crown plate', the inner top of the firebox. On the early locomotives this check on water level was achieved by three small taps or cocks, the top one positioned in the steam space, one on the preferred water level and one below in the water space between the correct level and the inner firebox top. Steam from the top one was OK; any water meant the water level was too high and could be carried over into the cylinders (known as priming). This could cause hydraulic damage, knocking out the end of a cylinder as water does not compress well! Steam from the middle one meant the water was lower than it should be, and steam from the bottom one meant watch out and stand by for a big bang.

All this changed in 1829 when Messrs Foster & Rastrick introduced the 'water level gauge', a sight tube of glass which gave instant reference to the water level over the crown plate. The loco 'backhead' or firebox back in the cab was the mounting position of the gauge, some early examples such as *Firefly* having a gauge with both taps and glass, and as there was no cab to protect the driver and fireman, one was mounted on each side of the firebox.

By the mid-nineteenth century, experiments were happening thick and fast to determine the efficiency of the locomotive boiler. The experiments concentrated on the evaporation properties of the fuel, it being determined that coal was only 66 per cent as effective as coke, and the critical dimensions were evaporation areas of tubes and firebox, areas of grate, volume of smoke box, size of blast pipe nozzle and design. Even in the construction of a boiler, an important finding was that in the desire for a large heating surface, care should be taken to avoid too little space being left between the tubes by cramming in too many.

Up to 1840, Stephenson had been very aware of a general problem that affected many contemporary locomotives, apart from the smoke problem with burning coal and the effects of the use of the more efficient coke. This had led to continuing problems with burnt front tube plates and tubes, damaged smoke boxes and chimneys, all due to the unused heat escaping up the chimney. His solution was to make the boiler longer, so he introduced his long-boiler design in 1841 and this quickly became the latest phase for those quick enough to realise its benefits, which included less clag in the smoke box and a reduction in the smoke problems and spreading of grit around the countryside.

The importance of feeding the boiler was not forgotten, and from the various pump methods came, in 1859, the invention of the 'injector' (see the complete story later in this book) to maintain the safe water level. These principles carried on throughout the life of the locomotive (see Chapter 22).

There were many designs of locomotive boiler: large; small; taper boiler barrel; straight boiler barrel; round-top firebox; 'Belpaire' firebox; wide-bottom or narrow-bottom firebox; with or without thermic siphons; with or without a 'feather' or passage across the firebox; combustion chamber at the firebox end of the barrel for long-flame coal or without the chamber for Welsh Dry Steam coal. One thing they all had in common throughout the locomotive world was the dozens of 'stays' securing the inner and outer shells of the firebox.

The individual 'stay' was about 5 or 6 in. long, threaded both ends for about 1¼ in. and reduced in the centre section to about ½ in. The stay could be in steel or copper, all batch-tested for tensile strength, selected stays being tested to destruction and the results recorded. Gripped by both ends in the tensile test apparatus, the stay was stretched and 'necked' in the centre, usually breaking at about ⅜ in. diameter. The top of the firebox (or crown) was also stayed, with either longer screwed versions or with a riveted and shaped 'girder stay'.

The front tube plate was also stayed with longitudinal stays, threaded about 2 in. in diameter by about 4 in. at both ends, with a smaller central diameter, stretching from tube plate to backhead. On a boiler drawing, the carefully spaced small circles covering the firebox indicate the position of the hundreds of stays to be used in construction. The short stays were machined on automatic lathes which could take up to six or seven long bars at a time, rotating to an index setting for the various operations to produce a completed stay. Over the years, many millions must have been produced and are still produced for the preserved heritage locomotives running today. With developments in alloy steels, it is doubtful if such rigorous testing procedures are followed today in stay production for the quantities now required.

A problem which was really conditioned by the thinking of the time in those very early years was caused by the number of axle boxes thought to be essential to afford the necessary support for a crank axle. In many of the early designs there was no 'frame' as we understand it today. The boiler itself became the 'frame', even to the extent of the drag box hook being attached to the rear of the firebox, and operating through a slot in the rear buffer beam. The design of Firefly, Gooch's passenger locomotive class, included no less than four inner frames as well as the outside 'skirt', all supported by the boiler. The four inner frames were securely riveted between the front of the firebox and the back of

A locomotive firebox. This photo shows the backhead, with provision for valves, water gauge, etc. The large central top opening is for the regulator. The large nuts around the top of the box secure the ends of the heavier cross and longitudinal stays. There are various other holes for washout mud plugs and washout covers.

The side bracket is the 'casing bracket' which supports the back end of the boiler, allowing it to expand along the top of the loco frame. The boiler shown is riveted but modern boilers are usually welded. The jury is still out on whether riveting is better than welding (the author thinks it is!). (See Section 'T' for Pressing Firebox & Boiler Plate components.)

the smoke box and carried by specially shaped brackets. Thus the driving crank axle had six supporting axle boxes, which made for a very rigid assembly, and as such contributed to both bearing problems and structural problems with frames and axles.

Mention could be made of the effect of such a rigid bracing between firebox and smoke box on those early locomotives. A modern boiler is only really rigidly attached to the frame at the smoke box end; the firebox, on a GWR plate frame loco, is allowed to slide on top of the frame, stopped from dropping through the frame by the 'casing brackets' which are very securely collar-studded to the firebox sides. Thus, hot or cold, expansion or contraction is allowed for and covered by the sliding action of the casing brackets on the frame top.

Movement of one of the early boilers, braced by four rigidly riveted inner frames, must have been very restricted and uneven and leaks caused by such stresses must have occurred. Such problems were recognised very early on, and Isaac Dodds of the Sheffield & Rotherham Railway applied in 1839 the (later universal) method of securing to the smoke box and allowing the boiler to slide on the frame-top by the attachment of brackets to the firebox sides, and modifying any inner frame member.

Stemming from the original wooden frame reinforced by iron plates of the early formative years of locomotive development, the wood was steadily replaced and reinforced with more and more iron, with three really distinct designs of frame emerging. One was the well-known 'sandwich frame' of the GWR, which was really an outer skirt only, of wood sandwiched between two iron plates (remember there were four solid iron frames between smoke box and firebox); secondly the iron 'plate frame', later to become steel, of course, and beloved of the GWR; and thirdly the 'bar frame' which, exported to America in the early years, conditioned much of later American practice. This design led to simplification of access under the locomotives so constructed. With the demise of the sandwich frame, the plate and bar types became the two rivals in locomotive design.

Before the opening of the GWR, the various firms then in business had a really thriving market as many countries could appreciate that here was a new and powerful transport motive power source. The firm of Robert Stephenson, which had been the first in the business, had such an order book that locomotives were 'contracted out' to increase the numbers produced for export by other firms. Among those early contractors, the firm of Edward Bury had a good lead and market, and the adherence by Bury to the bar frame, in preference to the plate version, contributed in no small measure to its ready and widespread acceptance in the expanding markets 'across the pond'. This was the nation which in thirty years' time was to be torn apart by a vicious civil war, a war in which the railways were to play a vital part. However, at the time of the 1830s and 40s the concentration was on getting steam and the iron roads to as much of that vast nation as possible. The American locomotive industry was born, and what an industry it turned out to be.

Above: Riveting the throat plate for a boiler barrel.

Left: The drilling frame for drilling and tapping for firebox stays.

Rolling a plate for a boiler barrel.

Brazing return bends on superheater units.

Inside a smoke box; the large (blue) pipes carry steam to the cylinders while the central large (white) pipe carries exhaust from cylinders.

The double boiler of a Fairlie design locomotive.

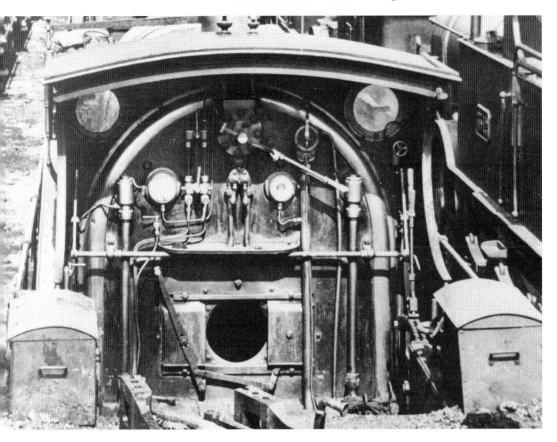

Above: The backhead of a GWR broad gauge boiler, *c.* 1860.

Right: A view of the backhead fittings of an 1890s Dean goods locomotive. Shown are the basic fittings found on any locomotive. Positions may change and more may be added, but the 'fire hole door' (centre bottom) stayed where it is shown. The coil spring sets are over the rear wheels and axle boxes. The centre fitting at the top is the regulator. The multi holed plate to its right is the vacuum brake control. To the left is the water gauge. Valves to left and right of this are the feed clacks; the pipes underneath take water from the injectors. The two-wire handled wheels under the regulator control the steam feed to the injectors. The lever in the rack on the right is the reversing lever, which controls the setting of the valve gear.

A broad gauge loco backhead from *North Star*, 1840. Very simple, with no fittings except pet cock, regulator, and water gauge. Note there is no 'safety box' around the gauge glass! Very dangerous if it shatters; scalding water and steam would spray onto the footplate. Reversing lever runs in the curved rack on the right.

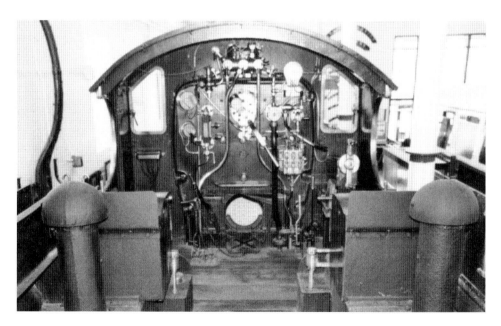

Reversing screw. Serves the same purpose as the lever on the previous photograph. Allows forward and reverse movements and control of the steam entering the cylinders. A graduated scale and pointer shows at what percentage of the piston stroke the steam is cut off, and the pointer runs in a slot in the top plate. Photo taken from tender coal space. Note 'mushroom' vents on water tank.

8
THE REGULATOR AND BOILER DESIGN

Either at the centre top of the firebox backhead, or positioned either side of the backhead, is a lever which must be lifted, pushed or pulled to operate a controlling valve, and is under the control of the driver.

In the design of the early locomotive boilers the valve was located immediately behind the regulator control handle gland and was of a disc design with a rotary action. It was apparently difficult to maintain and was a problem to keep steam tight, although nominally in a good steam-collecting position above the crown plate of the inner firebox, in the steam space.

Most locomotive boilers had a 'dome' on top of the boiler barrel, where in some of the early locomotives a collection pipe conveyed steam to the disc regulator valve. The valve itself, redesigned with a vertical or horizontal sliding action, was then positioned within the dome and in the ideal steam collecting space, controlled by a rod from the backhead-mounted handle. The steam so controlled was conveyed to the cylinder valve chest via a pipe from the regulator through the steam space to the front tube plate-mounted manifold, from which steam pipes went to the cylinder valve chests.

As locomotive design progressed, the prominent dome was dispensed with, thus smoothing out the boiler top and leaving only the chimney, safety valve and whistles. The regulator valve was now positioned in the smoke box and combined within the design of the distributing steam manifold, controlled by an even longer rod from the handle on the firebox backhead in the cab. The regulator valve developed into either a 'sliding' or a 'poppet' valve design. (The latter like an IC engine valve.)

There was a further development, quite early in steam locomotive design; this was 'compounding'. Locomotives were designed for exhaust steam from a cylinder, still retaining some pressure, to be used to operate another cylinder. In lbs/square in. pressure terms, the second cylinder was of necessity considerably larger in diameter than the first cylinder, giving a bigger area of piston for the exhaust steam to do efficient work. It was a system used with some success, but not all railway companies used it in their locomotive designs. The valve gear was modified to undertake the additional transfer of the exhaust steam at the correct function of the mechanism. Incidentally, another use of exhaust steam was to operate an injector for the boiler feed water. (This is detailed further on in the 'Injector' notes.)

On the subject of the steam itself, the hotter and more gas-like it is, the better. As an example, if you look at a boiling kettle, when the water starts to boil check the end of the spout. It appears that there is a gap between the steam you can see and the end of the spout! That 'gap' is the ideal condition of invisible steam. The steam you can see is 'wet' steam, and is already condensing back into water droplets. This still conveys power to the locomotive, but is not an ideal state.

The combined manifold/regulator valve was now further developed to include provision for a series of tubes to carry the controlled steam, en-route to the cylinders, back through special tubes in the boiler to give it that reheat and ensure it was in a gas state at the cylinders, there most efficient. Thus arrived 'superheating', and the new design manifold became the 'superheater header'. The object of superheating is to raise the temperature of the steam and thus its 'expanding' properties without raising the actual pressure. If the working pressure of a locomotive is exceeded, then the safety valve blows, or if, as in the early years, fiddling with the gauge, for example, screwing it down will increase the pressure, and continuing will result in an explosion!

If the steam to be used is in contact with the water in the top section of the boiler, then as the temperature increases, the boiler pressure increases. So to increase the temperature without increasing the boiler pressure, it is passed in isolation from the water in the boiler through the tubes of the superheater. This phenomenon was noticed very early on in the life of the steam locomotive by, for example, Daniel Gooch, who recorded that steam at the regulator appeared to increase in temperature when reaching the steam chest valves, and that the only way this could have occurred was in its passage through the pipes from the boiler, where they passed through the smoke box. But it

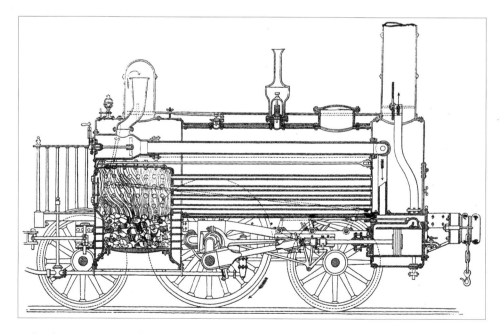

Boiler design, *c.* 1830s. The basic design established by Stephenson. Note the disc-type regulator and the steam-collecting pipe in the rear dome.

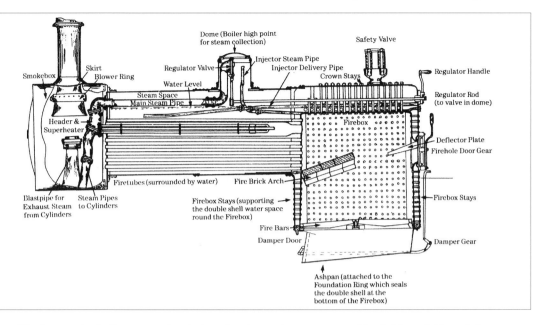

The locomotive boiler – a sectional view showing main components. The brick arch 'draws' the fire and directs heat through the firetubes to heat the water in the boiler. Steam exhausted from the cylinders (plus residual smoke from the fire) is discharged via the chimney, thereby causing a draught which 'draws' the fire. To aid combustion, the draught is also controlled by the damper gear. On the bottom right is the ashpan, attached to the foundation ring that seals the double shell at the bottom of the firebox.

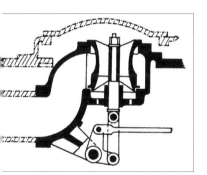
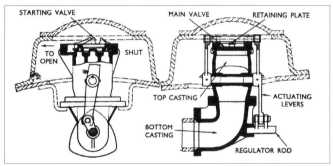

Boiler design, *c.* 1930s. The basic design shows very little change. Note the vertical regulator in the dome and the 'superheater' arrangement.

was some years before this discovery was exploited and superheating came into official general practice.

Note: In the Casting section of this book (Chapter 23), two castings are shown: a superheater 'header', and a smoke box-mounted combined regulator valve and 'manifold' for the main steam pipes to the cylinders. There is also a very heavy design of superheater header which combines the regulator valve. These latter were for the larger boiler designs.

9

THE SAFETY VALVE AND
PRESSURE GAUGE

The early boilers of Savery and Newcomen worked on pressures only just above atmospheric, but developments showed that increasing the pressure was essential as soon as Watt and his contemporaries entered the equation. Double-acting cylinders required a bit of push behind the steam to move beams and push wheels, and the dangers of exploding pressure vessels became obvious! The solution was weights of some kind over a pressure relief hole in the top of the boiler, with sufficient control to ensure the pressure could never rise above the safety limit of the boiler material. From the original cast iron boilers, looking like kettle bodies, wrought iron sheets were soon riveted together to make a cylindrical boiler. An orifice with a weight on top was the obvious answer, and once again the designers got to work on a further problem with the control of steam.

As with every other innovation, designs came thick and fast, and soon separated according to the requirements of the stationary boiler and the locomotive boiler. The lever safety valve was among the first attempts, an arm with a weight on the end, pivoted at one end holding down a valve, an extended end holding a weight that was calculated to be lifted at the required safe boiler pressure. This became the usual valve on the stationary boiler. A tried locomotive valve was the 'deadweight' valve, but this soon also became a stationary boiler fitting, the valve held down by a series of thick metal rings to the weight required. This was tried by Stephenson on his six-wheel locomotive of 1838.

By the 1860s, a spring-loaded valve had been introduced – the Ramsbottom design. This design also had a lever arrangement that allowed the valve to lift against the action of a spring, which could be adjusted to lift at the required pressure by operating and setting a nut, pre-set in the workshop.

A valve design which caused some problems was the 'Salter spring balance' design. This valve also had an arm holding down the valve, the end of the arm extending with, and held down by, a spring balance, the pointer of which ran in a slot against a pressure scale. And therein lay a problem! Drivers were very quick to realise that more power meant more speed, and more speed thus required more pressure, so screwing down the wing nut served a very easy purpose. Thus a static engine, in steam and waiting, could build-up quite a pressure as the water got lower, no pump action with no movement! If someone had fiddled with the pressure gauge, the result could be nasty! (Two valves were then used – one out of the driver's reach)

The Salter had a comparatively short life but the Ramsbottom design soldiered on well into the twentieth century, by which time the 'pop' safety valve had come into almost universal use. Except, that is, on the Great Western, which as with other things had its own ideas! The author spent a very short time as an apprentice on the safety valve gang, grinding in the twin valves, setting and locking spring-loaded valves by means of a 'test rig', and pumping up the pressure as indicated by the rig test gauge.

EARLY SAFETY VALVE DESIGNS

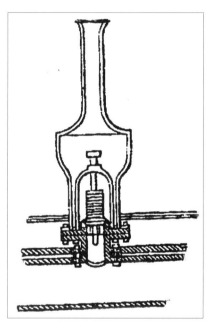

Right: Stephenson, 1838.

Below: Gooch, *c.* 1850.

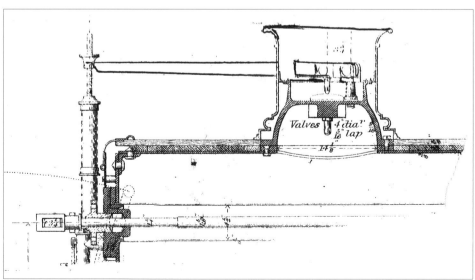

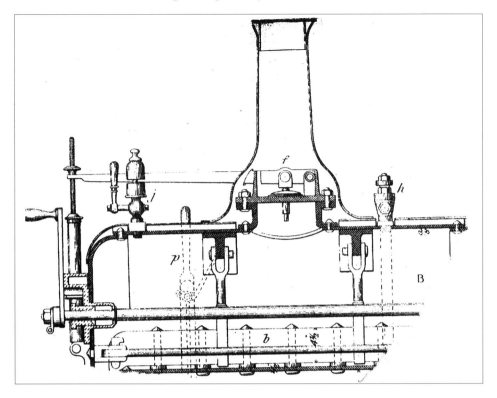

Fairbairn, 1850.

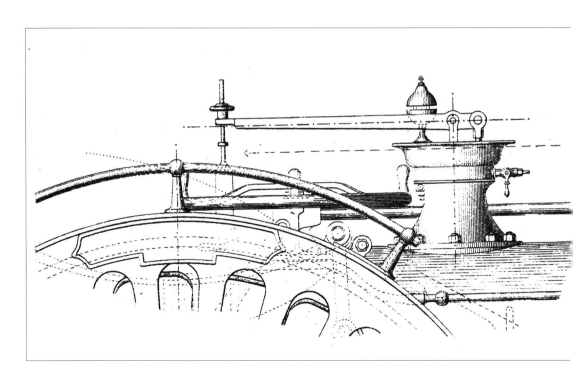

Crampton, *c.* 1850.

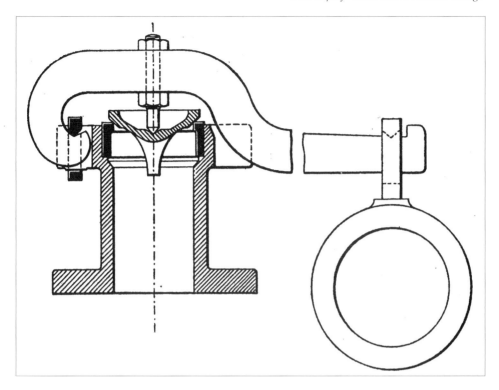

Above: Lever Type (Messrs Yates & Thom), a stationary boiler type.

Right: Dead weight type, a stationary boiler type.

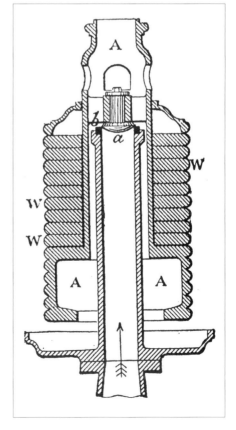

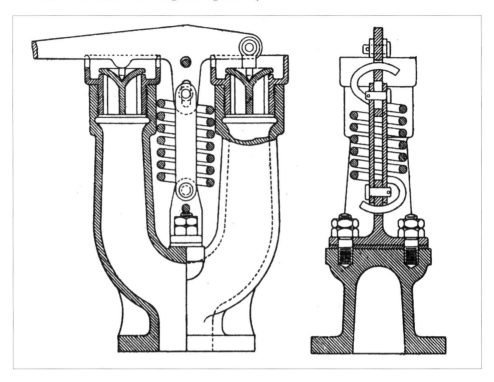

Ramsbottom, a locomotive type.

A Great Western valve inside its brass cover.

This page: Ramsbottom-designed safety valve, introduced in 1855.

Great Western valve with flanges for top feed boiler water 'clack' valves.

The Bourdon steam pressure gauge – an early invention and a welcome replacement of the Salter spring gauge.

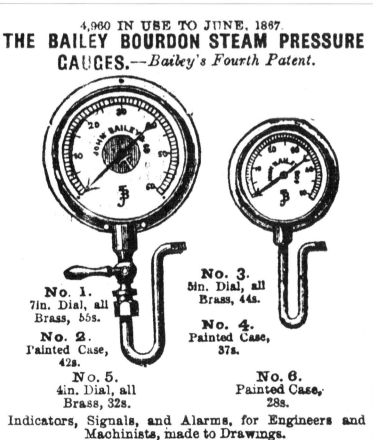

4,960 IN USE TO JUNE, 1867.

THE BAILEY BOURDON STEAM PRESSURE GAUGES.—*Bailey's Fourth Patent.*

No. 1.
7in. Dial, all Brass, 55s.

No. 2.
Painted Case, 42s.

No. 3.
5in. Dial, all Brass, 44s.

No. 4.
Painted Case, 37s.

No. 5.
4in. Dial, all Brass, 32s.

No. 6.
Painted Case, 28s.

Indicators, Signals, and Alarms, for Engineers and Machinists, made to Drawings.

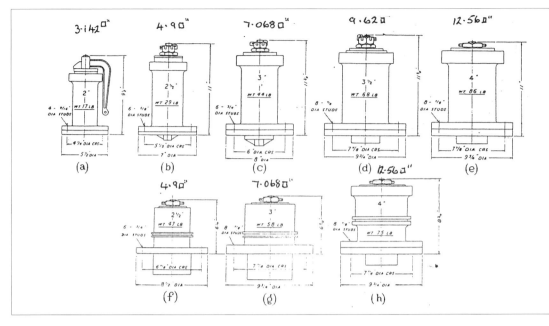

Above: Standard Ross 'POP' safety valves. Top, from left to right: (a) 3.142 in., (b) 4.90 in. (c) 7.068 in., (d) 9.762 in., (e) 12.56 in.. Bottom, left to right: (f) 4.9 in., (g) 7.068 in., (h) 12.56 in.

Left: 'Who screwed down the Salter?!'

Very early in the locomotive saga, setting the safety valve on the top of the dome was widely practiced. This became frowned upon as the dome, with the steam-collecting pipe or regulator within, became shrouded with wet steam blowing off. One of the practices of the early years also becoming frowned upon was the belief by drivers that the fireman was not doing his job unless the safety valve was blowing. As early as 1832, a Frenchman, the Comte de Pambour, carried out some experiments and found that up to 25 per cent of steam, water and heat were lost through a blowing safety valve. The Great Western design 'whisped' before blowing, not so fierce as the 'pop' type. A driver could only really tell the state of the pressure by the feel of the valve lever, so a positive visual check came in the 1850s with the introduction of the Bourdon glass-fronted, circular pressure gauge. Pressure tended to straighten a curved, flat brass tube which operated a pointer mounted in the centre and sweeping around a circular scale, with which we are all now well acquainted.

10
THE DEVELOPMENT OF VALVE GEAR

From the steam year 'dot' (around 1712), when Newcomen introduced his 'atmospheric' pumping engine to a sceptical world (of course, these newfangled ideas won't last!), the steam entering the cylinder had to be controlled. Starting the ball rolling, or the piston moving, a manually controlled valve was introduced to allow steam into the cylinder to push the piston up; when the valve was closed, another valve was opened to allow a jet of cold water into the cylinder to immediately condense the steam. The partial vacuum thus created sucked down the piston and expelled water from the attached pump barrel, the cycle repeated continuously to maintain pumping. Steam had arrived.

Having someone manually operating the steam and water valves did not last long, and soon trip levers were attached to the moving rods to operate the valves virtually automatically, although still watched over by an attendant whose job was now easier. Steam was at virtually atmospheric pressure, so the 'valves' were of a simple rotary plug construction where movement through 90 degrees fully closed or fully opened the valve. The real work of the engine was being done by the vacuum created and not by steam, which itself was only the means of creating the vacuum.

Incidentally, while the name of Newcomen is immortally linked to the atmospheric principle, the originator of the principle was a man called Savery, almost unheard of, and certainly unrecognised when the name is mentioned. He evolved a shallow, say up to 18 ft, method of 'pumping' or extracting water by means of two hollow vessels, each in their turn filled with steam which was then condensed, and the vacuum thus formed sucked up the water. This was certainly not the first time (and it will certainly not be the last) when the originator is forgotten and the developer gets all the credit. Savery died in 1715 but his patent was still in force, and so Newcomen was forced into a 'partnership' of sorts.

By 1725 Newcomen engines were in general use, several interested groups from Europe coming over to see how it was done. An engraving of 1726 shows the form of valve gear using tappet valves as opposed to the rotary plug valves of the early years. By the time of the expiry of Savery's patent in 1733 the engines of Newcomen were in very widespread use, although Newcomen did not live to see some of the really big versions which later developed, having died in 1729. One of the large engines, if not the largest, was produced at Coalbrookdale around mid-century with a 6 ft 2 in. diameter cylinder 10 ft 6 in. long and weighing 6½ tons.

Technology was still in its infancy, and a major problem was in the machining of the components, particularly, as mentioned previously, the great difficulty of truly boring out the cylinders. It would be very interesting to know the variation in diameter through the length of the big cylinder at Coalbrookdale! Control valves were still independent of the cylinder and mounted in the pipework; with a cylinder of doubtful internal finish filled with hot steam which was suddenly condensed by a jet or two of cold water, efficiency was low to say the least. In all of these engines boiler pressure was very low, averaging about 16.72 lbs per square inch, not much above that of the atmosphere.

A number of engineers of the period were becoming interested in the use and facility afforded by the new steam engines, and John Smeaton (he of Eddystone Lighthouse fame) was also hooked, and in 1772 produced a list of engine components. A problem with the atmospheric engine was that, while it was ideal at this period for operating pumps, it was almost impossible to obtain a smooth rotary motion due to the very mix of steam and vacuum on which it relied. The engines were often used to operate some of the machinery now evolving, machinery which nevertheless still had a lot of wood in its construction, by raising water to tanks which when released operated water wheels that gave a far smoother rotary motion to the allied machinery.

It was at this period that James Watt (1736–1819) came on the scene. He was commissioned to repair a model of a Newcomen engine, and succeeded in not effecting a repair but actually getting it to work, a previous repairer having failed to do this. Studying what he had done, Watt concluded that the process of cooling the steam with a water jet sprayed into the cylinder was a most ineffective way of achieving an end, leaving the cylinder both wet and cold before once again receiving the hot steam. The idea of a separate condenser was born and the effectiveness of the engine leapt upwards.

A further idea was that of admitting steam to the top end of the cylinder as well as at the bottom, thus introducing 'double acting', although due to the exceptionally low pressure, a measure of atmospheric pressure assisted by the weight of the pump rods was still a factor of design and would continue to be until the eventual demise of the Newcomen engine. Having introduced a double acting principle, the top of the cylinder was required to be closed. This was achieved by the use of a cylinder cover with a central gland or 'stuffing box' for a piston rod to pass through. Thus the steam engine as we now know it was taking shape.

The design of a suitable valve gear to work the now double-acting engine was a move which Watt considered to be a work of genius, and to this end his 'parallel motion' was devised, operating in the form of a pantograph. A problem which Watt experienced – indeed all innovators have the same general problem – was that of actually financing his improvements to the engine. The first backer was a Mr Roebuck, who was a difficult type of man, and while differences were being sorted out the backer went bankrupt. Watt then visited Boulton at the Midland Soho Foundry, and to cut a long story short, Boulton took over from Roebuck and a more amicable partnership developed.

Technology was improving all the time, and Wilkinson's development of the boring machine meant more accurate cylinders. Around this time, the Newcomen/Savery patent was due to run out, and an application was made to extend it. Thus protected, a further twenty-five years took the Newcomen system to the turn of the new century, 1800. A further patent granted in 1782 protected the 'double acting' principle of the engine, but along with technology other engineers were developing in their own experiments. The parallel motion gear patent also covered an introduction, still not fully appreciated, of a step toward 'expansive working', where the steam is cut off before the end of the piston stroke and allowed to expand within the cylinder. In this early application it was noted that the engine still worked satisfactorily, although the atmospheric pressure and weight of the pump rod still played a major part. A saving in fuel costs was also noted. These costs were to play an important part in the developing costing systems related particularly to pumping engines, and later applied to the mobile steam designs.

While parallel motion lasted until the end of the stationary beam engine, another innovation (particularly applicable to the future of the steam locomotive) evolved in the North. In 1799, William Murdoch devised the eccentric, and from this simple way of operating the tappet valves came the smoothly operating slide valve; its 'D' shape covered and uncovered the inlet and exhaust ports most effectively as the rotary motion of the eccentric became linear motion for the valve movement.

While an innovator himself, Watt was still opposed to using steam by itself and at greater pressure, and on the eventual expiry of his patent the way was open for others to step in. Among his competitors was Matthew Murray, who stood back and took a long look at the way the valve gear operated on the big beam engines and at the position of the pipework and associated valves and valve gear. There was new thinking in the air. The slide valve and the eccentric could replace a mass of rods and levers. Gone was the need for tappet-operated valves at each end of the cylinder. Why not have steam ports and ways integral with the cylinder, making for one small slide valve operating over steam ports, thus simplifying the whole concept of engine valve gear? Why not associate all this with double-acting steam at much higher pressures and not associate it at all with atmospheric pressure?

Thus all the ingredients were in place for the next move in the steam saga, the move toward mobile steam in some form. However, static steam and the beam engine were to last for upward of another three quarters of a century, and indeed increased in intensity as the century progressed.

Although existing engines on the Newcomen atmospheric system still continued to hiss and gasp at many locations around the country (why change something that still worked and would last quite effectively for its particular application?), higher-pressure steam alone would dominate the new mobile thinking. As well as the slide valve and eccentric, the driving 'crank' was already well established by the turn of the new century.

While James Watt was a far-seeking innovator – indeed he had forty years earlier proposed the application of the steam engine to the propulsion of a carriage for ordinary road use (and his patent of 1784 describes such a carriage) – he seems to have had an obsession with the condensing system for the use of steam. So, while thoughts of mobile steam were filling the heads of other experimenters, Watt appears to have ignored the trend and concentrated all his efforts on the improvement of the existing system. It had been established many years before in the scientific world that 'nature abhors a vacuum', but Watt pressed on until his death in 1819.

It would be left to others to develop steam power divorced from atmospheric implications. The first of the long line to do so was Richard Trevithick, who, along with Vivian (another name lost in the mists of time), patented a vehicle that utilised the expansive power of steam alone. This vehicle was first tried on a plain highway as opposed to a rail system; it resembled an ordinary stagecoach and may be recognised as the first application of an inside cylinder and the separate crank axle.

William Murdoch, the great friend of James Watt, constructed a model of a true steam carriage of the non condensing design in 1784, the same year as Watt's patent. According to a biography of Murdoch, who at that time was in charge of mining engines at Redruth in Cornwall, the little model was tried out on the pathway leading to the church. With its spirit lamp alight under the boiler, it apparently roared down the path, where it almost collided with the Reverend, and being after dark, was taken as an emissary of the Devil himself, shaking the poor gentleman to his boots!

A second full-size attempt by Trevithick in 1802 was patented and successfully pulled 10 tons of iron a distance of 9 miles at about 5 mph. This single vertical-cylinder locomotive running on the tram road at Merthyr Tydfil was reasonably successful but it did tend to slip. Although steam was now the sole propelling force, the locomotives of the period still followed the look of the established beam engines, with the vertically operating cylinders and overhead 'rocking' arrangements. However, these early attempts were concentrated mainly on the question of adhesion, to the extent that in 1811 Mr Blenkinsop added a third rail in the form of a rack into which a gear meshed and then pulled the locomotive along without slip but with considerable rattle. This engine, pulling a load, could ascend a gradient of 1 in 15 with a load of 15 tons, something the Trevithick engine could not do. It also pulled 94 tons on the flat and had a maximum speed of 15 mph.

The rack rail was taken a step further in 1812 by the Chapman brothers, who devised a method (still used incidentally by some river ferries in Britain) of picking up and moving along a chain secured at both ends of the track. By the year of the momentous Battle of Waterloo (1815), locomotive adhesion problems had been overcome by the work of Mr Blackett of the Wylam Colliery Railway. He had experimented and found that by establishing the load on the locomotive wheels and evenly distributing it, a certain number of loaded wagons could be pulled on smooth rails without slip.

Having sorted out that hiccup, attention turned to locomotive cylinder and valve design in the attempt to make starting and control easier. It was often very difficult to start a single-cylinder engine as the cranks and associated valves were in the wrong position, so the engine had to be barred along manually until the valves were in the correct position. It was found that at 90 degrees cranks and cylinders solved that particular anomaly, but the drive was still taken to the wheels by further gears that got noisier as they inevitably wore. Chains were also tried to replace gears, and while they worked well enough, they still wore and rattled.

Again, in the year of Waterloo, we find the name of Stephenson along with Dodds (another lost individual in the saga of steam), who together patented a method of utilising crankpins actually on the wheels, although the axles were still coupled by a rattling chain. The benefits of the crankpin were thus established, introducing a regular feature of the locomotive as we now know it.

By the 1820s the form of the locomotive and its main features which we now take for granted – a knowledge of the exhaust 'blast' and blast pipe; the boiler components of smoke box, barrel and firebox with associated flue tube; the ability to move forward or backward; the distribution of weight on the axles; and the effectiveness of adhesion using smooth wheels on smooth rails, the 'D' valve and the eccentric – were all there.

Attention was now to centre on the correct use of steam entering the cylinders, and the best ways of getting it in quickly and out again when it had done its work. The quest for an effective valve operating gear was on in earnest. The opening and closing of a locomotive's valves, or 'valve events' as they are known, opens up a vast and fascinating aspect of the steam locomotive. The rotary plug valves of the early beam engines, independent of the cylinders and clicking away as the rods moved, were in essence a century and more ahead of their time when the independent 'poppett' valve appeared. At the turn of the eighteenth century, the plain 'D' valve had made its appearance and required greater understanding than the simple plug valve.

Associated with the eccentric, the 'D' valve required very little movement to pass from fully open to fully closed. The hollow of the valve passed over three slots in the flat face of the valve seat, completely isolating them from the surrounding steam. The two outer slots admitted 'live' steam from the boiler to each end of the cylinder in turn, while the wider centre slot allowed the used steam from the cylinder to escape as the sharp blast up the chimney. In so doing it also caused a draught through the fire, so making it burn brightly. The problem now set for the engineers was that of making all these 'events' happen at the correct time and position of the piston during its stroke.

In the sequence of events, the valve progressively opens one end steam port to admit steam to one end of the cylinder, while at the other end of the cylinder it flows back through the port of entry and out of the exhaust port or slot. Mention was made earlier in these notes of Watt introducing 'expansive' working of the steam. This entailed the valve closing early before the end of the piston stroke, then allowing the steam that had entered to still do work by its own expansion. The first 'D' or slide valves could not do this as they were made to exact size and thus admitted steam for the full stroke of the piston. By adding what was called 'lap' to the valve this expansive working was introduced, but in a limited form only as the expansion from the point of steam 'cut-off' during the stroke was fixed by the amount of lap. Many experiments were carried out to determine a correct amount of lap.

While lap appeared to solve one problem, it introduced another. To maintain the correct events for the valve motion, a compensation had to be introduced for the steam's early cut-off, as the lap effected not only the cut-off but also the admission of steam at the other end of the cylinder. Therefore the valve had to open earlier than it would normally have done without lap, and so 'lead' was set by moving the eccentric for much earlier opening of the valve. (In a similar way the cars and motorcycles of our youth [mine at any rate] had an 'advance' and 'retard' lever on the ignition.)

To give the required lead, the eccentrics had now to be moved from the traditional position 90 degrees in advance of the crank to some other position in excess of 90 degrees, and this angle became known as the 'angle of advance'. There are ways of determining the amount of increase but we will not complicate these jottings by going into detail. Suffice to say the complications of valve gear design were only just beginning! There was no way in the early valve gears for steam to be used with 'variable expansion', in which steam is cut off during the stroke by altering the valve travel to suit the demand, in much the same way as one changes gear in a car to suit the requirements. The locomotive could only move forward or backward or stay still with the gear, whatever its design, in 'neutral', the driver being unable to 'notch up' or 'notch back' in later terminology. The seeds of the Watt patents were all in evidence and awaiting the first shoots to bring them to maturity. Who would provide the start?

The early engines using a form of cam or the early eccentric to operate the valve now ran into a major problem. It was found that the single eccentric with a virtually direct connection to its associated valve could be set to run forward, but when it was required to reverse or go into 'back gear', the engine had difficulty in starting and in actually running. Back to the drawing board! Valves without lap were difficult enough, but valves with lap were even more of a problem. Mr Wood, the engineer of the Killingworth Railway, devised a way of allowing an eccentric to be set on the axle to enable backward running as easily as forward motion, and although prone to disarrangement, complicated and very abrupt in its action, it worked.

This invention allowed the eccentric to be moved physically around the axle to one of two positive positions, located by a slot in the eccentric that followed a pin to one or other of its extremities, one end for forward and one end for backward running. This was somewhat of a reversion to the old 'tappet' arrangement of the atmospheric engines, but it utilised the eccentric and was a step in the right direction. It became known as 'slip eccentric gear'.

Once established and found to work, for all its shortcomings, it was soon subjected to variations and modifications. Hackworth on the Liverpool & Manchester Railway devised a variation for his inside-cylindered locomotive, the eccentrics actually sliding sideways to lock on pins or studs on the axle. Considerable force was needed to move the eccentrics sideways and a separate hand gear was required to move the valves themselves when starting. It was all very complicated. A Fenton, Murray & Jackson design variation required five handles and a foot pedal to operate. The latter slid the eccentrics, two handles moved the fore and back 'grabs', two shifted the valves and one was the regulator itself. The plot thickens and the problems multiply.

During the 1830s it was becoming more and more widely recognised that steam could be used 'expansively' and not for the full stroke of the piston. Several experimenters were trying various ideas; one of the first was of using the gabs differently, closing together the open jaws to form a 'link', and different valve designs to match were introduced.

As soon as the benefits of expansive working had been realised, all designers and manufacturers hopped 'on the bandwagon' and started once again with gear to operate their valves expansively, eliminating full steam for the complete piston stroke, but being able to control the point of actual steam cut-off during the stroke. This was possible due to the valve design, where the valve overlapped the steam ports of the cylinder valve face. 'Consumption of fuel per mile' was the measure of effectiveness of this method of working.

While the 'slip' eccentric solved several problems, it introduced complications which became unacceptable. The driver had to really concentrate on which levers to move, where to facilitate reverse, and, with no cab cover, in driving rain and darkness it was

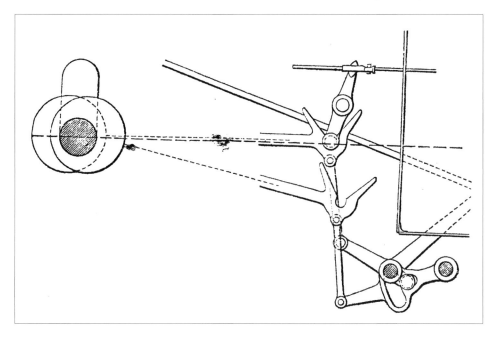

Hawthorn's is an example of what would develop into the 'Radial Gear', i.e. the Joy gear of 1879.

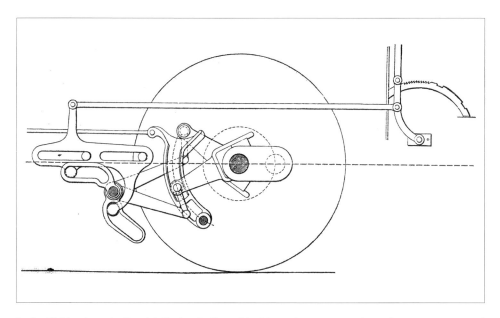

In the 1854 volume by Daniel Clarke, *Railway Machinery*, he commented on what was now termed 'Link Motion'. 'The last and most perfect embodiment of Gray's principle of the variation of travel, for working expansively, is to be found in the "Link-motion". Nothing but an impulse of genius could have given birth to this exquisite motion; and though in its first conception by Mr Williams, at one time of Newcastle, it was rude, and even impracticable, the idea was there, and it had only to be cleverly worked out by Mr Howe of the Forth Street Works to render it, in conjunction with the lap of the valve, the most felicitous acquisition to the locomotive." (Melling's, too, is a form of what developed into 'Radial Gear'.)

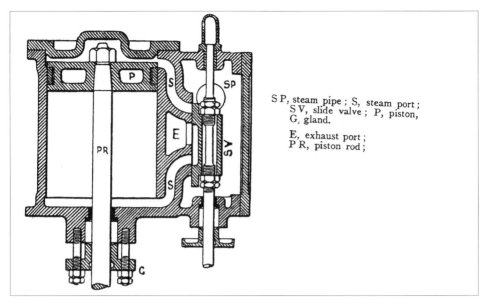

S P, steam pipe ; S, steam port ;
S V, slide valve ; P, piston,
G, gland.

E, exhaust port ;
P R, piston rod ;

A cross-section of a cylinder and valve with 'lap' – 'consumption of fuel per mile' was the measure of effectiveness of this method of working.

easy to become very confused. Some drivers took to the gear naturally, but there were some who never quite mastered it, and the enthusiasm which had greeted its introduction soon evaporated.

Abandoning the slip eccentric was not undertaken lightly, but an inevitable new line of thought was to accompany what was in effect something of a reversion to the use of the fixed eccentric. The difficulty of working as well in back gear as in fore gear returned with the fixed eccentric, and thoughts were centred on the eccentric rod and its attachment to the valve spindle. As early as 1818, J. & C. Carmichael of Dundee had faced this problem and their early experiments had produced, by the 1830s, a simple solution. This entailed a way of moving the valve to obtain steam entry at the opposite end of the cylinder for reversing, by the movement of one lever only. At the end of the eccentric rod, where it connected to the valve spindle, two 'V'-shaped forks or 'gabs' were set, one facing down and one facing up. To reverse, the lever was simply pulled back, thus disconnecting one jaw. The other jaw, while locating over its pin, actually moved the valve itself to its required position.

With only one lever to move, the driver's lot had improved but the system included some difficulty in preserving the 'lead' of the valve for reverse gear. Various designs were tried out, including one by Forrester in 1834 that had the one eccentric of the design, but included a forked eccentric rod working vertically upwards. Both rods had outward-facing 'gabs', one facing forwards and one backwards, and while it was effective in use, the noise and clanking of its operation made it quite notorious.

This gear thus outlines another requirement which was rapidly being recognised. While the 'gab' ends were still essential, thought was being given to taking the actual forked eccentric rod on a step further, and making it two separate rods. Two separate rods would mean two separate eccentrics per cylinder and so arrived, in the 1830s, the four-eccentric system which we recognise today. In the old phrase, the actual inventor or deviser of the four-eccentric system is 'lost in the mists of time'. It may be that several engineers working on the problems of 'valve events' came to the conclusion at the same time, but what is known is that the Hawthorn Brothers of Newcastle were the first to apply four eccentrics to one of their locomotives in 1837.

While this complicated manufacture, and certainly increased maintenance, it was all well compensated by the 'precision and certainty of action' of the valve gear. The gear itself now faced a number – a very great number, we could add – of variations of mechanism to utilise the new-found effectiveness. Rods and levers were employed in profusion to operate gabs working downwards, gabs working upwards, one gab down and one gab up; all manner of systems were devised. All the big names of the period are in there! Stephenson's developed a balancing form of gearing, while Bury & Co. used the underhung system of two gabs per cylinder working upwards. Buddicom, working for the Paris–Rouen Railway, had the one upward and one downward gab system. Messrs Sharp, Roberts & Co. dived in with such enthusiasm that when their design is analysed and the complications examined in detail, it is found that one of the two transverse shafts by which one pair of gabs were moved could have been dispensed with altogether and the other shaft used for both purposes.

However, development was now progressing rapidly and inevitably in these conditions there are those who are thinking far ahead of current achievements. Melling, who held several railway-associated patents, derived a mechanism which avoided the use of the eccentric altogether and, along with others acting probably independently, dabbled with what was to become known as a 'radial valve gear' (the best-known 'modern' equivalent being that by Joy, of which more later).

This gear derives its motion from a pin set in the connecting rod, the movement of which describes an ellipse. A problem with the form of the curve associated with the movement of the connecting rod was that due to the angularity of the rod, its slowest movement is at a period of rotation when the valve should move more quickly. Melling overcame this by utilising the connecting rod of one cylinder to operate the valve gear of the other. Remember, all this was occurring in the 1830s! Remember the old saying 'there is nothing new under the sun!' Still on the theme of 'nothing new', Stephenson experimented also with the piston valve in 1832, but as one of those ideas ahead of its time, it didn't catch on. Another non-starter of the period, again by Stephenson, was a 'double valve'. A variation on the slide or 'D' valve, this version had two valves on one spindle, each valve operating in the usual way but over ports at the ends of the cylinder, giving very short steam-ways on a long-stroke cylinder. With reference again to the eccentric-less valve gear designs, Stephenson summed the whole thing up by one of his favourite sayings, 'the danger of too much ingenuity', which applied very aptly to a design by Hawthorn of 1838 that included a long parallel slotted link which was rocked by the connecting rod pin, adding to the clatter of the rest of the gear.

All of these innovations were associated with the plain 'gab' gear, and, to quote another well-known phrase, used this time by Al Jolson many years later about the new 'talkie' movies: 'You ain't seen nuttin' yet!'

One innovation of the Stephensons' which did affect the design of valve gears was one introducing the steam chests, up until then on top of the cylinders in a vertical position between a pair of inside cylinders. This gave a new look to the valve gear layout in that it now dispensed with an intermediate shaft by bringing the valve spindles to the level of the crank axle. A further simplification brought the 'gabs' to be attached to the ends of the valve spindles, and the pins as part of the eccentric rods. This was the most effective design to date, being the most direct and with the fewest parts.

Despite the vertical steam chests, gabs on valve spindles or on eccentric rods, gabs working upward or downward, still the locomotives could only move forward or backward or stay still. The next thoughts to be translated to action were those concerning the variable use of steam to suit requirements and to use the expansive qualities of steam more effectively. Here once again, the field was wide open and inventions flowed in thick and fast once the concept had fired imagination.

The 'D' slide valve, at that time (the early 1830s) in common use, still had virtually no 'lap', only a minimal ¹/₁₆ in. or so to ensure that the valve adequately covered the steam ports so that the catastrophic entry of steam to both ends of the cylinders at once could not happen. With this plain valve, steam entered one end of the cylinder at the same time as the exhaust opened to dispose of the used steam from the other side of the piston. Thus steam was attempting to push the piston one way while being resisted by the used steam on the other side of the piston, which could not get out fast enough. Hence a considerable and undesirable back pressure resulted.

While an amount of back pressure is desirable as a 'cushion' at the extremity of the cylinder and piston stroke, it plays havoc with the efficiency of the locomotive should it be excessive, which in these early cases it most certainly was. Thus the emphasis was moving from getting steam into the cylinder to that of getting it out rapidly when used. So little had this been understood that when short-stroke locomotives had been introduced for 'high-speed' running on the Liverpool & Manchester Railway in 1836, the leap in fuel consumption was blamed on the short-stroke itself on the grounds that it embraced a 'mechanical' disadvantage.

By 1838 experiments were well underway, with various lengths of 'lap' up to ½ in. being tried on the Liverpool and Manchester engines. The locomotive *Lightning* was subjected to valve alterations that increased the lap from virtually nothing to ⅜ in. Thus the lap allowing steam into the cylinder at the beginning of the stroke found the exhaust port open ⅜ in., providing rapid clearance of the used steam from the other side of the piston. Speeds were notably faster, but the main improvement was in the consumption of coke, which fell by around 25 per cent.

1840 saw the locomotives *Rapid* and *Arrow* having lap increased to ¾ in., while the stroke of the valve, 3½ in., remained the same. Fuel consumption dropped from 40 lbs to 32 lbs of coke per mile, a saving of 20 per cent, pulling the same trains. If such savings could be made by simply adding an amount of 'lap' to a valve, what other methods could be used to effect further savings? Thoughts now turned to methods of cutting off steam in addition to the cut-off afforded by a considerable 'lap' amount. Could it be cut off to suit the demand on the locomotive? For example, full steam to get the train moving, then a reduction once the dead weight was rolling. It certainly could!

Experiments by John Gray at this time resulted in the first variable expansive valve gear. True, it rattled and was all slots, pins and friction, but it worked! Steam admission could be varied between 82 per cent and 46 per cent of the stroke and allowed to expand for the remaining stroke distance. *Cyclops*, the first locomotive fitted, showed a further economy of 12 per cent in fuel used. The valves had ⅞ in. lap outside and an experimental ⅜ in. inside (the latter known as 'exhaust lap'). Without going into detail, this preserved the 'lead' of the valve, which was then constant for all for all variations of cut-off. A further experiment with *Rapid*, again on the Liverpool & Manchester Railway, increased valve lap to 1 in. and valve travel to 4½ in., showing a drop in consumption again of 25 per cent. This had the effect of softening the blast by reducing the back pressure and allowing the coke to remain on the fire bars and not dragged through the tubes into the smoke box! Coupled with the design of blast-nozzles, the search for variable expansion valve gear was on in earnest.

Once the principles of 'variable expansion' had been established and Gray's efforts had been shown to work effectively, engineers and designers went to their drawing boards and got down to the task of designing according to their own pet theories. It must be admitted that there were some strange pet theories, but most of the designs actually worked, even if only after a fashion. There were two avenues to be explored in the quest for variable expansion and it depended on the point of view of the designers which route was travelled. The first route was that of obtaining the desired expansion by means of the valve gear rods themselves, externally to the cylinders and steam chest. The second was to experiment with the actual valves themselves. Double and even triple valves were tried in the quest for variable expansion, this second option being the 'internal theory'.

Around 1840, designs for variable expansion proliferated, some still with the lingering thought of one eccentric, although the use of two was by now well established, and some still dabbling with twin fork ends of the 'gab' design. With the latter, Mr Cabrey of the North Midland Railway came up with a design which extended the circular seat at the bottom of the gab jaw into a long straight slot. Applied only to the foregear gab, it certainly worked but the problem was that the 'lead' rapidly increased as the valve travel shortened.

We can see by this design that thoughts were heading in one direction, and the next inevitable step was to join both gabs face to face, open jaw to open jaw. This mode was tried by Crompton as an example, but some designers were still stuck with the single eccentric idea. Designs by Fenton had the eccentric moving on a spiral path along the axle! Another idea by Dodds of Newcastle had the eccentric moved sideways along the axle by an arrangement of wedges. All worked, but the friction and manual effort required to effect expansion meant that these designs did not catch on; although Dodd's idea saw more use than that of the others.

We come now to a period of great significance in the valve gear story. The inevitable consequence of the face-to-face gab design was described by a period writer as 'nothing but an impulse of genius could have given birth to this exquisite motion!' The two 'V' shapes of the face-to-face gabs had become a parallel slotted link, and the link motion was born from the thoughts of a Mr Williams. This typically flowing Victorian phrase was written some years after the design concept had been introduced, the first attempts being not too successful, but all could see the potential exposed by the slotted link. Williams' first efforts consisted of a straight link with a parallel slot, suspended by lugs not rods, from a pair of eccentrics which rocked the link with its sliding block attached to the valve spindle. The idea was grabbed by Howe (of the firm of Robert Stephenson) and altered to a curved link, the link itself moving up and down the sliding block as opposed to the Williams' version of moving the sliding block within the link. 1843, the year of the opening of Swindon Railway Works, saw this link motion introduced to the railway world and, as the 'Stephenson gear', adapted widely by British makers but with more reluctance worldwide.

During this period, and still associated with the gab motion, there were many and varied attempts to achieve variable expansion by redesigning the common 'D' or slide valve. There were indeed designs, and one by Nasmyth is a good example; it combined a slotted link, two gabs (one up and one down), and a double valve, one of the latter working on the back of the other. The use of the double or superimposed valve may be split into three methods or classes. These are tappet valves, screw-set valves and lever-set valves. The Nasmyth version quoted above is an example of the latter, as the double valve mentioned was set at the Works and not affected by the 'notching up' when running, nor could it be adjusted in any way outside of further attention at the Works.

An example of the tappet valve system is that introduced in 1840 to the French St Germain Railway. This comprised of an ordinary 'D' valve with connecting holes to a plate mounted on its back. Cams and fingers controlled the movement of the plate, checking the plate and covering the connecting holes before the lower valve had completed its full stroke. Originally designed for stationary engine use, its application to the locomotive, particularly at high speed, was not really a success even though the top plate and thus the cut-off could be adjusted while running. Slackness of fit and the continual jarring of the cam mechanism required very high maintenance and as such greatly increased costs. It was yet another example which could not survive.

An even more complicated valve was patented in 1842 by Messrs Lagarman & Dequoy of Lille, to overcome a snag with the St Germain valve. The mechanism only operated the valve system of cut-off for half the stroke, and the 1842 patent covered control for the complete stroke.

It also introduced the curse of valve gear design – complication, which in turn leads to increased friction, more moving parts and increased rattle. To ensure cover for the completed stroke, a second holed plate was interposed between the valve and the first plate, leading to three valves working in conjunction. To operate the second plate, another eccentric was required! Once again, too much ingenuity had been applied to effect a result. It worked, but that is all that can be said in its favour.

Valves working on valves seemed to be the 'flavour of the month' around 1842, and the work of Mr Bedries (whose name repeats through the railway patent book) included a design of expansion valve which combined a cylindrical valve operated by a left- and right-hand opposed screw thread which controlled steam to an ordinary 'D' valve. The cylindrical valve was in two pieces on one spindle, the turning of which brought the two pieces closer together or separated them depending on rotation of the spindle. There were problems with this design, modified again by Mr Meyer of Mulhausen, who reintroduced the valve actually on the back of the main 'D' valve, but still operated by the opposed screw threads. The modification introduced another source of movement to valve gears, in this case the use of a lever attached to and deriving its motion from that of the crosshead.

Yet a further modification to the Meyer valve, itself used with considerable success in France, was that effected back across the Channel by Nasmyth, Gaskell & Co., who included the separate screw-operated portion as part of the actual 'D' valve, a move which reduced the fatigue factor associated with screws. On all of these designs the actual fore and back motion of the valves still relied on the open-jawed gab worked by the usual eccentrics. One of the most significant moves, however, was that of introducing the relative movement of the crosshead to that of the eccentric. This factor was ripe for further development, and, coupled with the vastly superior slotted link *á la* Stephenson, developments were progressing.

Almost immediately after the benefits of the slotted link were realised there developed two methods of its adoption, and realisation of the extreme sensitivity of the use of the link in what is really a heavy engineering environment. Of critical importance is not only the way the link is supplied within the mechanism, but the length and positions of the attached rods of eccentric lifting and/or support arrangements. The two methods mentioned above are firstly, the link is suspended from a fixed point as a 'stationary' link, in which the mechanism lifts the link vertically over a sliding block which controls the valve spindle. In the former stationary link it is the sliding block which is moved up or down within the curved link, both versions of link giving the necessary 'expansion' cut-offs to the valve travel.

Design of valve gear now entered a fascinating stage as it was found that the positioning of eccentric rods on the link and even the length of the rods themselves had a dramatic effect on the 'valve events'. Even the suspension of the link was a critical location relative to rods and moving block. Very careful work on the drawing board followed any proposed design and a mechanism nominally designed by Gooch in 1843 was claimed to be virtual perfection. Why the gear was designed is somewhat of a mystery (the first of several). The Stephenson link motion was known to work well and Stephenson was known to be a fierce opponent of the broad gauge! Was it to avoid the question of using Stephenson gear? As in the case of the Stephenson gear, was the name attached that of the designer, and who actually designed the Gooch version? Daniel Gooch's brother was reputedly the first to actually use the design on the London & South Western Railway in 1843, and Daniel Gooch had the services of the ingenious Crompton and of Surrock, both to become quite renowned engineers in their own right when they had departed from the Great Western. Was it mostly their work? We shall never know.

The gear was, however, very successful and was applied in its perfected form to the *Great Britain*. This was at a time when opposition to the broad gauge was beginning to bite, and *Great Britain* was used in experiments on resistance before the Gauge Commissioners. Starting with valve lap of 1 in., ½ in. lead and a valve travel of 4¾ in., it was desired to effect cut-off and expansion earlier in the cycle, but to retain as near as possible to the point when release occurred. This was achieved by increasing the lap to 1¼ in. and the lead altered to ⅜ in. It is recorded that this greatly improved performance.

Gooch gear employed the stationary link, just swinging on support hangers, and was rocked by two eccentrics. Expansion was controlled by moving the radius block up or down in the link. The Stephenson gear was of the shifting link type, in which expansion is effected by moving the link itself over the radius block, the link also being rocked by two eccentrics for forward and reverse movement.

There were still those who were beavering away in the background, convinced that rocking either type of link should not require the services of two eccentrics; one should be sufficient. So, in 1844 along came Mr Egide Walschaert of the Belgian State Railway.

Mention was made earlier in these notes of the very significant step taken in valve gear operation when the motion of the crosshead was used in conjunction with that of the eccentric. This step, once established as quite operable, delighted the hearts of the exponents of gear driven by one eccentric only. One eccentric could now be abandoned for a simple outside crank, for less friction than an eccentric, far less weight and equal effectiveness.

The first effort by Walschaert was really an additional step away from the use of the 'gab' as the link resembled two face-to-face gabs with a slot at top and bottom and an enlarged central opening. The eccentric rod was fitted with two pins, one pin at a time being located in either the bottom slot for forward gear, or the top slot for reverse. The central opening was necessary to give freedom to the movement of the pin not in use. In consequence 'notching up' in the true sense of the word was not possible, and there was literally no 'mid gear'-position.

This example of Gooch Valve Gear is preserved in STEAM, the museum of the Great Western Railway at Swindon. It is from the broad gauge 8 ft single *Lord of the Isles*. The 8 ft driving wheels from the locomotive are also displayed at the museum.

As with all innovations, it did not take long before modifications were introduced to improve the performance of the gear. Subjected to modifications in 1848 and again in 1849 by Van Waldegg, the need for the enlarged central slot in the 'link' was disposed with, and a true link added to the format. The link was now rocked by the attached eccentric rod, which did not need to be lifted or lowered as with the former design. The main components of the gear had now established themselves in both name and use, and modern Walschaert gear has the same names, although slightly differently arranged. In many instances, in its worldwide use, the single eccentric is now superseded by an outside crank, but the motion of the crosshead is still used as an adjunct to the crank and still essential for correct operation.

As valve gears continued to develop, so the locomotives themselves became bigger and heavier, and steam pressure continued to increase. It soon became apparent that the plain 'D' or slide valve was becoming a problem, brought about by increased sizes and steam pressures. The steam in the valve chest waiting to be directed by the movement of the valve acts directly on the back of the valve, thereby pressing it down onto the valve face. Increased pressures and size meant greater difficulty moving the valve on its face, and consequently greater friction when it moved. Some way of relieving this pressure on the valve was required and the result was the 'balanced' slide valve. Balancing entails some method of positively reducing the area of the back of the valve on which steam pressure is applied. This was achieved by mounting directly above the valve a flat, polished 'pressure plate' parallel to the valve face. The back of the valve was grooved either in a square or a circle enclosing an area at the back of the valve. Into the grooves were set spring-loaded, ground and polished iron segments (square) or a solid ring (circle) which were held against the pressure plate by the action of the springs. In this way steam was sealed away from the areas enclosed by the segments or ring, and could only apply sufficient pressure to keep the valve against the valve face. The pressure applied was such that the valve could still lift as required to allow trapped water to escape before it could result in a knocked-out cylinder, the segments or ring compressing into its groove as the valve lifted.

A development of the design introduced by Stephenson in 1832 which was virtually unaffected by steam pressure on its back, but which did not catch on, was the piston valve. This valve operates in a cylinder in exactly the same way as a slide valve, having the same attributes of 'lap' and 'lead'. As with the slide valve, it was subjected to many innovations and different design features during its development, all changes seemingly performing well according to the design objective. Any form of valve gear can use any form of valve, and the number of designs of piston and slide valves must almost equal the vast number of associated valve gears.

The 'radial' type of valve gear has already been mentioned; it derives its motion from the elliptical path followed either by a component of the engine itself, such as the connecting rod, or even one eccentric. An example of the latter is that by Hackworth in 1859. This had a short eccentric rod working vertically, its end terminating with a die block working in two vertical guides. The valve spindle was pinned to the rod at a point between the block and the eccentric. The guides could be moved around a pivot point, thus tilting the ellipse travelled by the valve spindle pin in the short eccentric rod, thereby altering the valve travel.

Marshall patented a variation on the John Wesley Hackworth gear during 1879, but probably the most famous is that of Joy, which is distinctive in having no eccentric or crank, its motion being derived solely from a pin positioned about one third of the way along the connecting rod measured from the crosshead.

As with the Hackworth gear, a swivelling guide is the only component moved during 'notching up' and lightness and simplicity were the main advantages claimed. The disadvantages include a potential weakness in the connecting rod where the pin is located, and from which all movement is derived, thus putting additional loading on the connecting rod. The movement of the frame relative to the wheels when running upsets the valve events, and thus negates an advantage of theoretically greater accuracy of valve events, which includes quicker opening than comparative link motions.

Another valve motion which does not use the now familiar curved expansion link is that of Baker. While still a form of Walschaert gear, it replaces the link with levers, one of which is a 'bell crank' or right-angled lever. The use of such an arrangement eliminates any form of sliding surface (as with link and block) as all components are swung or pivoted on pins, which may be readily and cheaply renewed. Baker gear was the popular choice during the American years of steam, and was also used worldwide but did not find much favour in a Britain dominated by conventional Walschaert and Stephenson gear.

From a gear with no link to a gear with two links (and thus more friction) – we now look at Jones's variation of Walschaert. The ordinary Walschaert gives constant lead for all cut-offs, but the Jones version has a horizontal curved link in which runs the top pin of the combination lever, thus giving variable lead, the other link being in the usual vertical position.

In later years, particularly with the development of the really gigantic American locomotives (some built to loading gauge dimensions bigger than the original Great Western broad gauge and still on 4 ft 8½ in. gauge track!), a requirement for increasing power output at high speed with economical performance introduced a development known as 'limited cut-off'. The method of achieving this was to increase the 'lap' of the valve, thus shortening the cut-off even more and giving more expansion time. The largest lap possible and the largest valve travel are the ingredients. Above about 60 per cent cut-off, it was difficult to actually start the train moving with the cranks in certain positions. Once again, a fiddle around the valves solved the problem, with secondary small ports in the valve liners which allowed steam to enter the main steam passages in advance of normal. As speed built up, these auxiliary ports became inoperative.

With all valve gears using slide (or 'D') valves, and the higher pressure piston valves, the valve events in terms of admission of steam and its subsequent exhaust per stroke are inevitably tied together. While rearrangements of lap and lead will alter the events to a greater or lesser degree, in all cases one alteration for admission has a direct effect on exhaust and vice versa. Over the years, with the steam locomotive well established, the advent of the motor vehicle on the roads of the world introduced a new concept of valve operation. With 'inlet' and 'exhaust' also required for the internal combustion engine, cam-operated valve gear and poppet valves became another experimental course for the locomotive engineer.

Applied to marine and stationary steam engines quite successfully – indeed, James Watt engines had a form of them in the early years of high pressure steam – the 'poppet' valve was resurrected for the steam locomotive by Dr Hugo Lentz in 1905. Very successfully introduced, the poppet valve became a standard on the Austrian State Railways, but the First World War interfered with its general application elsewhere.

While operation of poppet valves can be through the conventional Walschaert-type valve gear, thus becoming 'OC'- or 'oscillating cam'-driven, the 'RC' or 'rotary cam' dispensed entirely with the conventional rods, eccentric- or crank-operated, and relied on a smoothly rotating camshaft, as in the internal combustion engine. Designs by Capprotti and Cossart were introduced in the 1920s, but were still in effect a 'halfway house' to the ideal, some problems continuing from 'link' gear days, all requiring redesigned cams or additional components. However, this was a step in the right direction, with inlet and exhaust events separately controllable within limits for the first time.

The Great Western Railway experimented with a 'Capprotti'-geared locomotive (*Caynham Court*) during the period (again interrupted by a world war), but the locomotive remained a 'one-off', the experiment being monitored but not continued. The locomotives of the Great Western Railway continued with their Stephenson link and Walschaert adaptations until the end of official steam.

DEVELOPMENT OF VALVE GEAR – ANCIENT AND MODERN EXAMPLES

The following is a simplified outline of some of the other designs of valve gear up to the official demise of the steam locomotive itself. There are a number of existing books detailing the operation of all variations. Although the Stephenson and Walschaert valve gears were the designs used almost exclusively by the railways of Britain, there were a number of other designs on the market, some evolving much later in the development of the steam locomotive.

The two mentioned are examples of what were known as 'link' motions, where a slotted link or quadrant is used, but in the quest for the best system for controlling the steam entering and leaving the cylinder many others were tried, along with the developing locomotive itself.

A very early contemporary of Walschaert and Stephenson designs was the 'Gooch' gear of the Great Western, which existed in the broad gauge Great Western era. Another contemporary, the 'Allen' gear, used a straight slot link. In some respects the Allen has an advantage over both Stephenson and Walschaert. The next three described are known as 'radial' gears.

The 'Hackworth' gear, invented in 1859, uses straight rocking guides and an eccentric which works vertically and to which the valve rod is pivoted. Twenty years after came a variation of the Hackworth in the 'Marshall' gear, with a different arrangement of operating rods but still with the vertically operating eccentric. This variation was followed by the 'Joy' gear in 1879. Dispensing with the eccentric altogether, this was again a follow-on design based on the principle of the Hackworth. Curved guides

Reversing gear – a replica of Stephenson's *Rocket* locomotive of 1829.

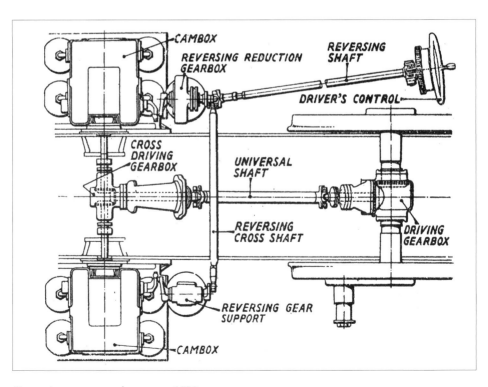

Caprotti rotary cam valve gear, *c.* 1920s.

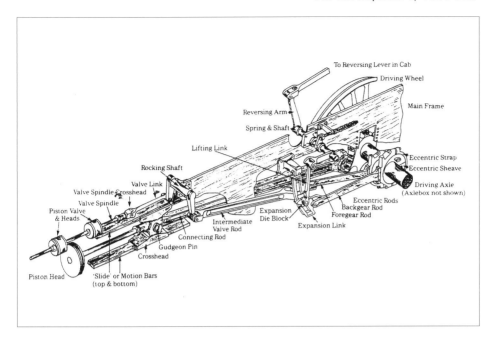

Stephenson valve gear, Great Western two-cylinder locomotives. Sectional view of right-hand main frame, illustrating the 'inside' valve gear and 'outside' piston and crosshead.

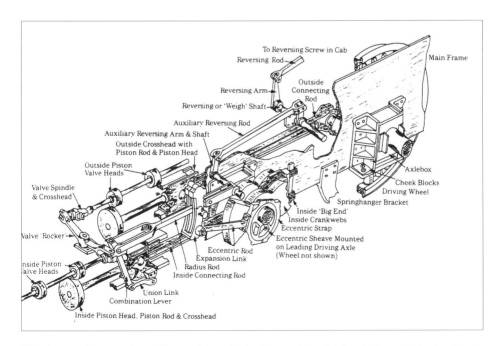

Walschaert valve gear, Great Western four-cylinder locomotives. Sectional view of right-hand main frame, illustrating the 'inside' valve gear for the 'inside' and 'outside' pistons and crossheads.

controlled a combining link activating from a connecting link obtaining its motion from a large pivot pin located actually through the locomotive connecting rod. Another gear which does not use the link and is popular in America is the 'Baker' gear. This, like the modern Walschaert, utilises the motion of the crosshead for its operation through levers and a bell crank to control the valve spindle. These give fixed lead for all 'cut-offs'. 'Jones' gear (1922), again a Walschaert variation, gives variable 'lead' for all cut-offs. Steam is not always entering the cylinder for the full stroke of the piston. This gives good economy of coal and water, and the gear gives a known 'cut-off' point depending on operating conditions. Full steam for starting can be reduced once moving by adjusting the cut-off point, using the steam expansively. Again, following the Walschaert design, 'Beames' gear (around 1924) saves the breakage problem of the Joy connecting rod pin connection by using a return crank and gear on the outside to operate inside cylinders and valves through a rocker arrangement.

All the gears previously described control one valve for one cylinder. With the use of horizontal rockers, two sets of gear can control three or four cylinders, two outside the locomotive frames and one or two inside. There are a number of variations of both Stephenson and Walschaert in addition to those listed. The adjustment of the valve gears listed may be by lever, a screw arrangement or by steam itself, giving a range of cut-off points during the piston stroke to suit the running conditions from stationary to full speed. The lever control worked in a toothed rack, the percentage cut-off position clearly marked, but, as with the experienced car driver who knows when to change gear up or down, the loco driver knew when to 'notch up or down' from his 'feel' of the locomotive. The lever in the forward position gave full forward motion and a full cylinder on every stroke, reducing back to the centre of the rack for virtually no valve movement from a stationary engine, and moving backward in the rack for opposite travel direction.

The screw version was hand-wheel controlled, a pointer moving over a marked top plate as the wheel was turned to its required locking position for the selected cut-off, as with the lever. The steam-controlled version was not widely used as it is recorded that it tended to 'creep' from its set position to full forward or back gear setting, thus it was not particularly popular.

The Second World War again delayed things and the premature end of official steam really sealed the fate of any development. A modern design of steam locomotive with computer-controlled poppet valve events – what developments we missed out on!

11
VALVE GEARS AND THE VALVES

The many valve gears make a fascinating if confusing study, but what of the valves which they control? There are also a number of different designs.

The two main designs were the 'D' or slide valve, a flat valve working over a flat surface, and the piston valve, two valve heads on a single spindle working in a cylinder. Other designs which had some use were 'poppet' or cam-operated valves (working in a similar fashion to those of the internal combustion engine), Caprotti and Cossart being two examples.

Two other confusing descriptions are 'inside' or 'outside' admission. This has nothing to do with steam pipes inside or outside the smoke box but how the steam, already in the steam chest, is controlled by the valve.

The slide valve is kept flat against the valve face by the pressure of steam on its back, thus 'outside' the valve. A piston valve can be either 'outside' or 'inside' admission. 'Outside' admission means outside both valve heads, exhausting via the centre between the heads. 'Inside' admission (usually the case) means inlet to the centre sections, exhaust around the ends.

The piston valve, allied to Walschaert gear, may be easily identified by the connection of the 'radius rod' position on the 'combination lever'. Above the valve spindle link pin means inside admission, below the link pin means outside admission.

There are a number of variations within the basic Stephenson and Walschaert designs, each with benefits. For example, the eccentric rods may be crossed, thus being attached to the link in reversed position, i.e. instead of the bottom, now at the top. Differences depend on the duty of the locomotive. The advantage with a passenger locomotive is that it usually travels very fast forwards, but usually only comparatively slowly backwards, whereas a small shunting locomotive probably travels comparatively slowly in both directions during working.

There are complete books on the subject of 'valve gears'. This little note only really scratches the surface of what could be a complex study!

Setting valves on a standard British Rail locomotive, *c.* 1955. The special plant in Swindon's 'A' shop allowed the wheels to be 'inched' round at the push of a button to ensure correct marking and adjustment of the valve travel.

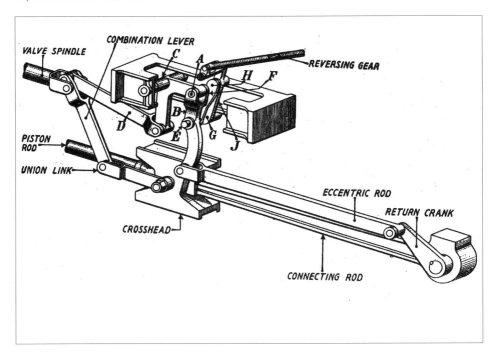

The Baker gear, favoured by the Americans.

THE ASSOCIATED VALVES

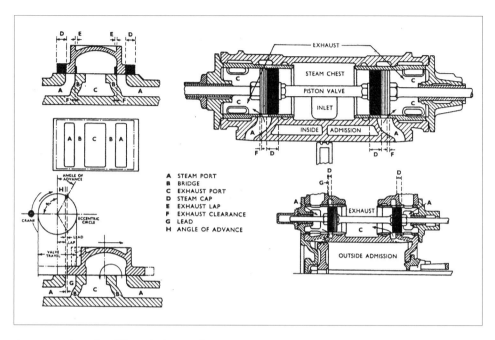

A cross-section of a slide and piston valve.

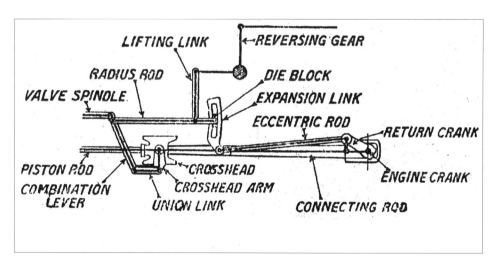

Modern Walschaert gear: outside admission.

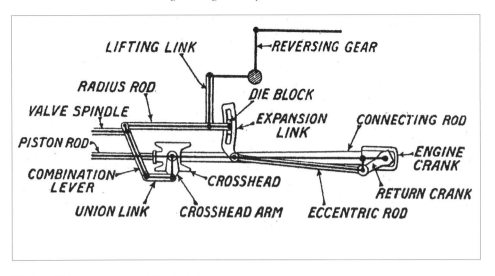

Modern Walschaert gear: inside admission.

12

THE INDICATOR DIAGRAM – A NOTE ON WHAT IT IS AND WHAT IT DOES

This little note just serves to introduce an instrument and procedure for determining the effectiveness of the steam used to power the locomotive. It needs to be just a note, as complete books have been written on the subject.

The 'lap' of the valve is explained by the previous descriptions, and the other important factor is 'lead'. It should be remembered that on reaching the end of the cylinder, the piston has, for a millisecond, got to stop on front or back 'dead centre' to reverse direction for the return stroke. 'Lead' is the amount the valve 'inlet' is open when the piston is in this position. This allows steam to enter and act as a cushion for the directional change of the piston just before the piston reaches the end of the stroke. Different valve gears give different results; some retain constant 'lead' and some variable 'lead' as the gear is 'notched' up or down as the reversing screw or lever is operated.

For a valve without lap, the eccentric that controls the length of stroke of the valve will need to be set on the axle at 90 degrees to the relevant crank. With lap, the valve will be delayed in opening at the correct position of the crank, so the eccentric would need to be in advance of 90 degrees to compensate. The amount is the 'lead' plus the amount of lap. The angle of 90 degrees plus lap plus lead is known as the 'angle of advance'. Note that if the valve is operated via a 'rocker', i.e. pivoted in the centre with the eccentric rod connected to the bottom and the valve spindle to the top, the eccentric has to *follow* the relevant crank.

The events which take place in the locomotive cylinder have to be as follows with any design of valve.

1. A period of admission of live steam up to the valve setting 'cut-off'.
2. A period of expansion of the steam up to the point of release.
3. A release period for the used steam.
4. A period of compression after the valve has closed.
5. A brief admission of live steam before the piston commences its working stroke.

The value must be such that it

(a) closes both steam ports when in its central position;
(b) allows steam only to one end of the cylinder at a time;

(c) opens to exhaust at one end of the cylinder, at least at the time of opening, to allow steam into the other end.

The 'indicator' instrument was not a twentieth-century innovation but was well established by several designs by various makers.

This note will not go into detailed analysis of results but will just describe the bare function: a diagram being produced on a paper drum which rotated as the loco cylinder operated on its normal function. It was easier to use the instrument on a static test bed, the loco running at required speeds but not actually going anywhere, but an outdoor run, against weather, etc., gave probably truer results.

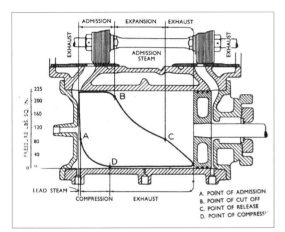
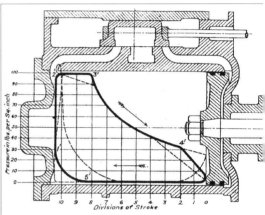

Indicator diagrams superimposed on locomotive cylinders, showing action of steam. On the left is an example of a piston valve. 'A' is the point of admission. 'B' is the point of cut-off. 'C' shows the point of release, and 'D' shows the point of compression. On the right is an example of a slide valve.

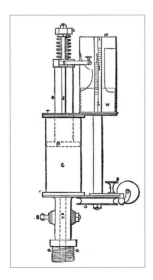

Messrs Maudslay's indicator.

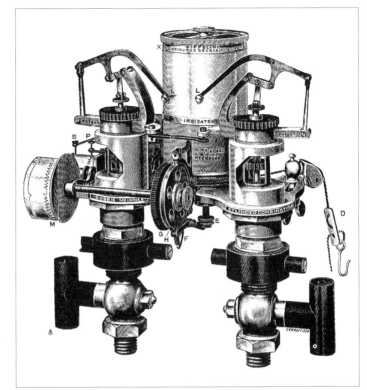

Dobbie McInnes' indicator for locomotives. The principle is still the same as the earlier versions, but this double example records both forward and backward strokes of the piston at regular intervals, on a paper roll, with speed and time.

Method of applying indicator. A draughty perch! American railroading *c*. 1890s.

Note: In use, the results from actual tests – and many are to be found in published books – only give a basic resemblance to the crisp shapes shown in the examples above, although the main features are identifiable.

13
LOCOMOTIVE TESTING AND THE TEST PLANT ON WHICH IT IS DONE

One of the sights fondly remembered by the author was that of locomotive testing on the static plant in the 'A' shop complex. Working for a short period 'on the bench' adjacent to the plant, the sight of a Castle class locomotive, firmly anchored at both ends, travelling at 75 mph, connecting rods just a blur yet going nowhere, is a sight never forgotten, viewed through the open door to the plant. The idea for a test plant at Swindon came from Mr Churchward, but he was not the originator; plants had been devised by others in this period, around 1900. A new locomotive or one which had been through a 'heavy repair' was required to be 'run in' before entering traffic, so while all sorts of information could be obtained from a 'static' test, and running the locomotive assisted with the 'running in' process, it was early decided that such information was limited as the actual 'in service' conditions could not be fully duplicated by the results so obtained. One benefit which (in the early years only) could be obtained when a locomotive was being tested was that the adjacent workshop air compressors could be switched off, as the rollers on which the locomotive wheels ran also powered a duplicate set of air compressors.

However, for a period the whole testing process wound down, until about forty or fifty years later, with a 'modernised' and extended plant, the sights that the author remembered came to the fore as new thinking to be applied to the new plant, and in the 1940s and 1950s the plant was used extensively. After Nationalisation, comparisons of the various locomotive designs assisted with the design of the 'standard' range of locomotives. With hindsight, the question arises; was it all worth it? The life of the 'standards' was to be cut short by 'dieselisation', and steam development stopped.

The life cycle of the test plants was not restricted to that at Swindon. The Americans came up with the same conclusions – recorded as follows.

The early 1890s saw the establishment of a test plant at the American Purdue University. After considerable expense from several installations, a first flush of enthusiasm from various major railway companies at the detail which could be obtained soon appeared to cool. An analysis of conditions in the running areas, damp rails, wind, condition of track, inclines, etc. led to, as recorded, 'the plants constructed gradually [falling] into disuse'. What a waste!

Information which could be obtained from a test included

1. Traction dynamometer record of draw-bar stress under any load.
2. A small dynamometer records the power required to move the valves.
3. Indicators show the steam distribution in the cylinder and pressure in the steam chest.
4. A calorimeter shows the dryness or otherwise of the steam.
5. A speed recorder denotes the speed attained.
6. Gauges indicate the rarification (vacuum) in the smoke box and ash pan.
7. The heat of the smoke box gases is ascertained with a pyrometer. Balancing was tested and valves adjusted, weight of coal and amount of water was measured. The results showed units of work per ton of coal per horsepower hour.

With different criteria now being established at the new plant at Swindon, this was co-ordinated with information obtained from actual running conditions and the special updated 'dynamometer-car' being towed or static when used with the test plant itself.

THE LOCOMOTIVE TESTING PLANT

The earlier Test Plant at Swindon.

The later Swindon Plant – extended and updated, no longer powering air compressors when in use. This is *c.* 1950, as remembered by the author.

A running test; immediately behind the tender is the early dynamometer car. The locomotive front structure is shielding instruments and testing staff monitoring the various recordings.

Opposite above: This shows the early Great Western test plant, *c.* 1900. The loco is a very early 'Dean Goods' with a round-top firebox. Dome and safety valve covers missing. [The usual Test Plant picture is of the modern plant with a 'Castle' Class at full speed.]

Opposite below: The American test plant at Purdue University, *c.* 1890.

14

LOCOMOTIVE WHEELS – DESIGN AND MANUFACTURE

The early years of the steam locomotive were forcing the development of the existing technology. Iron, brass and bronze could be cast and wrought iron could be worked in the realms of the blacksmith. At the time of the 1804 loco of Richard Trevithick, steel in bulk was fifty years in the future, so the engineers of the day, all on a steep learning curve, had to use what was to hand; thus wheels were of cast iron, not really an ideal material for the purpose. The little wheels of tram and plate way trucks, horse drawn, had always been made of cast iron, but the locomotive would require something stronger. However, cast iron was the material used for a number of years to come. The general casting procedure is basically the same as that illustrated in Chapter 23 of this book. All patterns of the period were of wood, although technology has advanced since this.

As the locomotives got bigger, wheels also became bigger, so it was found that wrought iron was now a better proposition. This iron could not be cast and wheels had to be fabricated, thus a new skill was developed by the blacksmith. A smithied wheel, and 7 ft diameter was by no means the biggest (illustrations show an 8 ft pair of wheels on the crank axle of the Great Western broad gauge *Lord of the Isles*), was built up by a team of very skilled smiths. Wheel sections were made, each comprising a portion of the outer rim, one spoke and a wedge of section to form the centre. Each section in turn was brought to white heat in the blacksmiths' fires and the sparkling sections were 'smith welded' together to form a wheel. A disc, again white hot, was smithied and welded over the centre or hub of the wheel on both sides.

There were at the earlier period no steam hammers (that awaited Nasmyth in 1854), so a form of 'drop hammer' is recorded in a notebook of the period. This formed a frame like a French revolution guillotine; a bottom block with ropes hauled a second block suspended above on the ropes, which dropped with a hammer blow onto the white-hot sections below on the bottom block, a good aid in forming the wheel sections.

An iron tyre was rolled to the section of a flanged wheel rim, machined and then shrunk onto the wheel. In the early years Gooch was concerned about the rapid tyre wear when running, so he had a bar of steel rolled in with the iron tyre. The steel made the wheel too hard on the wearing surface to be machined on the lathe with the carbon steel tools of the period, and grinding was the only way of machining the surface.

This was very dangerous in itself, as there were no bonded grit grinding wheels, only wheels made from natural stone, hand cut. A flaw in a rapidly revolving natural stone grinding wheel could cause it to disintegrate in use, often decapitating the operator.

The wrought iron wheel differed from the cast wheel in that the latter was cast as, very often, an elaborate disc; the fabricated version, which was considerably bigger in most cases, had spokes. The cast iron wheel must have worn quite rapidly as cast iron is a softer material which is much easier to machine than its wrought iron successor. Some of the wrought iron wheels must have been a nightmare to machine. One such pair of wheels made for a locomotive built to a Brunel specification (which itself was faulty to start with) for the Great Western were 10 ft in diameter. Making the wheel must have been difficult enough and there is a record of one of the contractors attempting a design to suit Brunel's specification having to hand-chip a section out of a workshop wall to accommodate an 8 ft diameter wheel on the face plate of the biggest lathe he possessed, which had been positioned too near the wall.

Mention was made earlier of casting with elaborate shapes but it must be stated that even cast wheels had spokes; those by Edward Bury had either a wrought iron tyre or were cast solid with the flange included. Adams had a complete wheel with a wood centre, followed by Mansell whose carriage wheels lasted out the century. Smith had a solid wrought disc wheel. Haddon & Wharton included wood inserts in their designs while Hague, Losh & Bell and Bramah & Fox had quite decorative spoke arrangements, all in wrought iron.

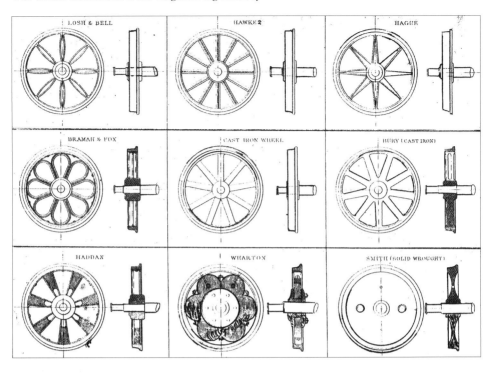

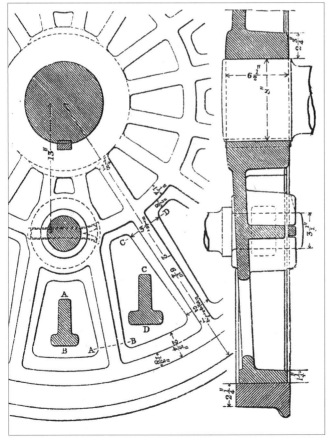

Above: 1850s wheel designs made in various metals, excluding steel.

Left: An 1855 design.

Hydraulic wheel press arranged with face plate for pulling tyres off wheels, *c.* 1893.

Lathe for large locomotive wheels, *c.* 1893.

Driving wheel pattern made by the author in 2006 for the rebuild Steam Rail Motor at the Great Western Society at Didcot. Cast in steel, 4 ft diameter. The basic method of casting is still the same now as in Trevithick's day!

The 8 ft diameter wheels of the broad gauge locomotive *Lord of the Isles*, displayed in Swindon's STEAM Museum (with Mr Brunel!). Wrought iron smith-made wheels.

A close-up of a crank on the axle, also smith-made in wrought iron.

Pearson's tank loco for the Bristol & Exeter Railway. It had 9 ft diameter driving wheel and dated from about 1873 –but the class was from the 1854 broad gauge.

15
LOCOMOTIVE SPRINGS – DESIGN AND MANUFACTURE

A note in this book later on explains how springs for locomotives were made but when and how were they applied? It appears that before about 1825 the early locomotives were not sprung, their axles running in fixed plain bearings. That is not to imply that no one actually tried to apply springing, but if they did they ran into a problem.

Many of the early locomotives, as shown by their illustrations, were either based on the vertical-acting 'beam' system or had cylinders working on rods or crankpins either vertically upwards or downwards. If springing had been applied to the axle boxes, which could be made to slide in guides to take advantage of the damping effect of springs, the designers were in for a surprise; as with the piston acting vertically and the axle box also free to move vertically, the driver was in for a very bouncy ride with each stroke of the system!

Subsequent locomotive designs from about 1820 had cylinders progressively coming down at decreasing angles until by the 1830s they were horizontal; indeed, drawings of Stephenson's *Planet* design (probably drawn after the locomotive was built) show the cylinder angle below the horizontal, up at the back toward the driving wheels.

Locomotives from this period to the end of commercial construction have cylinders on the horizontal and 'leaf' or plate springs, similar to those shown in the early illustrations. Initially each axle box had its own spring, but over the years developments led to the attempt, when balancing the weights over each pair of wheels, to link the actions of all the springs to obtain an even smoother ride.

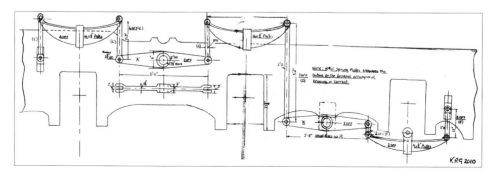

Compensated spring gear on a plate frame (1898).

A 'leaf' spring.

Coil springs, not often used for wheel sets.

Frames, wheels, tyres, axle boxes and springs – how they did it: the American way, *c.* 1890.
Top: Compensated spring gear on a bar frame. *Middle left:* Balanced cast iron wheels with
wrought iron or steel tyres. *Middle right:* A section of tyre with retaining rings. The tyre was first
shrunk on. *Above left:* A driving journal-box, with brass bearings in a cast iron or steel axle box.
There was an underkeep for an oil pad. *Above right:* Fitting an axle box.

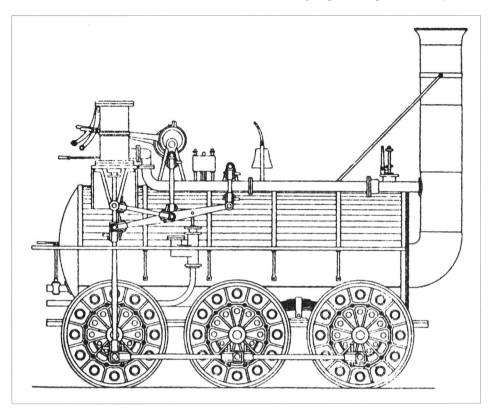

The *Royal George*, 1827. No spring on the vertically driven wheel.

By the late 1820s, with horizontal cylinders (for example, on the *Planet*) springing was a must, although 'balancing' attempts had not yet really caught on. Stockton & Darlington's *Royal George* as late as 1827 had cylinders acting vertically downward on a 0-6-0 wheel format. The cylinders acted on the rear wheels, which apparently were not sprung, but the centre and leading wheels had an 'upside down' spring acting between them.

16
LOCOMOTIVE AXLE BOX DESIGN

In the early years axle boxes and rotating axles were producing little heat as the speed of the locomotive was slow, so cast iron was the designed material, with melted tallow or whale oil as the lubricant, though vegetable oil was also used in the days before mineral oil became available around the 1880s. The first boxes were fixtures, firmly attached to the frame of the loco, the frame usually of wood. The frame section of these notes will show how the frame developed, and with it the provision for the axle box to move up and down under the later influence of the spring. On the early bar frames, the provision was by extensions under the frame, which were known as 'horns'. Thus, even with the later plate frame, the name stuck. The plate frame needed guides for the axle box so these were christened 'horn blocks', riveted or bolted to the plate frame.

As speeds increased, so lubricated cast iron bearings were running into heating problems. In response, a 'yellow metal' insert in the shape of half a cylinder was inserted into the top of the cast iron box, about 1½ in. thick at the top. By the 1850s thoughts had turned to using wrought iron boxes, and experiments with 'Muntz' metal (a zinc/copper brassy alloy) continued. It was found that wrought iron did not wear well, so chilled/toughened cast iron returned cast iron to favour.

Lubrication was by tallow and oil, with siphon tubes and a wick inserted in an oil reservoir in the top of the axle box. A tray at the bottom of the axle box retained the oil in the box, often with a pad which soaked up oil in bearing contacts.

With the introduction of volume steel following the designs of Bessemer, it became inevitable that steel axle boxes were not too far into the future. There were thus many designs of cast iron which all worked adequately until the general acceptance of the steel box. This developed into the steel box with white metal (a bearing material) on the moving faces that fitted the horn blocks and often with a large box 'tray' under the axle journal, containing a spring-loaded special pad that kept the journal lubricated.

The Great Western used a thick felt strip in the under-tray (known as a 'keep'), also spring loaded, but a very effective pad was the design known as an 'Armstrong Oiler', a large frame in the keep supporting a pad which resembles a floor mop, the frame and pad being one unit.

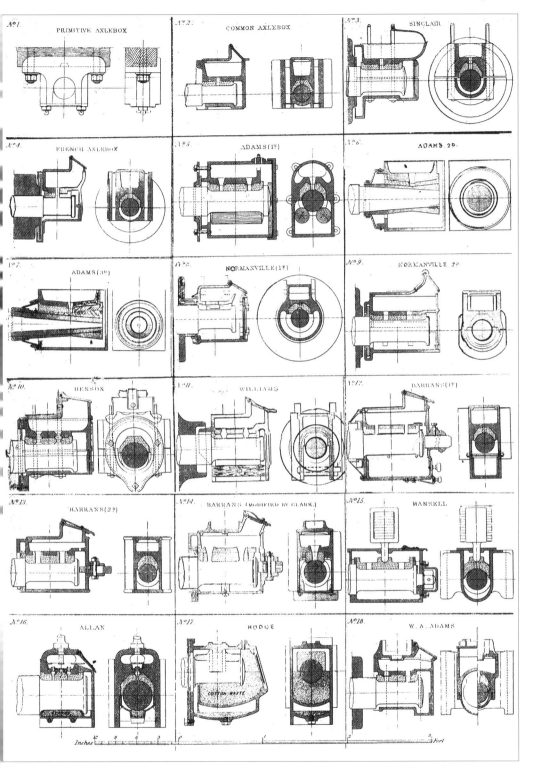

Various designs of axle boxes up to the 1850s.

Above: An axle box keep pattern. A coach axle box has a cast iron keep; the example shown is a BR version, from patterns made by the author to replace a broken version for one of the heritage railway groups. This is for an oil pad, and why it is such an elaborate design only the 'clever clogs' designer knows. A difficult pattern, difficult to cast!

Left: A 'horseshoe' or 'bridge' pattern horn block design, usually for the driving axle boxes.

A left and right pair of horn block castings also await machining. This design was usually for trailing wheel boxes.

Some recent problems with locomotives getting a 'hot box' when running were put down to the use of modern lubricating oils. Although the tallow and whale oil of long ago have gone, lubrication is still an important factor.

Two examples of horn block are illustrated, one a bridge or horseshoe pattern, the second a pair of castings for left and right horn blocks, both from the author's patterns.

Toward the end of official steam, when 'standard' locomotives had been added to the existing fleets, 'modernisation' included the use of Ball and Roller races in place of the traditional yellow-and-white metal plain bearings in many applications, including the axle box. This was an added expense to a system which had served excellently since the days of Trevithick.

17
LOCOMOTIVE LUBRICATION

Any engineering component which moves in some way creates friction, and to ease the problem of heat and wear some form of lubrication is essential. Over the years of transport development, particularly with the steam locomotive, the problems have always been with us.

It was found that two dissimilar metals rubbing together cause less friction than two of the same metals, but a lubricant is still needed. Early lubricants were animal or vegetable based, often leaving a sticky deposit or being to a certain extent flammable, and it was the later 1800s before mineral-based oils became available, some of those being equally flammable. The author remembers as an office boy in Swindon Works in 1945 watching an American locomotive go by (slowly, waiting to be taken off the goods train) with one of the tender axle boxes on fire, flames about 2 ft high. Somewhere there is always friction and heat! So the problem was still there.

Early lubrication methods were the simple hole in the top of a bearing and a quick nip around with the traditional oil can. Hidden frictional surfaces were difficult to get at, the cylinders no exception; steam alone is not a lubricant. Melted tallow was used, and as an example, the replica *Firefly* locomotive has the original system (authentic but not used) of special lubrication cocks screwed in the front cylinder covers, made by the author from original drawings. These have a trumpet-like spout, which turns down out of the way and can be turned around for pouring in the melted tallow.

Also screwed into the front cylinder covers, the 'Furness' lubricator was patented in 1871, being popular for a number of years until superseded by 'displacement' and 'mechanical' lubrication, though it will still be found on some smaller tank locomotives. The globe was filled with oil and the return stroke of the piston created a vacuum, sucking a little oil into the cylinder. (In the 1870s tallow was used.)

The 'Roscoe' lubricator was a 'displacement' type, connected to the main steam pipes, usually found on the smoke box sides of locomotives without superheating. Again, in the 1870s tallow was the lubricant but using oil, the Roscoe is still in use today. There were a number of others in the period, all to do the same lubricating work with different designs, but they all seemed to work. Ramsbottom, Loco Superintendent at Crewe, was responsible for No. 4 illustrated, No. 5 resembles a 'Furness', and No. 6 is a 'Roscoe'. No. 7, the 'Furness', is still in use, the one shown running on a preserved Saddle tank loco.

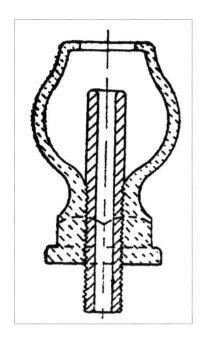 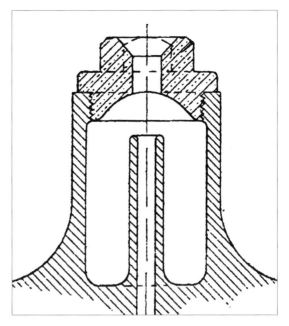

Above left: Simplest of all were the 'syphon cup' lubricators, which had universal application to the steam locomotive. A wick in the centre tube kept the oil flowing.

Above right: A 'machined in' design for a big end bearing. Syphon tubes were also used in the recesses in the top of an axlebox. They also could be grouped, several in a long box, with pipes leading to bearings.

Cylinder grease cocks made by the author for the replica *Firefly*, from original drawings. The bell nozzle turns upwards for pouring the melted tallow on a stationary locomotive.

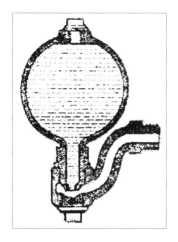
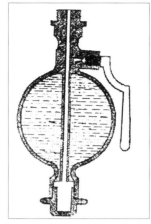
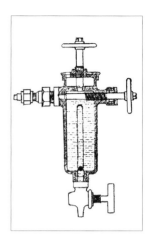

Above left: The Ramsbottom design.

åbove centre: A 'Furness' type.

Above right: A 'Roscoe' lubricator.

A 'Furness' design on a preserved railway running saddle tank. Mounted in the centre of the front cylinder covers and automatic.

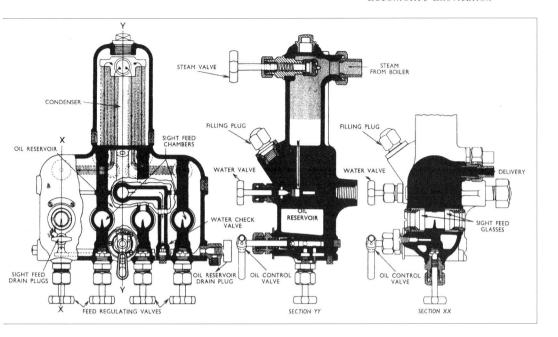

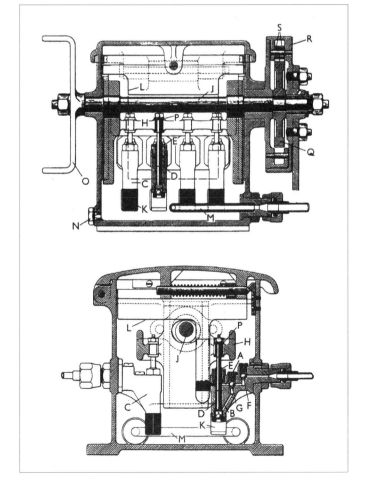

Above: A diagram of a Detroit hydrostatic side feed lubricator.

Right: A diagram of a Silvertown mechanial lubricator. A: Cavity; B: Passage; C: Supply Pumps; D: Pump Plunger; E: Packing; F: Ball Valve; G: Ball Valve; H: Driving Frame; J: Fixed Wheel Plate; K: Small Sieve; L: Fine-mesh Sieve; M: Warming Pipe; N: Drain Plug; O: Driving Shaft Handle; P: Thimbles; Q: Driving Wheel; R: Fixed Wheel Plate; S: Pawl.

ARMSTRONG OILER

For ...
of axl...
lubrications for
locomotives and
rolling stock

Armstrong oiler.

On most large locomotives built in the last, say, fifty years of official steam (although many are still running on preserved heritage railways), the No. 9 mechanical and No. 10 hydrostatic displacement lubricator condensed steam mixes with the oil which overflows, rising through the water and showing in a sight-glass tube or tubes. These are usually mounted in the cab under the eye of the driver. The mechanical lubricator is mounted at the front of the locomotive to be close to its activating lever. Nos 9 and 10 are from the 1957 *BTC Engineers' Handbook*. A very simple but effective axle box lubricator was secured in an under keep in the mop-like No. 10 Armstrong oiler.

18
LOCOMOTIVE BALANCING

In the early days, as with other locomotive finer points, the 'balancing' of reciprocating and revolving parts was in its infancy. It was well known that the balancing of oddly shaped components for machining in a lathe required carefully positioned counterbalance weights, otherwise the lathe vibrated, rocked, and swayed in quite a frightening fashion.

As early as 1810, George Heaton of Birmingham had been concerned with such balancing problems of machinery and took it upon himself to expound his theories (which were effective) on every possible occasion. From machinery his interest grew into the reciprocating and revolving masses of the developing steam locomotive, and in the 1820s and 30s he evolved a very simple example of what he was really talking about. His favourite ploy, during discussions in which he tried to influence others to his point of view, was to produce a pair of model locomotive wheels on an axle and roll them along a table top. Made especially with an 'off-centre' rim thickness, although the periphery was concentric with the axle, the resulting very jumpy movement drove home the point of his argument.

The need to balance was now being taken very seriously. As with any new idea, it seems to have taken a long time actually to 'sink in' to the heads of those who had the problem. One of the earliest applications was by Braithwaite and Milner on the Eastern Counties Railway, who in 1837 applied balance weights between the spokes of their driving wheels. The idea was taken up also by McConnell of the Birmingham & Gloucester Railway in 1842.

As with all innovations and new theories, no matter how well they apply in practice, there will be those who know better! Mr Bodmer (who also dabbled in valve gears) devised two pistons opposed on two crankshafts, the idea being that one mass balanced the other. The idea was sound. It did balance and it worked but was altogether too complicated. Mr Heaton went one better, with a second crank rotating a large counterbalance weight alongside the firebox. This also worked but was again too complicated and really dangerous, as 'Safety at Work' ideas were few and far between in those days.

It was to be 1845 before Fernihough solved the problem with a more scientific approach, where the forces in play were calculated at a known radius, taking into account the pistons, connecting rods, crank and other moving items. All of these attempts, no matter how successful, were not really followed up very quickly by other makers. Many

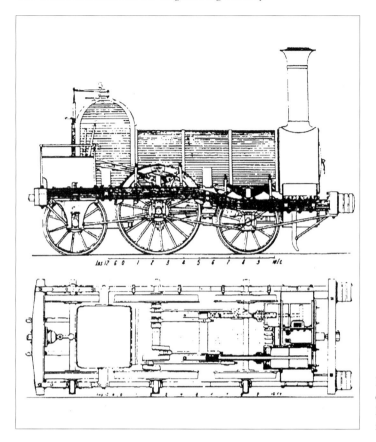

Bodmer's balanced engine for the South Eastern and Brighton railways, 1845.

still dabbled with longer wheelbases, centres of gravity as low as possible and even more rigid (and thus more easily breakable) coupling arrangements between locomotive and tender, to make one long, stiff unit.

In previous jottings we discussed how Crampton had solved, quite successfully, the problems of 'rocking and rolling' as he saw them. This had led to a very distinctive locomotive, of which when we now see a drawing or photograph we immediately say, 'That's a Crampton!' Taken to heart on the Continent, the Crampton was not really accepted or used very much in Britain. The French adopted it with rapidity and their later designs were influenced by Crampton's designs.

The French, as with much locomotive design, were always willing to try out new ideas that seemed to stagnate in Britain. Mr Nollau in 1848 devised a test for a locomotive entailing suspension from the roof until the wheels just cleared the rails. The in-steam locomotive was then subjected to various balancing tests, with varying weights attached to the wheels. A number of such tests were made, from a situation of no weights swaying and rocking the loco when the regulator was opened, to a virtually static position once the correct balance had been achieved. M. Le Chatelier continued these experiments at the New Orleans Railway workshops and much valuable information was produced.

An offshoot of balancing, which seemed to surprise everyone, was that when a fully balanced locomotive pulled a train under load on a normal run, there was found to be a recognisable saving in fuel used, as much as 18 per cent being recorded in the 'fuel per mile' statistics. Another locomotive problem had been solved virtually completely, but in one aspect it left a design feature, particularly with the Great Western, which remained ingrained for sixty or more years.

In the early years, when the six-wheeled locomotive of whatever wheel configuration was in vogue, and bearing in mind the 'unbalanced' state of the moving parts, we have seen that 'rocking and rolling' was a major problem. Going back even further to their four-wheeled contemporaries of the even earlier years, the cylinders, whether on top with all necessary connecting rods and valve gear positioned at the smoke box or firebox ends of the frame, were all 'outside'. In an earlier section I mentioned that the top-mounted cylinders also added to the balancing problem when springs were first used, and so cylinder positions began to come down toward the horizontal position, either at the back or front of the locomotive – but still on the outside. The six-wheeled version, introduced by Stephenson's *Patentee*, had reduced but not solved the stability problem.

With the very short wheelbases of the period, whether four- or six-wheeled locomotives, every stroke into the unbalanced mechanism caused a crabbing movement of the frame. An examination of the problem brought about the theory that if the cylinders were to be moved closer together, it could reduce or eliminate the crabbing motion. Thus the 'inside cylinders' format developed whereby cylinders were to be positioned between the frames.

I mention the 'frames' as we now think of them in the context of the 'modern' steam locomotive, but in those early days it was not as simple as that. Let us look, although slightly later, at Gooch's Firefly class as an example. The 'frame', in this case of the typical wood-and-iron sandwich construction, was merely a 'skirt' which positioned the pairs of wheels relative to the gauge and was in reality suspended from the boiler. The boiler itself was the main construction member and it carried the cylinders built into the bottom of the smoke box, as well as all of the valve gear, which was mounted on four inner frame members along with the main driving axle boxes and crank axle. The draw gear was also attached to the back of the firebox, and not to the frame, the coupling swivelling through a slot in the buffer beam. The four inner frames, each with its driving axle box, were attached by rivets to the back of the smoke box and front of the firebox, making a very solid, complete unit. (What it did for boiler expansion I leave to readers to imagine.) The boiler at this period, as with most components, was of wrought iron, for the cheap and plentiful supply of steel was still awaiting Bessemer.

That it all worked is beyond question. The Firefly class was the backbone of Great Western passenger traffic and a speed of 60 mph was a quite usual performance from these very successful locomotives. The class as a whole had a lifespan of about thirty years, some with the original boilers, a couple blotting their copybook by exploding due to the water level and safety valve problems discussed earlier in these jottings.

The positioning of cylinders as close together on the locomotive centre line as possible introduced yet another problem to the locomotive builders. Inside cylinders could only use their power through a crank axle, and as with the large wrought iron driving wheels, this was a job for the blacksmith. Remember that at this period there were no big power hammers. Nasmyth and his steam hammer were still in the future, so it was a job for big men with big hammers and the traditional coke fires.

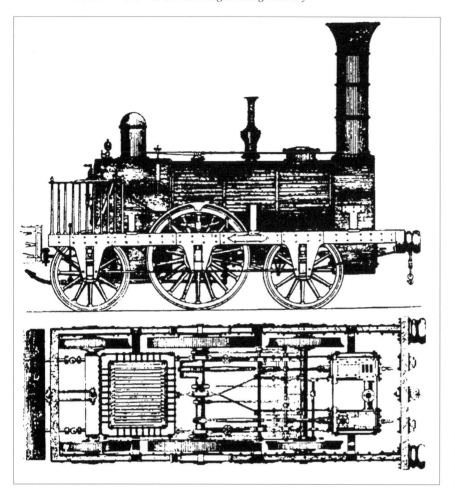

Stephenson's 2-2-2 patent engine of 1837.

There is a wonderful record of the 1840 period handling of locomotive components in a notebook written by James Nuttall, who probably worked on the *Firefly* at Jones, Turner & Evans Works at Newton-le-Willows. He describes in the notes, with sketches, how he built up a crank axle, the spelling of the notes actually written in his own dialect. One of his excellent sketches depicts a 'drop hammer'. Built in the manner of a French Revolution guillotine, it required the services of twenty men to haul up the 'tup' or hammer by uniformly pulling on ropes. One can imagine the red glow from the iron as the ropes were pulled and then released on a command from the chargehand. What happened if one was a little late in letting go of the rope can only be imagined! It would make a wonderful cartoon drawing, but probably quite deadly if it ever happened. However, the crank axle had been introduced and designers were stuck with it and its continuing problems.

Thus while the move to stop the 'rock and roll' effect by moving the cylinders into a position between the frames solved one problem to some extent, it also introduced several more! These had to wait until the true balancing of the moving components was achieved.

19

THE QUEST FOR EFFICIENT BRAKES – HAND, STEAM, VACUUM, AIR

Early locomotives such as Gooch's Firefly class of around 1840 had brakes which operated on one side of the six-wheeled tender only and these were applied by hand. Some of the earlier locomotives had no brakes at all and were stopped after reducing speed by baulks of timber thrust under or through the wheel spokes! This may have been acceptable in the early application of the steam locomotive to the horse-drawn tram roads for mineral traffic, but the introduction of the human passenger called for something better.

From quite early on in the locomotive development story, attempts at effective braking are listed. The number of trains continued to grow, speeds generally were increasing (it took a number of years for other companies to match the Great Western broad gauge in this respect) and with these increases, so increased the number of accidents. From mid-century there were numerous attempts to devise a satisfactory brake system which could be applied to the complete train, not just selected brake-fitted vehicles, often only on one side of the tender, and a whistle-signalled application of a handbrake by the guard.

Locomotive development was introducing increasingly heavier trains, and among the many problems to be countered was that of a heavily laden train breaking in two when a coupling failed. Thus, to be included in any design was the 'fail safe' requirement of brake application should the train separate. So, the field of experimentation was wide open. Theories were expounded, inventors burned the midnight oil, and proposals started to roll in, all awaiting the chance to prove themselves.

The quest for what is termed 'continuous brakes' started in earnest at the turn of the mid-nineteenth century. In 1857 a patent obtained by a James Harris introduced one of the main braking power sources – compressed air. In principle, a steam-driven compressor supplied air to receivers or tanks under each carriage and releasing the air applied a braking force. This was one of those patents where someone patents an idea or proposal and looks in vain for a producer.

There were really four methods of powering a braking system at this period: a straightforward steam brake, which of necessity was eventually restricted to the locomotive itself; the use of compressed air, and conversely the application of a vacuum operation; and finally, some form of hydraulic appliance; all of these found advocates as designs proliferated. A possible fifth method was some form of manual application, which was really not practical.

In 1860, Du Trembly and Martin patented a vacuum application, the system continuing through metal pipework with a flexible connection between each coach, a procedure we recognise today. This proposal remained a proposal only, but carried the potential for future development. A crude steam application created a partial vacuum to collapse the flexible end or sac of the brake cylinders, thus applying the brakes.

The whole potential of compressed air and of vacuum application was recognised and triggered the design and development of the two important 'power' source mechanisms. In one case, there was the steam operated air compressor – a piston compressor which, while it worked, was later developed for general engineering use into the much more efficient vane compressor. On the vacuum front, there was the requirement for an effective 'ejector' to create and maintain the necessary vacuum. The vacuum pump, which in modern times maintains a vacuum, came along considerably later, but in the early years a 'pump' of sorts competed with the 'exhauster', itself a forerunner of the ejector.

Prior to these power applications, there was the proposal of D. Clark around 1870, which was actually fitted to a train. This comprised a system of levers, each with a mechanical advantage when operated by a lowered weight attached to a chain which ran centrally along the complete length of the train.

Joined by links at each coach, the supporting pulleys also had the effect of increasing the pull on brake blocks of cast iron swinging on hangers on each side of each wheel. In tests, a 90-ton train, not including the engine, was stopped in 245 yards from running at 55 mph on a 1 in 99 gradient. The period six-wheel coaches could be fitted with the system at a cost of £17 each. While moderately successful, it did not really catch on.

A proposal by the same railway engineer utilised hydraulic power to operate the braking system. With this idea a 1½ in. pipe, always filled with water, ran the length of the train, flexible couplings joining the individual carriage pipes. Each coach was fitted with a 6 in. cylinder, its piston attached to a lever on a shaft, which by other levers pulled the brake blocks onto the wheels. Power was supplied by steam to the piston in a 'charging chamber' on the engine. This force compressed the water in the system and applied the brakes, the water incidentally being mixed with an anti-freeze solution. Again, this system worked.

There were of course worldwide attempts to solve the braking problem of trains, which increasingly were getting bigger and heavier. An example from the Great Indian Peninsula Railway utilised a vacuum to keep the brakes in the 'off' position. Breaking the vacuum allowed the spring-loaded brake gear to clamp around the wheels. This system also had a built-in safety arrangement, in that in the event of a train breaking in two through a failed coupling, the destroyed vacuum automatically applied the brakes.

There were many early contenders for the continuous brake development crown, but two suggestions were coming to the fore. These were the vacuum system and the application of compressed air. Among the names of the vacuum proponents we find those of Smith, Sanders and Westinghouse, all successful in their own way. Westinghouse was to leave the vacuum contenders and concentrate on the compressed air version, which had great success, to the extent of replacing Loughbridge's air brake, then widely used on the rail roads of America.

Such competition and variations of proposals and applications led inevitably to a requirement of a joint discussion between government and engineers to review the situation and come up with a proposal for standardisation on all Britain's railways. As a result of the talks, there came a proposal for a series of practical trials. Although at this period it was thought essential for a brake to be fitted to the tender and the rest of the train, whatever its length, the locomotive itself was not considered at all – it being thought that reversing the valve gear and opening the regulator would suffice. (I have very strong reservations on the use of such tactics unless in an acute emergency as such activity does not do the valve gear or other components any good at all!)

The effectiveness of the vacuum system was given a great boost when in 1877 Graham obtained his first of many allied patents and introduced the first practical 'ejector'. Although mention was made earlier in these notes that a brake on the locomotive itself was not really necessary, there were other engineers with more practical ideas. A locomotive running light needs better stopping power than a hand-screwed tender brake! Many engines of the period were already fitted with a steam brake devised by Roberts and later incorporating McConnell's improvements. On the Continent, Chatlelier's counter-pressure brake had also been in service for some time.

There were set out in the brake trial requirements papers eighteen specific essentials for a practical, acceptable continuous brake system. These in brief were that the brake had to be in charge of, and easily operated by, the driver. Action should be controllable from partial to full application depending on requirements for such application. It should be simple to maintain. If one portion of the system failed it should not affect the rest of the system regarding brake application. Vehicles making up a train may be various and must not affect coupling-up or braking. Any length of train was to be braked with uniform efficiency. Brake blocks should apply, and thus wear evenly, without undue wear on any part of the wheel tyre. Brakes were to remain 'on' when applied but capable of instant release when required. As a safety measure, access to operation by the passengers must not affect the overall safety of the train.

In retrospect, it is surprising to find that compensation payments in the non-braked or experimental years were reaching very high figures. For example, the year 1872–3 saw payments of £311,000 in compensation alone, while damage to rolling stock reached the astonishing figure of £650,000. Something obviously had to be done! The railway companies involved included the Caledonian; Great Northern; London, Brighton & South Coast; London & North Western; Lancashire & Yorkshire; Midland; and the North Eastern. With their approval, the Midland had placed a suitable length of track between Newark and Thurgarton on the Nottingham to Lincoln branch at the disposal of the Government Brake Commission. The braking systems to be tried out comprised Barker's hydraulic, Clark's chain, Clark's hydraulic, Fay's handbrake, Smith's vacuum, Steel-McInnes' reaction airbrake, Westinghouse's automatic compressed air and Westinghouse's vacuum. The trials got underway and to all intents and purposes progressed satisfactorily, all test requirements being covered. At the end of the day, however, it was clear that no decisions or selection of any of the systems had been made, the onus being put back on the designers to 'acquire additional brake power in what way seemed best to them'.

As with all experimental work, some designs seemingly based on a good idea inevitably proved impractical when applied. One such design had the brake blocks applied to the rail and not the wheel and was known as the 'sledge brake'. If applied with force, the blocks had the effect of lifting the wagon bodily off the rails, particularly if running light.

So, what was termed the 'Battle of the Brake' continued and in 1878 the Institution of Mechanical Engineers sought to end the confusion by appointing a Captain Douglas Galton to undertake another series of tests. While the first trials, inconclusive as they were, had examined the practical uses of the systems, these trials had a more scientific approach, to include determining the coefficient of friction between brake blocks and wheels, and between rails and wheels, strains on the engine drawbar and the time constraints of initiating and completing brake application. Coefficients of adhesion between wheel and rail related to speed; brake block pressures on the wheels were also the subjects of study.

These intensive studies, followed by experiments and modifications shown to be required to approach something like the requirements of the perfect brake, only led to the situation amounting to checkmate. The several parties with interests in a particular system had by now got the message that their system was on a par with several others. No 'standard' selection could thus be made, and individual railways were left to their own choice, as long as that choice fulfilled the criteria for safe braking.

An 1859 Act of Parliament required all trains carrying passengers to be fitted with automatic power brakes. The Railway Act of 1921, bringing all companies (with one or two exceptions) into the 'big four' net, generally endorsed the vacuum automatic brake as the standard for British steam trains. The perfection of the vacuum brake thus virtually achieved has led to quite complex – but easily operated – designs, some incorporating joint application of the locomotive steam brake and the train vacuum system through the operation of a simple lever-operated valve. A long struggle which paid off in the end.

The subject of brakes contains a clause! You have to know when to apply them. In the years prior to this book the railway system has suffered some horrendous crashes, signals not seen, not acted upon, etc. This was followed by a rush for some magical electronic device to solve the problem. The Great Western had this wrapped up eighty years ago! The following chapter tells the story, proudly presented for the Great Western Centenary in 1935.

20

AN EFFICIENT WAY OF APPLICATION – AUTOMATIC TRAIN CONTROL

An engine approaching an ATC ramp on a typical section of GWR standard track.

Above left: The shoe fixture under the front of the locomotive; the hardened shoe is spring-loaded. The 'lift' is about one inch.

Above right: The bell/siren equipment at the right-hand side of the cab.

Safety of travel on the GWR has been much enhanced by the adoption of a system of automatic train control, by means of which audible warning is given to the enginemen of the condition of distant signals, and in the event of one being passed at 'caution' the train is stopped automatically before it reaches the next signal. There is a steel ramp, 40 ft long and rising to 3½ in. above rail level, midway in the 4 ft opposite the distant signal, and connected to the signal lever electrically. When the signal is at 'caution' the ramp is dead; the action of pulling the lever to give a 'clear' indication of the distant signal completes an electric circuit and energises the ramp. On the locomotive is fitted an iron shoe, with a T-shaped end extending head-downwards to within 2½ in. of rail level. As the engine passes over the ramp the head of the 'T' comes into contact with it and is lifted 1 in. If the signal is at 'caution' the ramp is dead, and the action of lifting the shoe opens a valve on the vacuum-automatic brake apparatus and causes the brakes to be applied throughout the train, at the same time sounding a siren in the engine cab. If the signal is in the 'clear' position, the ramp is energised and the electric current, passing through the shoe, prevents interference with the vacuum brake, but rings an electric bell in the engine cab. This type of signal was first introduced on the Henley branch in January 1906 and on the Fairford branch in December of the same year. By September 1931 the whole of Great Western Railway main lines, totalling 2,130 miles, had been equipped – as well of course as all the locomotives liable to work over these lines.

21
THE VACUUM SYSTEM – THE AIR BRAKE AND THE STEAM BRAKE

The 'Ejector'. This works in a way similar to the boiler feed 'injector', steam passing through a series of cones to exhaust the air from the vacuum system. The 'injector', through a series of cones, forces water into the boiler.

The 'Vacuum Pump'. This stops the use of steam when the loco is moving by taking over from the ejector, being operated mechanically by the movement of the loco crosshead, thus economising on the use of steam.

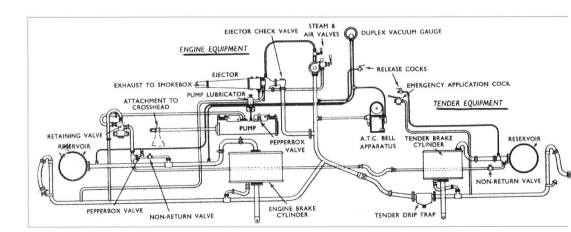

The complete system fitted to the locomotive and tender.

THE AMERICAN WAY

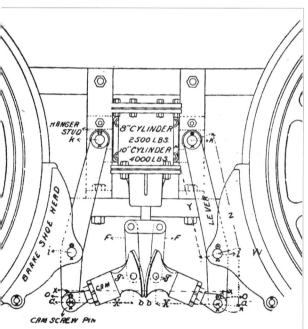

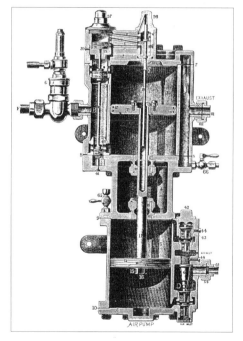

Top: An American locomotive of *c.* 1890, fitted with the Westinghouse air brake system. There were also several vacuum brake systems, but mostly air brakes were used. *Above left:* Driving wheel brake. One of these arrangements both sides of the loco. *Above right:* Brake air pump.

The Great Western's *King George V*, fitted with an air pump, on a test run prior to the visit to the Baltimore & Ohio Railway centenary exhibition in 1928. (The famous bell was presented at the exhibition.) The air pump was to match the common American braking system.

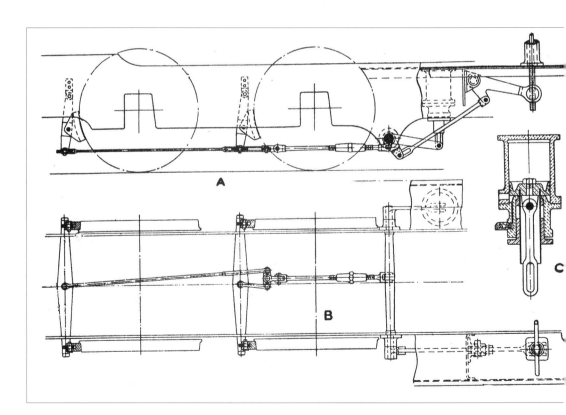

Steam brake/hand brake combination – independent use. 'A' and 'B' show the rods and shafts. 'C' shows the sectioned steam cylinder.

22

THE INJECTOR — GETTING WATER INTO THE BOILER

> The injector is without doubt the most simple, ingenious and best device ever employed for feeding water to locomotive boilers.

The above is itself, without doubt, the most quoted sentiment in any book on the steam locomotive, this from a 1903 American volume.

The 'injector' first came to the fore when patented on 8 May 1858. The inventor, Henri Jacques Giffard, is the, one must say, genius who came up with the outstanding and lasting principle of using the latent power of steam from the boiler itself. His ingenuity and technical education caused him to re-think the whole problem of feeding the boiler, eliminating pumps and pump operating methods, whether by hand or mechanical means, to that point benefiting any steam-powered apparatus. It must be said that all phases of the question were very thoroughly considered and theoretical solutions formulated before anything was actually made.

Such was his approach and thoroughness that the principles of the design of the body and the proportion and shapes of the cones and nozzles are recognised as almost the same to this day. Such was the theoretical work applied before construction of the prototype that it entirely satisfied all requirements of a continuous stream of water directed into the boiler against the nominal pressure within the boiler. There were no crosshead-driven pump rams, and no spinning eccentrics complicating axle space to operate the said rams. On some earlier locomotives (*Firefly* was one example) the pumps were operated by hand and located either side of the firebox; these were now no longer required, even if converted to axle-driven eccentrics operating vertically (see the *North Star* replica, Swindon's STEAM Museum), a must as increased boiler pressures increased the hand power required, and the long extension loose handle was always inconvenient to use.

The introduction of the Giffard Injector caused quite a stir among learned bodies, and even the public were concerned that the inventor had stepped beyond ethical limits in creating something very close to perpetual motion! Such was the considered opinion of the learned faculty of the Academy of Science in Paris that Giffard, with no opposition, was awarded the Grand Mechanical prize of 1859.

In England patents were granted to Sharp, Stewart & Co., and in America to William

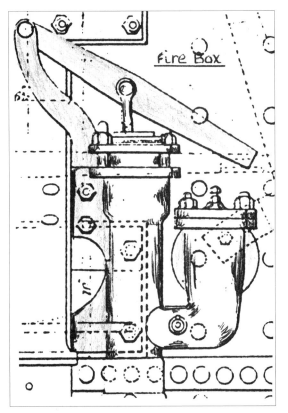

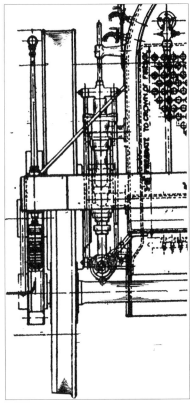

Above left: Hand pump, *c.* 1840, used with an extension lever. The illustration shows the 'hand pump' on *Firefly* with the stub handle onto which fitted the long extension. The pump in this case is a dummy converted so that the stub handle works the firebox dampers! The locomotive has a pair of GWR No. 6 injectors tucked away out of sight.

Above right and left: Eccentric-driven pump converted from hand operation.

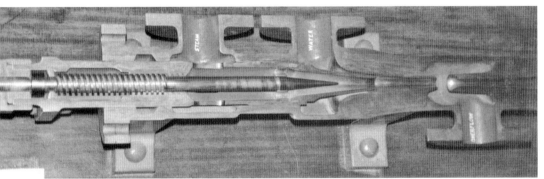

A sectional Giffard injector from 1858, to be seen in STEAM, the GWR museum at Swindon.

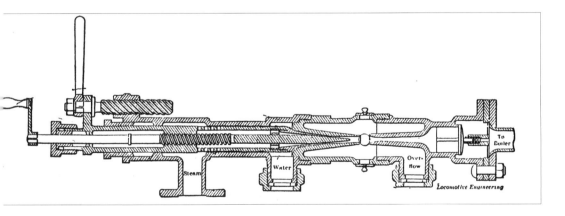

The Giffard injector, *c.* 1860.

A view into the smoke box of a 'condensing locomotive'. Note the 'Weir Pump' for boiler feed on the left and exhaust steam pipes.

Sellers & Co. of Philadelphia, Pennsylvania, manufacture thus starting in 1860, the latter soon coming up with their own version.

Having introduced this unique piece of apparatus to the engineering world, and showing how effective it was, questions then arose (and really continue to do so!) that, knowing that it worked, everyone wanted to know *how*! After pages of technical detail, listeners usually say, 'I accept all that, but I still don't know *why* it works!' We must thus just accept that it does and if we require, refer to the numerous arguments and theories existing over the years!

There have been many injector designs over the years, each attempting to improve on the principles of the perfect working injector clearly shown in the patent documents of Giffard's original. Shapes and sizes have changed, but the principles remain the same.

One major problem eliminated at one fell swoop with Giffard's invention was that with the crosshead- and eccentric-operated pumps, the locomotive had to be moving for the pumps to operate. Conversely, with a moving locomotive the pumps were continually operating, and at speed the pressure build-up caused very serious hydraulic damage. As in the case of *Firefly* these locomotives had no brakes, only a handbrake on the tender (operating on one side only!) and there are recorded episodes where the driver, possibly in emergencies, clamped the tender brakes on, oiled the track and opened the regulator. The spinning wheels could not have benefited the track or the tyres! A very dubious practice, possibly much frowned upon, but who knows?

Very early on it was inevitable that avoiding and 'improving' on the patent should be attempted. Over the next forty years developments continued and by the turn of the century injector designs had consolidated into a combination of various functions and types of operation, which may be listed as follows:

Single set of cones	Fixed cones
Double set of cones	Open overflow
Adjustable and self-adjusting cones	Closed overflow

A further subdivision went as follows:

Re-starting	Non-lifting
Automatic	Lifting

The Giffard was of the open overflow, adjustable type.

Readers may see an original Giffard Injector, sectioned and exhibited in STEAM, GWR Museum, Swindon (see beginning of this chapter). Also, in the period up to the tail end of the nineteenth century a further injector variation was developed that economised on steam by utilising the exhaust from the cylinders, with complications of its own that we will look at later on. Yet another variation was known as an 'Inspirator', and differed from the injector in that the lifting and forcing jets and tubes are combined within the same instrument, while in the injector they are independent of each other.

The credit must go to Giffard for cracking the problem of forcing water into a boiler in steam against the pressure within that boiler – this was the solution to a long-standing problem.

The essential parts of an injector are (1) a steam nozzle; (2) a 'combining' nozzle where steam and water meet; and (3) a delivery nozzle for the combined water droplets and condensing steam into the boiler. In fact, the Marquis Mannaury d'Ectot must be credited with establishing the above principles in his patent of 1818 for a steam jet apparatus that delivered water from one tank and raised it to another tank. It took the essential work of Giffard to crack the pressure problem relating to boilers in steam.

An outstanding problem which Giffard solved was that of the Marquis' patent. The amount of water lifted by an injector must not be sufficient to overcome the incoming steam and must then be controlled. The solution was providing a space around the combining nozzle to allow excess water to flow freely out. Thus, on starting the injector by opening up for steam, the overflow water may be reduced until the flow stops; thus the injector steam and water are combining as they should, and in balance. The Giffard injector had to be quite finely adjusted to achieve this and a bump on uneven track would cause the injector to stop, entailing re-setting it all over again. Slight design modifications, while retaining the original principles, overcame this problem, enabling the injector to restart by itself; this was all in the course of later developments, which proliferated once Giffard had introduced the main principles which were shown to work.

There were many differing designs before even the turn of the century, each claiming of course to be the most simple to maintain and the most efficient. Whatever the claims, it was apparent that they all worked! Some of the late Victorian-era injectors are American designs. Such a proliferation worldwide was not confined to the locomotive, but found an essential use in marine, stationary and road engine boilers for all applications and was taken to heart by the American rail roads.

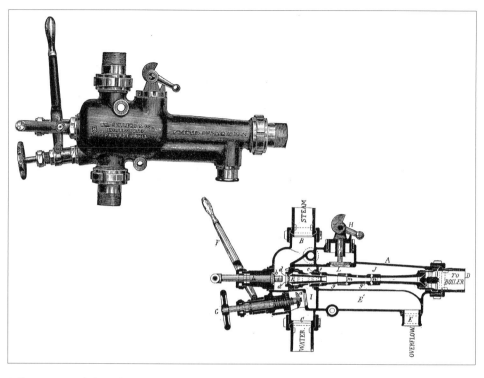

Sellers' injector, left, and a section of Sellers' injector, right.

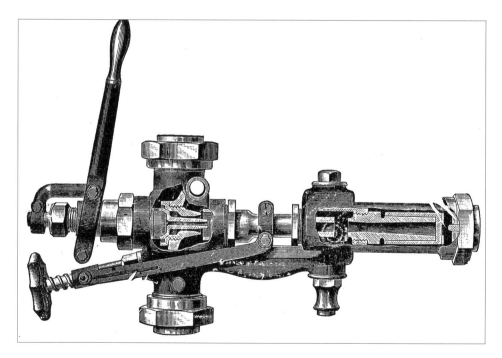

Little Giant injector.

Let's take the Sellers injector to start with. A first version appeared in 1876 and went through several modifications during its life time. It was self-starting and required no regulation of the water supply to prevent overflow above 40 lbs steam pressure; it was easily maintained and repaired.

An injector introduced in 1880 was stated to be 'so extensively used in this country (America) that no introduction is necessary'. This was the Monitor injector, which appeared in various designs and was classed as 'the most efficient and reliable'. There is a very interesting sequel to the 'Monitor' story. During 1957 the British Transport Commission issued a *Handbook for Railway Steam Locomotive Engineers* (many readers probably have a copy). This volume contains diagrams of various locomotive components in sectioned form with explanations of how they work. On page 60 is a diagram, Fig. 26, and a description which reads, 'One of the latest types of injectors is the "Monitor" type, as shown in Fig. 26, in this arrangement will be noted …' Should we ask who received an award for designing the latest injector? Perhaps not! (see Plate 2)

From 1875 comes the 'Little Giant' injector. This was a very simple design and was the only injector having a moveable combining tube for adjustment to suit varying steam pressures.

During the 1880s Mack's injector appeared, once again easily maintained, the parts being 'easily removed for cleaning or renewed if worn by the action of impure water', the latter not doing the boiler much good either! (See Plate 1.)

Toward the end of the century there were several injectors, all claiming to be 'the latest design'. One of these was to Korting's design, by L Schute & Co. of Philadelphia (see Plate 1). This very compact design has two steam jets, one above the other; the lower one is proportioned as an 'ejector', i.e. an arrangement which gives suction but discharges against a moderate pressure only. Thus the forcing jet is supplied with the required amount of water dependent on the steam pressure. A slow continuous movement of the lever will start the injector. Two injectors that appear to be the same were the Ohio and the Garfield, a slight variation between them being the internal methods used to hold cones and jets in place, both claiming easy access for maintenance (see Plate 1).

The Dodge (see Plate 4) was a single-lever injector, the lever controlling both forcing and lifting jets, another claim being that it fed water to the boiler at a hotter temperature than any other on the market. It was made by Fitchburg of Fitchburg, Massachusetts.

The Lunkenheimer automatic injector (see Plate 2) was claimed to start promptly if it cut out and 'will start promptly at all pressures between 30 and 250 lbs, and higher on lifts not exceeding 18 ft', which is quite a claim. A single movement of the lever will start the injector immediately. It was made by Lunkenheimer, Cincinnati, Ohio.

The Metropolitan 1898 Model Locomotive injector (see Plate 2) takes us up to the end of the nineteenth century and shows the development range over the forty years or so from the Giffard patent. It was a double-tube design that lifts the water (remember the marquis' design of 1818) and delivers it to the forcing apparatus, which discharges it into the boiler. The write-up states: 'Impossible to secure in any other form of injector … features recognised by experienced rail road men … for the proper and effective performance of the loco injector under all conditions which exist on the modern high-pressure locomotive.' This double-tube arrangement delivers the water in the proper quantity to the forcing tube under pressure, where it passes through the forcing tube, boosted to overcome the boiler pressure.

This injector will deliver very hot water through a great range of steam pressures without adjustment, and was the first (as claimed) with pressures above 200 lbs and with heated water or cold.

One very simple injector the author has come across is the Brownley Double Tube injector (see Plate 1), used on the Manhattan Railroad of New York. It was claimed to give better results than any other injector tried, very powerful and economical on steam. It was of one-lever operation, and works between 15 lbs to 350 lbs per square inch, an impressive range; it was also of the under/over tube arrangement. We must ask ourselves, 'Why are all the rest so complicated if this design works so well?' Perhaps once again we shouldn't ask!

A variation of the injector was the 'inspirator' and the Hancock inspirators (see Plate 3) of 1874 and 1894 show the marked differences between the inspirator and the injector, its development and an example of the type. With the inspirator the lifting and forcing jets and nozzles are independent of one another. The lifting side and the forcing side jets and nozzles have independent overflow valves. The operating lever has two connecting levers, and its slow positional movement opens or closes the internal valves in a required sequence to lift the water, pass it to the forcing jet and thence to the boiler.

Incidentally, it will be seen that the designs all followed a recommendation that the injector should be mounted in an accessible position in the cab. All of the early ones illustrated have the controls, whether lever or wheel, mounted on the injector itself. The modern injector, being possibly more reliable, is now mounted out of sight under or outside the cab, although Stroudley did this as early as 1872. Shows how reliability has improved! As long as the overflow can be readily seen from the footplate, that is all that is required for operation and most are now remotely controlled and hidden.

We have looked at the complicated and the simple injector, the latter with only one control lever, but the most simple of the lot seems to be the British Batesmith Injector of around 1904, advertised in *Cassier's Magazine*, a monthly publication of current engineering developments. This design has no built-in controls at all (see Plate 4), being hidden and controlled remotely. There is no other technical detail in the advertisement, so what its range was is not known. Once again, why are all the rest so complicated?

A similar injector with no built-in controls at all (see Plate 4), under the Penberthy patent, also on that advertisement is an 'Ejector', or 'water raiser' with lifts up to 24 ft, bringing to mind where we started with this look at injectors – with shades of the Marquis Ectot patent of 1818, or even Savery of 1702.

As the injector developed, thoughts increasingly turned, with a modern approach, to the inevitable word 'economies'. The injector used fresh steam from the boiler and with economies in view, and without reverting to crosshead- or axle-driven pumps, the sights were focused on the exhaust steam; usually most of it was blasted up the chimney and away. Could this be utilised?

Around 1895, when the Great Western Duke 4-4-0s appeared, it was already used in part to heat the feed water of the tender, an economy in itself, but the Duke class still retained crosshead-driven pumps (shades of the later Firefly updates) to feed hot water to the two large clack boxes on the sides of the boiler barrel.

Clack boxes, an important item associated with boiler feed, had, to various designs, appeared in numerous locations; the front of the barrel, the backhead, the sides of the firebox, but in all cases raised questions of where to introduce warmed or cold water into a hot boiler. The question was solved in 1911 by the introduction, where practical (at least at Great Western), of the 'top feed' and trays above the tubes in the boiler. All credit to Swindon for this development, which had already been tried without success by Germany and France.

Having diverted waste steam to heat water, the next step was to extend its uses and what better than an 'exhaust injector'. While a good idea, the practicalities raised problems of their own: first, exhaust steam was already finished with, so although used at low pressures for the very large cylinders of 'compound' locomotives, it was available on the 'simple'. Having done its work, normally in the cylinders, it would now be also full of cylinder lubricant, which remembered from Swindon erecting shop days, started life in a repaired loco's cylinders just like treacle, to be followed by a lighter oil in operation. That would have to be removed from the steam by an arrangement additional to the injector. A further arrangement would have to cover operation when the loco was stationary or with regulator closed to ensure live steam was accessible, preferably cutting in automatically. Also, in very hot, tropical countries, the injector would have to lift or move hot water, so a low position below the level of the water tank would reduce the lifting requirement. Incidentally, exhaust injectors are mentioned, but not detailed nor illustrated, in books published around the late 1890s.

An exhaust-type injector was developed by Davis and Metcalfe. It would take water temperature up to 140 degrees Fahrenheit with boiler pressures up to 250 lbs/sq. in. and was entirely automatic and restarting in action, covering all of the above requirements. It is started by simply opening the live steam valve and the exhaust steam function is practically instantaneous. It is described in E. A. Phillipson's 1938 book, *Steam Locomotive Design: Data and Formulae*.

For working in hot climates the 'hot water injector' of Messrs Gresham & Craven is a good example. Feed water at an initial temperature of 140 degrees Fahrenheit, boiler pressures of 180 lbs/sq. in. and a delivery temperature of 240–260 degrees Fahrenheit are covered within a wide range of pressures, and the injectors are capable of high lifts. The following short table explains the type of injector and capabilities:

Type of Injector	Working Pressure Range		Maximum Initial Feed Water Temperature
	Maximum - lbs/sq inch	Minimum - lbs/sq inch	
Standard	180	40	95°F
High Pressure	300	50	90°F
Simplex	200	40	120°F
Special Hot Water	225	40	140°F

Mention was made earlier in these notes of the 1957 *Handbook for Railway Steam Locomotive Enginemen*, a volume issued really far too late in the story of the steam locomotive, at least for official use. It did, however, contain the 'last gasp' details of locomotive component design before the loco itself became official history.

Apart from details of the 'latest injector design' previously mentioned (see Plate 4), the last of the exhaust injectors are also detailed. These took the listing for various designs, internally slightly differing and each one improving on the one before. They were designated 'H', 'J', 'H/J', & 'K'; K being the latest design introduced. Henri Jacques Giffard certainly started something that the preservation groups are thankfully continuing. So come on you youngsters! Join a steam preservation group and get your hands dirty! Beats staring at a computer screen!

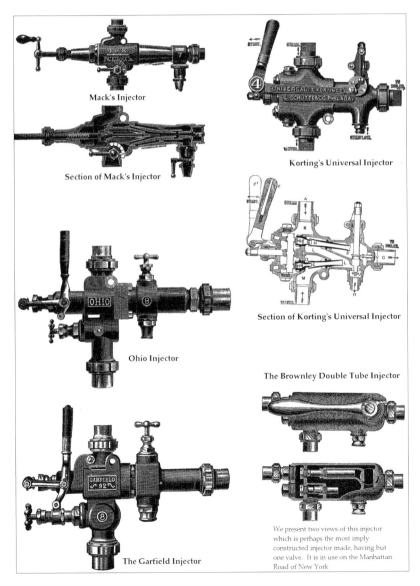

Mack's Injector

Section of Mack's Injector

Korting's Universal Injector

Section of Korting's Universal Injector

Ohio Injector

The Brownley Double Tube Injector

The Garfield Injector

We present two views of this injector which is perhaps the most imply constructed injector made, having but one valve. It is in use on the Manhattan Road of New York

Plate 1 Drawings showing the Mack's Injector, Korting's Universal Injector, .Ohio Injector, Garfield Injector and Brownley Double Tube injector

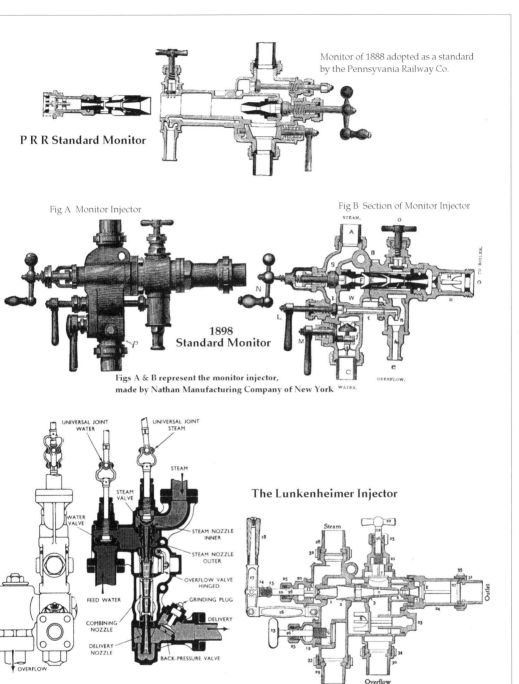

Monitor of 1888 adopted as a standard
by the Pennsyvania Railway Co.

P R R Standard Monitor

Fig A Monitor Injector

Fig B Section of Monitor Injector

**1898
Standard Monitor**

**Figs A & B represent the monitor injector,
made by Nathan Manufacturing Company of New York**

The Lunkenheimer Injector

Plate 2. Left: live steam injector, monitor type, British Transport Commission of 1957. One of
the latest types of injectors. Right: The Lunkenheimer injector illustrated here is an automatic,
single-tube machine of the fixed-nozzle type. By 'automatic' it is meant that, should the machine
stop forcing (due from interruption of steam or water supply), the injector would restart without
attention as soon as the supply is resumed.

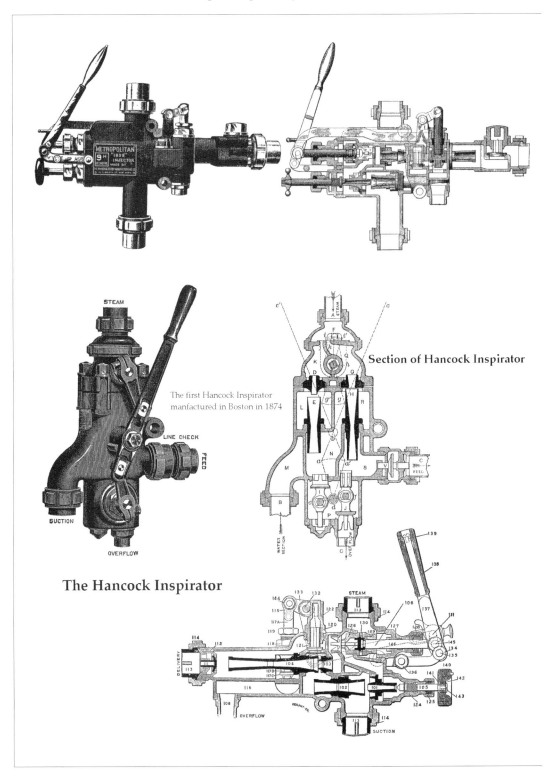

The first Hancock Inspirator manfactured in Boston in 1874

Section of Hancock Inspirator

The Hancock Inspirator

Plate 3. Above: The Metropolitan 1898 injector. Below: A sectional view of the latest Hancock locomotive inspirator of 1894.

Right: Plate 4 Advertisements and diagrams showing the Batesmith, Willcox and Dodge injctors.

Below: Plate 5 Diagrams of injectors taken from the 1957 *Handbook for Railway Steam Locomotive Enginemen.*

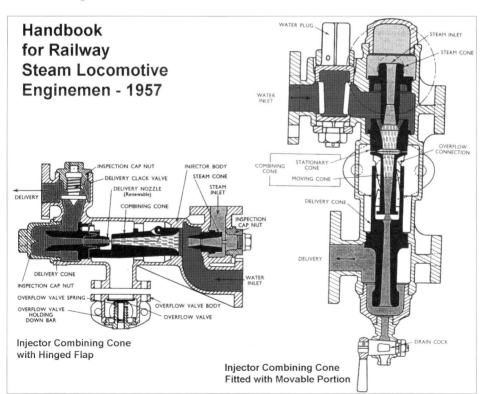

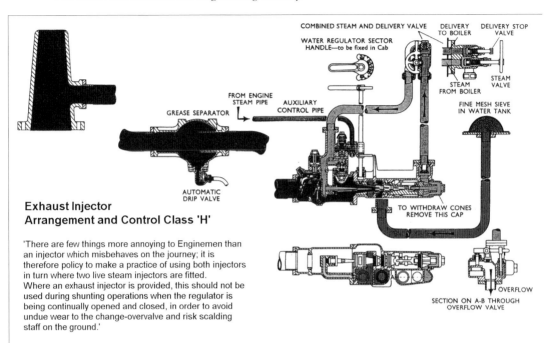

Exhaust Injector
Arrangement and Control Class 'H'

'There are few things more annoying to Enginemen than an injector which misbehaves on the journey; it is therefore policy to make a practice of using both injectors in turn where two live steam injectors are fitted. Where an exhaust injector is provided, this should not be used during shunting operations when the regulator is being continually opened and closed, in order to avoid undue wear to the change-overvalve and risk scalding staff on the ground.'

Exhaust Injector Class 'K'
(Improved)

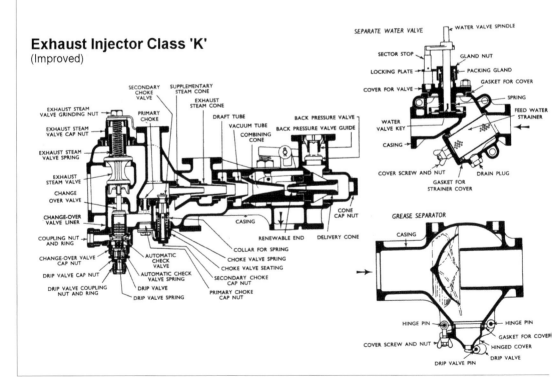

Plate 6 Diagrams showing the 'H' (above) and 'K' (below) types of exhaust injector.

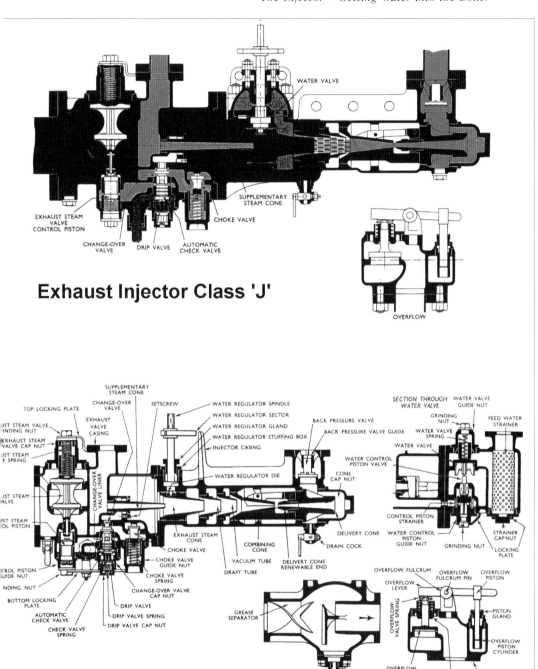

Exhaust Injector Class 'J'

xhaust Injector Class 'H/J'

Plate 7 Diagrams showing the 'J' (above) and 'H/J' (below) types of exhaust injector.

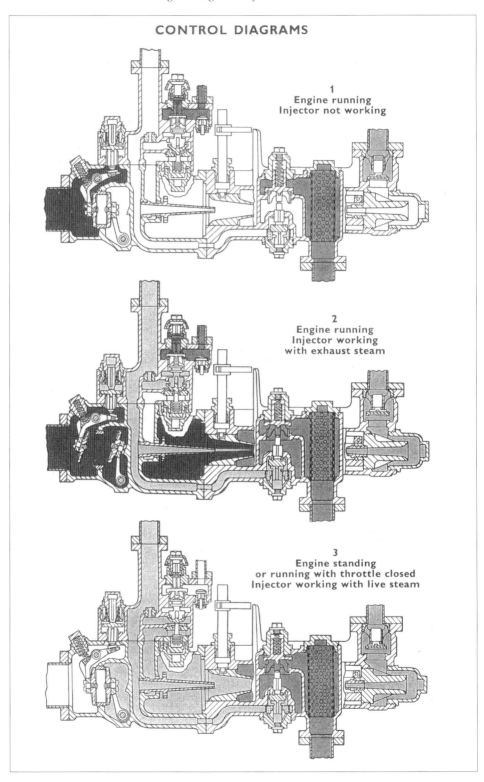

CONTROL DIAGRAMS

1
Engine running
Injector not working

2
Engine running
Injector working
with exhaust steam

3
Engine standing
or running with throttle closed
Injector working with live steam

Plate 8 Three diagams showing the 'K' type of exhaust injector..

Exhaust injectors provided an economical method of injecting water into the boiler by utilising a small amount of exhaust steam from the cylinder for this purpose. Exhaust steam which would otherwise go to waste also heats the feed water, so that a hot delivery to the boiler is obtained; therefore, for most economical results the injector should be at work when the regulator is open, the feed being regulated by the water regulator handle on the Fireman's side of the cab.

The 'H', 'J', 'H/J' & 'K' types of exhaust injector are shown in Plates 6–8. When the regulator is open, the injector works with exhaust steam in conjunction with a supply of supplementary live steam. With the regulator closed, additional auxiliary live steam is necessary to take the place of the exhaust steam.

On all four types of exhaust injector mentioned, the changeover from exhaust to auxiliary live steam is provided automatically, being governed by the pressure in the steam chest. Earlier types do not have the automatic control. The injector detailed in the

The hand pump on *Firefly*. (Now a dummy, the stub lever operates the firebox dampers, through the bottom of the pump barrel.) The back flange will be screwed to the mahogany boiler lagging, giving the impression of feeding into the side of the firebox. Great Western No. 6 injectors are mounted under the footplate.

Live steam injector mounted in front of the cab, Swindon STEAM museum.

Exhaust injector mounted under the footplate level, Swindon STEAM museum.

previous section obtained the feed water from one of two sources – either from tanks carried actually on the locomotive, or from the tender towed behind. Both tanks on the locomotive (either 'saddle', 'pannier' or 'side' depending on the loco design) could be filled from the top by means of a 'water crane', a manually controlled swinging pipe with a flexible leather hose or 'bag' inserted into a large filler hole on tank or tender.

There was another way of filling the tender. The capacity of tank or tender was limited, particularly for the larger non-stop journeys of the passenger trains, so to enable a locomotive to obtain water without stopping, a series of 'water troughs' were positioned at strategic points on the various routes. These troughs, located in between the rails, were about a third of a mile long, and an elaborate pumping and balancing building was constructed at the line-side adjacent to the trough. In certain locations where very hard water was the only water available, a water-softening plant was included in the ancillary equipment, the whole system requiring routine attention and maintenance to ensure the troughs were always full. The tender had two bar handles, one either side of the ends of the tender-tank; one controlled the handbrake and the other controlled a 'scoop' arrangement under the tender water tank. The scoop was lowered over the trough – the locomotive at a slower speed to avoid hydraulic damage from the pressure of water – and the tender tank filled from the trough.

The author's father, who was a foreman supervising the trough maintenance as part of his duties, told an interesting tale. It appears that on one occasion a cleaner in the Running Shed preparing a locomotive turned the wrong handle on the tender, winding down the scoop instead of releasing or applying the handbrake. The locomotive went out into traffic with its scoop down, the scoop hitting the first track crossing it came to. The noise 'woke up' whoever was on the footplate and the scoop was immediately wound back up. But the damage had been done, and had gone unreported. The blow had knocked the scoop out of alignment so that when lowered in use it ripped out a long length of trough!

Incidentally, the inside of a tender tank had a number of transverse baffle plates with a hole in each large enough for someone (usually the apprentice) to crawl through when maintenance was undertaken. A large slotted 'gauge' was positioned at the front of the tender with a pointer connected to a very large 'ball float' arrangement (similar to a toilet tank), which operated the water level pointer against a scale on the gauge. It was the duty of whoever had crawled in to assemble the float gear to make sure it operated correctly. Up at the front of the tank alongside the coal space it was very restricted, so anyone too large had quite a job!

The tank had a pair of mushroom-shaped air vents to allow air into the tank when water was withdrawn, which occurred when the injectors were in operation.

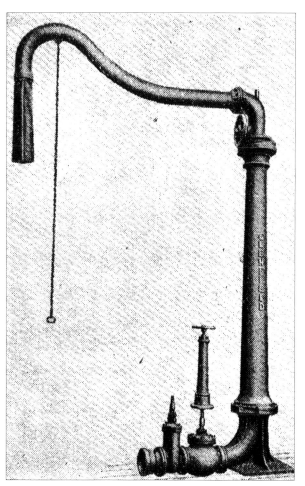

Above left: Glenfield & Kennedy water crane with anti-freeze device.

Above right: A Great Western-designed water column or 'crane'.

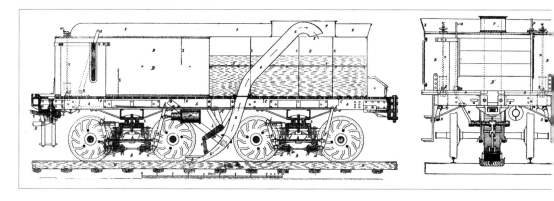

American tender water pick-up gear and water trough, *c.* 1890.

The scoop handle and water level gauge. The two small handles are the controls of the water valves for the two injectors.

The handbrake handle.

The scoop.

The water dome and filler cap.

23
CAST COMPONENTS AND THE FOUNDRY –
HOW DO THEY MAKE LOCO CYLINDERS?

THE FOUNDRY

Although not recognising the furnaces, moulding sand and the technology, the general conditions have not changed a great deal, still looking basically the same over 100 years.

There are many steam locomotive components which begin as a casting from a pattern rammed into a moulding box and cast in one of the wide range of metals available – various steels, cast irons and the wide range of yellow metals, the brasses, bronzes and leaded gun metals – all having the properties required for the specific application of the finished, machined casting. Component sizes can vary from a simple maker's plate to the complex shapes of cylinders; the maker's plate in brass, the cylinders usually in cast iron. Steel was used in cast form for locomotive wheels and particularly in America for locomotive frames, resulting in very complex castings (see Chapter 5 – Mallet Frames).

The basic principles of casting have not changed since the first locomotives were made. Materials have developed. The sand used for the moulds would now be unrecognisable to the early founders, but it still serves the same purpose. In the early years, including the 1940s when the author was an apprentice, the 'binder' used to keep the sand particles together was horse manure. How that would be viewed by the current 'Elf & Safety' people doesn't bear thinking about!

Whatever the design of the casting, a 'pattern' is made, which is really a 'model' of the required casting. It is a special type of model with special 'built-in' allowances. All metal shrinks a certain amount on cooling, and there will be certain faces of the casting which have to be machined, so sufficient size must be left on the relevant casting face to enable machining to size to take place. The pattern will be rammed with sand into a special moulding flask or box, so it must be designed in such a way that it can be removed from the moulding box when rammed, without pulling the moulded sand to pieces. Thus the pattern must be carefully thought out to include sufficient taper on the relative faces to enable clear removal from the moulding box. Incidentally, the pattern maker only gets a drawing of the finished component with sizes indicated; he does not get a drawing of the required pattern, which he has to determine himself.

Some patterns may be made solid, in selected seasoned wood (although other materials are now used as well), but many castings are required either hollow or with carefully positioned holes. These must be included in the design of the pattern, the hole itself made with moulded sand prepared in a 'core box', the internal shape of the box the shape of the required hole in the casting.

An example of a solid pattern could be a fire bar for the boiler firebox. Complex examples of a 'casting with holes', shown in illustrations on pages 203–208, are from patterns made by the Author for (i) the replica broad gauge (full-size) locomotive *Firefly* now in steam and running at the Great Western Society at Didcot. Shown are patterns for the cylinders which weigh approaching half a ton each. Note the pattern is in two halves, split on the centre line; (ii) a clack valve for a small industrial 'modern' saddle tank loco (page 203).

SMALL CASTINGS

The previous notes showed how the injector started to force the water into the boiler against the pressure within the boiler. In a similar fashion, the early hand-pump or the eccentric axle-driven development did the same job. What stopped the water being forced back through the injector or pump? This was the 'clack valve', attached to the boiler and with a non-return function. In the early designs this was a ball that was seated in the valve, pushed off its seat by the water going in and returned to its seat, thus sealing the boiler, when the injector or pump was stopped. It was reputedly named from the noise the ball made during its operation. The ball was later replaced by a winged valve design.

There were several places on the boiler and its firebox to which the valves could be attached and all were discussed and argued about as the ideal position at which cold water (in later years the water could be heated) should be introduced to hot water and steam under pressure. Each position had its objectors and its advocates.

The early hand-pump feed went into the bottom of the firebox, just above the footplate. Some designs had the clack valve at the front of the boiler barrel near the smoke box. Many locomotives had the feed into the backhead, two valves on either side

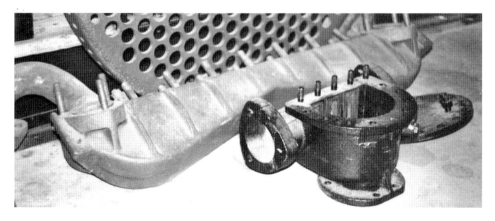

A couple of medium castings. In front is a regulator valve body. Just behind is a superheater header to which the superheater units were attached.

from the later injectors. The Great Western feed was on the top of the boiler in a number of designs, a combined safety valve with a pair of feed clacks, one either side of the valve. To eliminate some of the shock of a sudden spurt of cold water into a boiler or firebox, a horizontal tray was positioned at the top of the steam space under the valves which dispersed the intake of water, combining it quickly with, and assisted by, the steam.

From little saddle tank locos to the 4-6-2 *Tornado*, clack valve designs incorporated a safety feature by including a 'stop valve' within the clack valve design to isolate the valve if required. This was added in the light of experience!

GETTING THE WATER INTO THE BOILER – *FIREFLY* C. 1840

The set of patterns at the back is the hand-pump pattern. Clack box patterns and components are at the front.

A set of moulds.

The clacks as cast await machining. This early design has no emergency stop valve.

A CLACK VALVE C. 1940

Original valve on the boiler.

Valve stripped as there were no drawings.

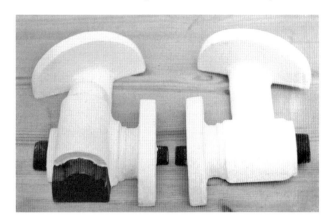

Patterns for the body, made from drawings based on the stripped valve components.

The associated 'core boxes'. The solid cores made in these boxes will form the holes through the casting when set in the mould.

Using modern-style small moulding boxes. Two halves of the mould secured together await pouring. The box or flask of wood is removed from the solidified halves, which are then secured together with the 'runner' (square) for the molten metal and the 'riser' (round) in position. Molten metal showing in the riser indicates the mould is full.

The old method, using a metal moulding box showing runner (left) and riser (right). The casting is retained in the moulding box until sufficiently cooled.

Pouring into a modern-style mould. The crucible is supported on an overhead crane hook, and moved along the line of prepared moulding boxes. This is casting in 2010 but Trevithick would still recognise the process.

MAKING CYLINDER PATTERNS FOR THE REPLICA *FIREFLY* 'INSIDE' CYLINDERS

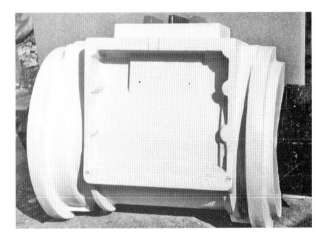

Core prints awaiting the finishing touches – filling and sanding (a 2 ft rule shows the size). The core prints on the ends of the cylinder pattern are of two different sizes to ensure the bore core goes in the correct way round.

Pattern for *Firefly* cylinder. This is a completed half with 'seats' and instructions for 'other hand' use. The seat for the exhaust core print can be seen at the top when it is moved for the other hand cylinder.

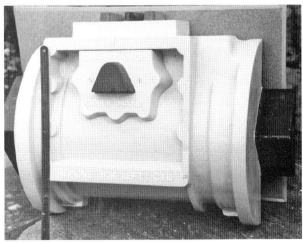

Completed half with 'other hand' instructions. The exhaust core print and shaped flange boss are shown. This is transferable to the other hand pattern.

The half core box for the cylinder bore. The black ends are the 'core prints', additions to the actual core to support it in the mould. The red 'prints' support the steam passage cores. Two half cores make one core.

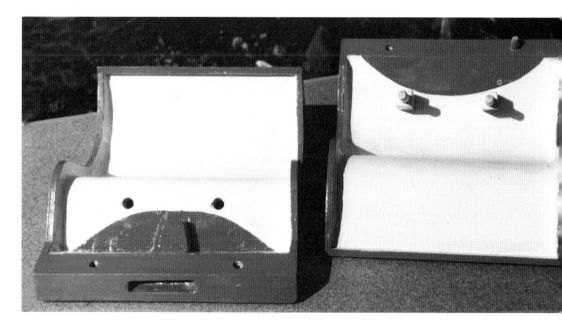

A steam passage core box. A second box was made for the other, different length core.

The core shape of the exhaust passage core. The long, curved face follows the curve of the cylinder wall.

The core box to produce the exhaust passage core.

FIREFLY CYLINDERS – CASTING

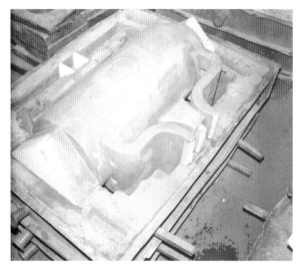

The moulding boxes at the foundry await closing and then casting. (The metal is brought from the furnace by an overhead crane carrying a large crucible full of molten metal.) The bottom box (drag) is pictured. The core prints and passage cores are clearly seen in position. Note the pouring gates and filters at the top left of the box.

The top box (cope).

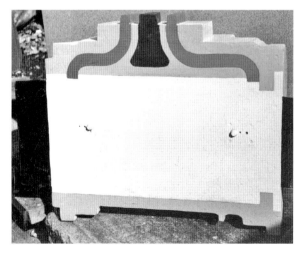

Bore and core positions shown on the joint face of the pattern. The red passages are inlet and exhaust. The slide valve directs exhaust steam to black passage to chimney via the blast pipe. (This was not strictly required, but painted for information as the patterns were displayed for a time in Swindon's old railway museum).

FIREFLY CYLINDERS – CASTINGS, COMPLETED, MACHINED AND SHOWN WITH STEAM CHEST IN POSITION

'Inside' cylinders – design and drawings from *c.* 1840.

FITTING THE CYLINDERS

The left- and right-hand cylinders are attached permanently to a centrally placed prefabricated steel frame.

OUTSIDE CYLINDER CASTINGS

The sole surviving example of the forerunner of the current 'Multiple Diesel Unit', the three-vehicle combination for local and rural travel, was a unique vehicle rebuilt at Didcot.

Conceived at the beginning of the twentieth century and following the first in 1903, the 1908 version with ninety-eight fellows opened up the rural areas by station-hopping along the many branch lines then existing on the GWR as examples.

Although extremely successful, being responsible for increased traffic between the many 'halts' or little platform stations which were introduced because of that traffic, it soon became obvious that they were *too* successful. They were not powerful enough for the amount of traffic generated. The steam rail motor was in effect a long (about 70 ft) railway carriage with a powered four-wheel bogie at one end, and while it could pull an additional coach as a trailer, the growth of farm traffic – cereals, milk and livestock – proved too much when required to pull wagons as well. There was also a further problem. At a number of small businesses which were developing along the lines, it was often required to deliver and shunt wagons, empties in, full ones out. This the rail motor could not really do, so a separate wagon move with a separate locomotive was required. If anything on the unit required repair, the whole coach was taken out of service.

So, although interrupted by the build-up and then tragedy of the First World War, the steam rail motors had the powered ends removed, and became trailer cars themselves, pulled by small tank locomotives which could be controlled by the driver from either the loco or from the other end of the coach itself, known as a push-pull set. A new concept of rail motor using diesel power came into the Great Western in the 1930s and the old rail motors were progressively scrapped, the last trailer conversion going about 1934.

Although withdrawn from trailer service, some became stores vehicles and the last one survived in this capacity, becoming a mobile office conversion for the author and a small team introducing Planned Preventive Maintenance schemes over the Great Western system for about five years from around 1955, continuing when the author moved on, back into the Works at Swindon.

It is strange how things turn full circle. On retirement the author joined the Great Western Society and was extremely surprised when on visiting, he found the coach was on the list for rebuilding, now the only survivor. He immediately joined the 'friends', eventually making the patterns for the cylinders, steam chest, wheels, axle boxes, horns and valve guides shown. The casting procedures would be recognised by the original builders and indeed as far back as Trevithick himself.

A Foundry scene and procedures of 1901 are included in this chapter. Nothing basic really changes! **Note:** The steam rail motor is now fully operational at Didcot.

Steam rail motors await their fate outside Swindon Works 'A' shop, *c.* 1930.

The engine unit for the Great Western Steam Rail Motor of 1908 being rebuilt by the Great Western Society at Didcot.

SMALL CASTINGS USING A 'PLATE' PATTERN

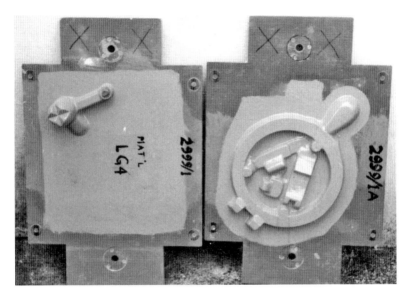

A plate pattern was for machine moulding but could be used on the moulding bench for a 'one-off' or small run. The plate protects some of the finer detail of the pattern. This pattern was for the 'port hole' windows in the cab of the Hall/ Saint conversion undertaken by the Great Western Society at Didcot.

The pattern was made and the castings machined and fitted by the author. The outer-ring frame of the window formed a 'ring gate' which fed the rest of the components when the metal was poured. (A second plate pattern, not shown, formed the backing ring of the completed window.)

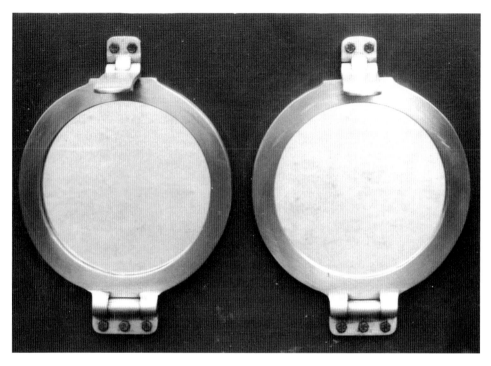

The completed window-frames of the two windows await the springs fitted to the top locking catches and the glass. Mounted on a plywood backing to show how they worked. The material is leaded gunmetal (LG4).

Diagrams from a Foundry Correspondence Course of 1901.

REPAIR OF LOCOMOTIVE CYLINDERS

First of all we have to determine what could go wrong with a cylinder semi-permanently attached to the frames:

(a) **Hydraulic damage** – trapped water in a cylinder will not compress and while the loco is running, smashes a cylinder cover, often breaking out part of the cylinder in so doing. (Use of the drain cocks before moving should avoid this problem.) Often a different grade of iron was used to ensure the cover broke first, before the damage to the cylinder occurred.

(b) **A stress crack** – somewhere in the cylinder casting.

(c) **Uneven wear in the cylinder bore** – leaving a 'step' in the bore caused by the extremity of the stroke at the front or back piston ring. The same could happen with a piston valve chamber and piston valve. The face of a slide valve seat will also wear. A counter-bore at each end of the cylinder was often used to prevent 'stepping'.

(d) **A broken piston ring** – often jams and scores the bore. Pieces of a piston valve ring can also find their way into the cylinder itself via the steam ports, thus scoring and damaging the cylinder bore.

So – how did they cope with the problems?

(a) In the days of official steam, cast iron welding was avoided if possible as it was a very difficult procedure. A broken cylinder or its cover would be replaced by new items as a matter of course. In the sixty or so years since, technology has improved so attempts would now be made if repair was considered even remotely possible, as this is certainly cheaper than a new cylinder.

(b) Apprentice years often trigger memories. In the erecting shop there was a 'circuit' of repair procedures. A locomotive came in for a 'heavy' general repair. First on the circuit were the stripping pits, every fitting being removed from below the frame, the boiler removed, the frame cleaned and moved to the 'frame gang'. The cylinders were retained in place and the author recalls a cracked 'between the frames' cylinder block, a distinct open crack across the top of the steam chest. The usual procedure was then followed. The crack, about 7 in. long, was immediately the work of a fitter and apprentice with a pneumatic portable drill, the traditional 'post and arm' arrangement set up on top of the steam chest. Blind, closely spaced holes were drilled (like a honeycomb) for about 3 in. all around the crack to a depth of about ⅜ in. and 'tapped' for ⅜ in. diameter, and a steel screwed rod was screwed tightly into each hole and cut off almost flush with the surface. A welder arrived, a screen was placed around the crack and a layer of weld material was laid over the surface of the crack and steel. The welded repair then usually lasted the life of the locomotive, the steel rod 'inserts' allowing ordinary steel arc welding to take place, thus forming a permanent patch.

(c & d) There were two methods of dealing with a worn or scored cylinder bore. A cylinder was usually designed as quite a hefty casting with sufficient metal to allow at least one re-bore. This was done by using a portable boring machine which could be fitted directly to the front of the cylinder using the ring of studs which secured the front cylinder cover. It was driven from a compressed air line coupled to an adapted portable drilling machine, a very useful power source. There were also similar machines for re-boring piston valves and facing slide valve seats.

Having been opened out to its limit, further machining allowed it to be opened out sufficiently for a 'liner' to be inserted. This entailed a fascinating process. A liner was machined with a slightly larger outside diameter than the machined bore. Positioned by the cylinder, a large tank of liquid carbon dioxide (CO_2) was surmounted with a small hoist to which the liner was attached, lowered into, and allowed to soak. On withdrawal it had shrunk sufficiently to be carefully pushed into the cylinder bore. On thawing, it gripped on expansion so tightly that the only way to remove it would have been to machine it out.

A demonstration of the effectiveness of the process was made with a piece of rubber hose or an apple. Immersed and frozen, they broke and shattered like porcelain when struck or dropped.

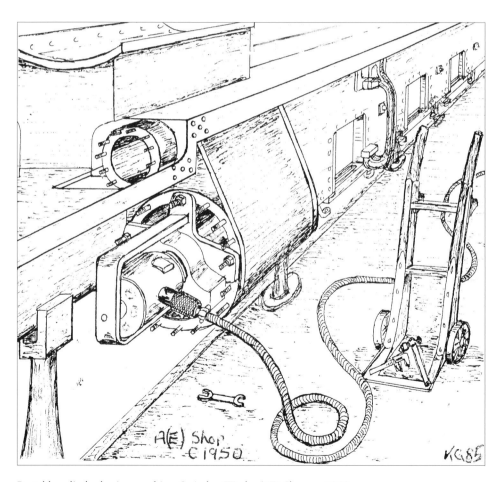

Portable cylinder boring machine, Swindon Works A(E) Shop, *c.* 1950.

THE AMERICAN RAILROADS

The American rail roads were early exponents of *in situ* cylinder boring and valve seat facing. It was probably easier due to the American locomotive design, which favoured outside cylinders and valve gear of whatever design. In Britain, four- and three-cylinder locomotives had the cylinders grouped together across the frames, but the American designers opted for outside the frames, and for four-cylinder versions just made the locos longer: pairs of cylinders, one behind the other, all very accessible, particularly with the valve chests on top of the cylinders and the valve seat, with the slide valve, horizontal. (See also Chapter 28) In Britain, particularly with the GWR, two-cylinder locomotives with the cylinders between the frames had the valve seats vertical in a number of loco classes which used the slide valve.

The Americans widely used a hand-operated rotary facing machine for valve seats; the design was available in two sizes for use on other suitable seat-facing requirements. Lining cylinders was also well established with the US rail roads. Having bored out the cylinder, there were four basic methods of lining. One had the liner to the exact length of the bore between the cylinder covers, which hopefully secured it in place. A second had it forced in hydraulically with a danger of cracking the cylinder. In a third method, the liner was held in with screws into the steam space each end of the cylinder. A fourth attempt had the cylinder preheated to expand, questionable with cast iron 'but it all worked'. The liner was pre-machined to include the steam ports in each case.

Some of the earlier designers and the Americans were well to the forefront in this respect and developed some outstanding and unique ideas. Mr Samuel Vauclain, of the Baldwin Locomotive Works, developed one such idea for a four-cylinder/two-cylinder compound locomotive that on first sight looks like a 'normal' two-cylinder version. On closer examination, it proves to be a four-cylinder compound with two piston rods, one working above and one below each crosshead. This used the cylinder arrangement of a high- and low-pressure cylinder working one above the other. It was built in 1895 by the Baldwin Locomotive Works for the Philadelphia & Reading Railroad. A 'Wootton' type boiler (again a typical variation in design), 26 in. stroke by 13 in. and 22 in. diameter cylinders. Wheels, 84¼ in. driving pair and 54¼ in. diameter trailers. (Compare this to the last broad gauge locomotive of the GWR of only three years before as an example of innovation and design progress!)

Baldwin Vauclain compound. Passenger No. 385, Philadelphia & Reading Railway.

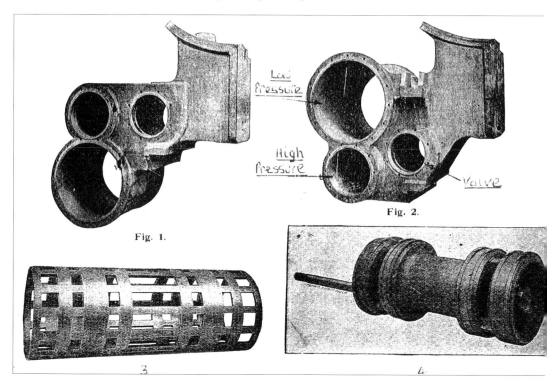

The American way. Cast cylinders – two versions of 'Vauclain' design. Figs 1 and 2 are two designs of compound, piston valved cylinder castings with half smoke box saddles. Fig. 3 is a fully machined piston valve liner. Fig 4 is a piston valve.

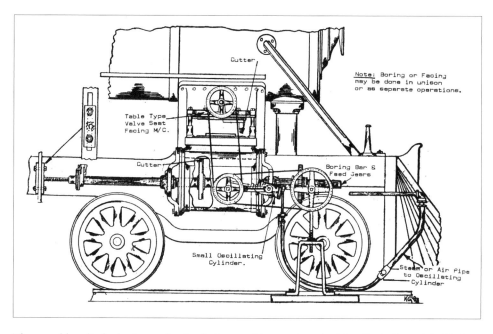

The portable cylinder-boring and valve-facing machine used on the New York Central & Hudson River Railroad, *c.* 1900.

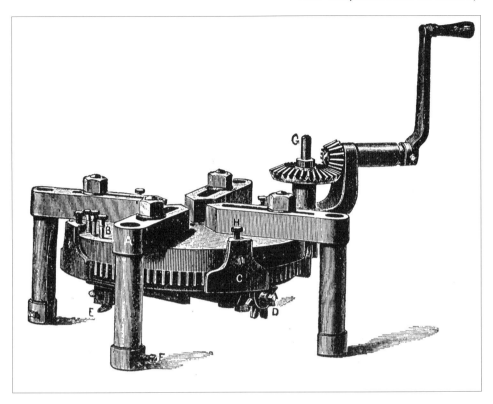

Hand-operated valve seat-facing machine. With this machine you can face a valve seat in about a quarter of the time required to do it by hand. If the machine is in good order it leaves the surface almost perfectly true, therefore the seat requires very little filing or scraping.

24

OTHER COMPONENTS – HAND FORGING, DROP STAMPING AND STEAM HAMMER-PRESSING

We have looked at casting as a technique – another important one was forging. This has nothing to do with swindling the Bank of England, but is a way of working metal by hammering either mechanically or by hand when the metal is red/white hot. (The author remembers as an apprentice always spitting on the metal when collecting anything from the blacksmith's shop. If it hissed you didn't pick it up – you learned the hard way in those days!)

Railway works had quite a range of 'Hot Shops' – blacksmiths, stamping, steam hammers, spring shop, often a small press shop or an area usually in the carriage and wagon works for forming the metal sheets and shapes around windows etc. for the covering of the wooden-framed coaches. Sheet metal in a soft state was pressed cold.

There is a 'classic' photograph of the steam hammer shop at Swindon Works with a team forging a locomotive connecting rod from a block of metal under a large steam hammer, which was controlled by the hammer driver, usually a skilled operator who could vary the blow to suit the work. Equally skilled was the operator guiding the metal under the controlled hammer blows, the hammer rising and falling in rhythm with the twisting and turning of the metal. The finished rod, now 'in the black', would be taken for finishing to the machine shop.

The blacksmith's shop in any carriage and wagon and the Loco Works were lined with the typical blacksmith's forges and most had a small steam hammer in the working area. Again as an apprentice I watched a hammer driver, in this case a war-recruited female, crack a walnut under the hammer, such was the touch she had for controlling the blow. Apart from the steam hammers, any blacksmith's shop, like a foundry, didn't change in appearance over the years, although the steam hammers would have replaced the original 'Oliver' or tilt hammers, pivoted beams with a large hammerhead on the working end over the special anvil, and tripped at the back by a revolving shaft operated by a water wheel or a steam engine. Mentioned earlier in these notes was the description by John Nuttal of a rather crude hammer operating like a French Revolution guillotine, pulled to the top of the frame by ropes. Over the years as the steam hammers got bigger, so the form of the drop hammer got bigger, now with better control.

Such items as brake block hangers and spring hangers were produced by the biggest drop hammer in Swindon Works. In the early years, these and similar items would have been forged by the blacksmith, but such was development and technology that such items could be produced in one bang by the 8-ton 'monkey' or 'tup', the big top block which contained half the shape (like a casting mould) of the item to be made, the other half of the die being in the bottom block. A solid block of sparkling white-hot steel would be drawn from the adjacent furnace and placed on the bottom block; the top block would be allowed to fall from a predetermined height up its frame, depending on the power of the blow required and the size of the required component. In one hit, the item would be formed. Very quickly removed from the die, it would have a skirt or ring round it (like the ring around the planet Saturn). It was then, still glowing, taken adjacent to a 'scragging press' where it was forced through a shaped plate which neatly removed the skirt, and then placed aside to cool. The operation of the big drop hammer could be heard all over Swindon during the night in the war years, when it was apparently hammering out the components of tank turret rings!

Incidentally, in the stamp shop the hammers were all mounted on really built-up ground so stability was a problem. The big hammer base block, on which the bottom die was set, was apparently a 68-ton casting, the biggest casting ever made in the Works, the whole mounted on a 25 ft cube of blue bricks. The stamping shop has now long gone of course, but the block casting is still there – still hidden below ground level and built over. A puzzle for archaeologists in the years to come, perhaps.

Among the limited number of items produced by pressing at Swindon Loco Works were the components of locomotive boilers. In the early locomotive years, such items as tube plates, throat plates, and inner and outer firebox backhead shapes would be produced manually by heating and beating the plates over cast iron formers, but again

The spring shop. This is the leaf spring section.

Repairing by oxyacetylene welding a pin location on a spring compensating beam.

The Godfrey oxygen jet cutting machine. A 1920s oxyacetylene cutting machine shaping a Smith and steam hammer-forged connecting rod.

The stamping shop, Swindon Works. The biggest drop hammer, the 'Tup', is shown here. Weighing 8 tons, it was hauled to the top of the frame, a white-hot steel block was placed on the bottom die, and the Tup was released like the blade on the French guillotine. The resulting blow squashed the white-hot metal into the shape of the die, half the shape in the falling Tup and half the shape in the anvil bottom block. Still red-hot, the resulting shape had a squeezed-out 'skirt' between the two half-shaped dies. It was then taken to an adjacent 'scragging press' and forced through a shaped plate which trimmed off the skirt, leaving a shape such as the brake hanger below, which then only required a slot machined for the brake block and drilling when cold for the various pin-holes. It was fascinating watching the operations as an apprentice. The steel blocks seen on the rack await their turn in the adjacent furnace. The finished items, already 'scragged', wait on the trailer for transport to stores or machine shop. (Photo Eric Bradle)

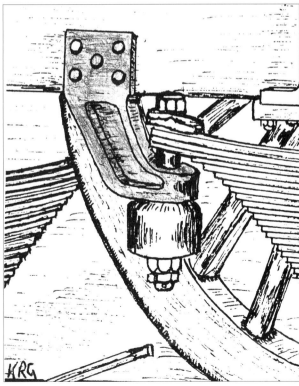

A 'spring hanger bracket'.

Left: A brake hanger.

Below: Forging a connecting rod under a steam hammer.

Making a coil spring. A bar of white-hot steel is removed from the small furnace on the right and hooked under a loop on the machine mandrel. The mandrel rotates and also moves from left to right, thus winding the steel bar around itself at the required pitch of the spring coils. The completed spring is then quenched in an oil bath.

Making a boiler throat plate; the plate is taken from the furnace on the left then positioned under the press. Note the finished throat plate on the floor.

A tube plate – another product of the press, the blanks pressed out and drilled for the boiler tubes, which were expanded rather than welded or screwed into the various holes. The large holes are for the superheater tubes, the centre hole at the top for the main steam pipe from the regulator. The smallest holes are for the longitudinal boiler stays, linking to a similar plate the other end of the boiler barrel.

as technology grew, the press tool developed. Heating in an adjacent furnace, the plates would be handled with long 'T' grips, slipped into the press, and out comes a completed shape, all sides curved round uniformly. The backhead was of steel plate, as were the throat plate and front and back tube plates. The inner firebox was of copper in the Great Western days and the boiler was all riveted. Nowadays boilers are all steel and welded! Certainly cheaper, but better?

The spring shop had the appearance of the blacksmith's shop but dealt solely with spring-making – any type, size or shape! The usual locomotive spring was of multi-plate design, with the plates held in a box-like buckle around the centre of the stack, held by a rivet through the centre. These usually took the main springing of the locomotive, but for certain applications coil springs were used. Once the assembled, hardened and skilfully tempered (in oil) plates were assembled into a spring, it was positioned in a machine and 'scragged' or bounced 'X' number of times to check its future action in use.

Coil springs started life as a long spring steel bar, heated in the adjacent furnace and quickly inserted into the locking clip on a mandrel. The machine was started and the bar carefully guided as it wrapped itself around the rotating mandrel, making a symmetrical coil – each coil at the correct pitch from its neighbour. It was then removed and put into the tempering oil bath, then across to the machine to be bounced. Different size mandrels allowed different diameter springs to be made.

25
THE 'NUTS AND BOLTS' STORY

The title contains a phrase often used to describe the fine details of the workings of an organization or mechanism, but in these notes it means exactly what it says. From whence were the 'nuts and bolts' of the steam locomotive obtained?

It was not until the 1860s that the tap, die and twist drill as we now know them came into being. The introduction of the milling machine enabled rapid development into much more efficient tools. The blacksmith-made 'diamond-point' drill and the four-cornered tap (which if not used carefully just reamed out the hole without cutting a thread) became historical relics. Such were the problems of drilling holes that as many holes as possible were, in the early years, hot punched in the metal by the blacksmith. Also, in the early years up to 1841, when Whitworth described his unification proposals for a standard screw thread system (which still took time to be accepted and introduced), manufacturers made their own nuts and bolts. Therefore it became imperative to retain nuts and bolts from your purchased locomotive, and you lost a nut at your peril, as finding a relevant thread pitch and form could prove difficult.

Development raced ahead, and in the forty years to the turn of the century thread-milling had produced some marvellous examples of various pitch and form of multi-start large-diameter screw threads. Incidentally, in Birmingham Science Museum is a lathe with a hand-cut lead screw from the early nineteenth century, which, when built into a lathe, enabled others to be turned. A start the hard way.

Once pitches and forms related to diameter of bolts had become established, nuts and bolts settled into accepted common user items. In the steam years, the Works at Swindon was virtually self-contained and made everything required for rolling stock construction. Nut and bolt manufacture had settled well into a regular groove, with a nominal production flow pattern.

Very strangely positioned, literally at arms length from the Locomotive Works manager's office, was what was probably the dirtiest workshop in Swindon, the 'N' shop, which made 'black' nuts and bolts literally by the million. 'Black' nuts were so-called because they were made from as-rolled hexagon bar with a rough black and scaly surface. There were other nuts and bolts of other materials for special applications as well as 'bright' steel and all these latter were produced on the automatic lathes of the adjacent 'R' machine shop or other machining facilities within the Works. The 'N' shop contained punching and blanking machines, each hand-fed with steel bars heated to bright red for a length of one end and pushed into the continually running punching and blanking machines. The small furnace adjacent to each machine burnt gas oil, not a particularly flammable substance; especially when lighting up, a choking black smoke would fill the shop, pouring out of the open doors and broken window panes. Occasionally, a blackened figure would emerge from a doorway, take a couple of deep breaths, a quick glance at the sun and sky and plunge back again into the smoke and noise. The roar of the little furnaces, the clank of the machinery and the smoke and flame-filled interior must have resembled Dante's inferno to those who worked there. I only went to the shop once, on a maintenance quest with a fitter from the 'G' shop while I was an apprentice, but once was enough! To be sent to the 'N' shop to work was also a punishment for misdemeanours. I remember as an office boy the circulating tale of the fate of two office boys from the Locomotive Manager's office who, I understand, were accused of putting indelible ink in the office tea urn! I believe they were both on the list of acceptance for apprenticeships and were given the choice of dismissal or transfer to the 'N' shop until apprenticeship commenced. They chose the 'N' shop rather than miss out on the apprenticeship.

A nut or bolt blank produced by the 'N' shop really was a labour intensive item. A nut still had to be faced top and bottom, and tapped with the appropriate thread, and a bolt had to have its shank threaded to the required length. Some nuts had an application where the facing of top and bottom was not required, so these were only tapped.

Forming the third corner of a square with the 'N' shop and the manager's office, and across a narrow road, a corner of the 'R' machine shop was dedicated to the machining requirements of the black nut and bolt. Within the hierarchy of trades, certain jobs were decreed to be the work of the 'turner', and other jobs were for the 'machinist', and 'never the twain shall meet!' Basically, we could say that for work in which the cutter moved or revolved (i.e. milling, drilling, shaping and slotting), a machinist was employed, but for work which itself revolved (i.e. the lathe work), this was the province of the turner.

In this area of the 'R' shop two separate gangs were employed, one machinist and one turner; in my day, the machinist chargehand was Dave Simms, and the turner chargehand, very appropriately, was named Harry Turner. Bins of black nuts and bolts were moved on completion from 'N' shop across the road and into what was known as the 'Scraggery' for the final machining operations. Dave Simms' gang operated the screwing and tapping machines which were the first process, and the tapped nuts were passed in their bins across an invisible gang boundary into Harry Turner's domain for facing.

I am often asked, 'Why was the place called the "Scraggery"?' A dictionary definition of 'scrag' gives 'Anything thin or lean with roughness' but there were several applications of the word within the Works. In the spring shop, for example, a new spring was bounced or 'scragged' in a special machine. Next to the drop hammers in the stamping shop was a 'scragging press', used to remove the ragged protrusion formed when the die blocks of the hammer shaped the component. The hammer struck a tremendous blow as the dies came together, a blow which forced the white-hot steel billet to the shape of the die blocks, mating top and bottom. The blow squeezed out a thin layer of metal at the joint of the die blocks, and while still red-hot, the component was rapidly transferred to the adjacent scragging press, where it was pressed through a hardened shaped plate to the external periphery of the finished profile, so giving a smooth external shape. Among the components so made were the brake block hangers, quite large, and arranged under the biggest hammer in the shop. Incidentally, although the hammer has long gone, I understand that its base block, the biggest casting ever made at Swindon foundry and weighing over 60 tons, is still in position! (How do you remove it and what do you do with it when it is removed?)

However, to return to nuts and bolts – bolts were threaded individually in screwing machines, a horizontally held bolt blank fed manually by a capstan mechanism into a slowly revolving geared die head. Set to a stop or when the feed was manually retarded the die head opened automatically, the bolt was removed and dropped into a waiting bin. The process was repeated for each individual bolt. Nuts were tapped in multiple spindled vertical machines. A nut blank was placed under a long machine tap, the tap entered into the hole in the bank where it started to cut, and continued cutting while another nut was placed under the next spindle in line with the tap entered. I believe there were about six vertical spindles on the machine, the finished nuts ending at the top of the tap thread on the long smooth shank of the tap. When, say, half a dozen nuts were stockpiled, the tap could easily be removed and the nuts tipped off into the appropriate bin. The tap was then returned to its spindle and the process repeated.

Under the trade hierarchy system, the lads who tapped the nuts and screwed the bolts were machinist apprentices, and the bins of nuts (metal bins, say 18 in. by 10 in. by 9 in.) were moved to the turner apprentices for completion. The introduction to turning for the latter was usually a painful process. Each nut, to be faced on a machine so set, ranged from about ½ in. up to 2½ in., the latter from the large drag hooks and just about the largest tackled. The machine for this large nut was quite ancient and known as the 'killer' from the long horizontal lever, which closed a collett arrangement gripping the nut. The smaller nuts were the most painful ones. Each nut had to be individually screwed onto the mandrel nose of the machines. There were no spanners, so the nut was held in the fingers while the apprentice controlled the speed of the mandrel, the nut screwing itself onto the mandrel nose. Often the thread 'picked-up', and the nut blank revolved between the fingers when the sharp rag or 'flash' on the face to be machined nicked the fingers holding it. An applied bandage often then caught on the rag of a later nut, was whipped off the finger and deposited in the nut bin at the machine's base. Each nut was faced by operating hand-wheels which passed a little cutter across the face of the nut. A second wheel operated another cutter which either chamfered the outer corners of the machined face, or chamfered the start of the thread, depending on which face of the nut was being machined at the time. 'Stops' on the machine bed ensured uniformity, and the nuts were removed by operating a lever which reversed the direction of the mandrel, and a 'fork' gripped the nut so that it unscrewed and fell off into the waiting bin.

The permanent staff of the gang consisted of three females recruited, as in many other workshops, during the late war shortages. Peggy, Rose and Sylvia, although friendly and working within the group, were rarely chatted to by the apprentices. Harry Turner saw to that, and as they disappeared at tea breaks there was not much opportunity. One of the girls, I think it was Sylvia, was occasionally visited by her boyfriend, always under the beady eye of Harry, who frowned at such liberties and who ensured that he did not stay very many minutes.

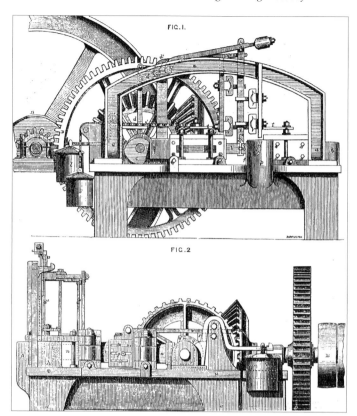

FIG. 1.

FIG. 2.

Left: The Engineer, 6 June 1856. Rothera's improvements in machinery for manufacturing bolts, screw-blanks, etc. Patent dated 8 October 1855. This invention consists in a novel arrangement of machinery for manufacturing bolts, screw-blanks, rivets, and other similar articles. Fig. 1 is a front view of the machine, showing more clearly the 'swages' and the cam for working the same, and also the 'yielding' motion, with lever and weight for allowing the bearing of the cam shaft to move. Fig. 2 is a side elevation, more particularly showing the apparatus for forming the bolt or screw-blank head, together with the cams for actuating the same, and also its own particular 'yielding' or giving-way motion.

Below: Nut making machine.

The girls were permanently working on the nut facing machines, but the apprentices 'graduated' from nut facing to the 'parting off' machines on which very simple work was done. Tubes for superheater return bends were parted off or cut from long tube lengths, and bars of bright steel were cut to length for other purposes. Nuts, bars, bolts and tubes were then taken into the adjacent stores for despatch throughout the Works and system. We, the apprentices, were always glad our stay in the Scraggery was comparatively short, about two months, before moving out into the 'R' shop proper and onto proper lathes. Replacements were always available in the continuous process of apprentice training, and the legends of the hardships and difficulties expanded and enlarged when talking to the lads who followed.

Nowadays the procedures would probably be condemned by Health and Safety at Work regulations. However tough they were, they certainly did not do us any harm. Steam work sixty-five years ago was tough, but having said that, I would not have missed it and have never regretted anything of my apprentice years.

26

Outlines of History – Events of Locomotive Design and Use in the Mid-1800s

All the early years of the Great Western Railway have been well and truly documented, and are really dominated by the activities of two men, I. K. Brunel and Daniel Gooch. Although outstanding as a broad-thinking engineer, the success and vision of Brunel did not really extend into the locomotive field. While beaten by the technology (or lack of it) of the day with his 'Atmospheric Caper' on the South Devon, his specifications for his first steam locomotives left much to be desired, being really quite impracticable.

His first batch of locomotives, usually referred to as 'freaks' by many subsequent writers, were the result of the attempts by the unfortunate manufacturers to whom the contracts were issued to produce a locomotive designed and built to the specifications as issued. It should be understood that Brunel did not supply drawings, only a specification from which the manufacturers were to design and build from drawings prepared by themselves. The 'engineering drawing' itself was in its infancy at this early period. His requirements, including a weight limit and an almost impossibly low piston speed, coupled with the unusual gauge of 7 ft, certainly gave sleepless nights to the designers!

To achieve any form of success the manufacturers had to deviate from what were already well-established design criteria, and such locomotives as *Thunderer*, *Hurricane* and *Ajax* were among the results. Two of them had wheels of 10 ft diameter, while the third, *Thunderer*, had a system of gearing giving an equivalent 18 ft diameter to the driving wheels. Another engine, *Vulcan*, had 8 ft drivers and was reasonably successful. The problems of manufacture were increased by the 7 ft gauge.

Prior to the orders being placed, the manufacturers, including such names as Mather Dixon, Haigh Foundry, Sharp, Roberts, Hawthorn's, etc., were already well established in the locomotive-making business. Indeed, locomotives were already being exported. The first to go to America, by the firm of Edward Bury, were so well thought of in principles of design that the 'bar frame' which they introduced formed the basis of virtually all subsequent American designs. The 'plate frame' of GWR practice was of secondary consideration. It thus follows that, with their makers, their workshops had been conditioned by what they were actually making, so that an order 'out of the blue' for broad-gauge giants immediately caused problems as they would not fit into the shops without difficulty. Most tracks were standard gauge, with a few up to, say, 5 ft 6 in., but 7 ft was a different matter entirely, particularly when the design called for wheels of 10 ft diameter.

Such problems that arose in design must have been communicated back to Brunel himself. He decided, and indeed it was becoming obvious, that he could not do it all himself. He needed someone to handle the locomotive side of things. Again, out of the blue came what must now be the most publicised job application letter in Great Western history. A young man named Daniel Gooch found himself for the second time without a permanent job, but currently in very temporary employment with his brother. He had heard of the possibility of a vacancy and had forwarded his application.

Brunel, who had a railway to organise and for whom time was running out regarding its opening date, seized the opportunity himself and went north to interview the applicant. Brunel was apparently impressed by what he saw and Daniel Gooch was duly appointed Locomotive Superintendent. Among Gooch's first jobs was to travel around the manufacturers, ostensibly to gauge progress on the building of the engines. It is safe to speculate that this was a cover for a more detailed look to ascertain what problems would be arriving with the locomotives themselves; problems caused by the original specification and the fact that it was now too late to do anything about it anyway! He records that he was 'not impressed by what he saw!'

Also well documented is the work undertaken by both Brunel and Gooch in the running sheds at London in an attempt to get improved performance from the locomotives as delivered. The 1838 inaugural journey to open the line took place successfully, but as Wellington said of Waterloo, 'it was a damn close run thing'. The first locomotives and their problems are well documented so suffice to say here that the directors were not overly impressed by the first efforts. So they went around Brunel to Gooch with instructions to design something more effective than the first batch of locomotives.

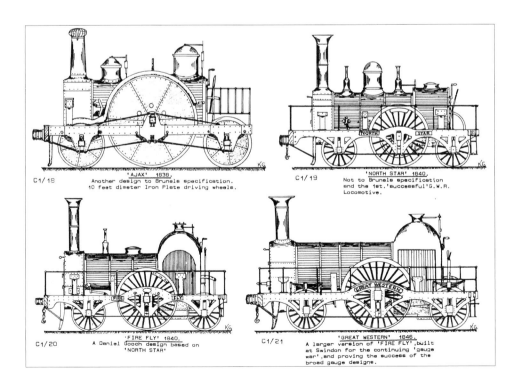

'AJAX' 1838.
C1/18   Another design to Brunels specification.
10 feet dimeter Iron Plate driving wheels.

'NORTH STAR' 1840.
C1/19   Not to Brunels specification
and the 1st.'successful'G.W.R.
Locomotive.

'FIRE FLY' 1840.
C1/20   A Daniel Gooch design based on
'NORTH STAR'

'GREAT WESTERN' 1846.
C1/21   A larger version of 'FIRE FLY',built
at Swindon for the continuing 'gauge
war',and proving the success of the
broad gauge designs.

Among the locomotives acquired in that first batch had been one which had not been built under the problematical Brunel specification but which was fortuitously available. It was built for an American railway that eventually could not pay for it and was altered by makers Robert Stephenson for the broad gauge Great Western; thus *North Star* was the one shining success in an otherwise dim galaxy. Working with Gooch at Swindon at the time were two men who were later to be recognised as outstanding engineers in their own right. Thomas Crampton was chief draughtsman and Archie Sturrock, brought from the north by Gooch, was the locomotive manager. With a team like that success was bound to follow, and using *North Star* as a guide a design was produced for the most successful of the early broad gauge passenger locomotives.

There were some relatively minor problems with *North Star*, a tendency to 'prime' being one of them, but a redesigned firebox with a haystack crown was an improvement. This was still at a time when the Great Western had no factory or facilities of its own, so orders were placed from the drawing board for a batch of sixty-two spread around seven manufacturers! Such was the confidence in the design that Gooch issued not only specifications (with more practical detail than those of Brunel), but sets of templates made for various components to ensure some measure of uniformity. Although interchangeability would not be achieved between manufacturers, nor indeed with most components between locomotives from the same maker, an 1830s step had been taken in the right direction.

At this time the six-wheeled locomotive was the vogue. For passenger service, the 2-2-2 with the central pair of very large drivers gave more power and thus weight, requiring a better support than the four-wheel design of a few years earlier. Other wheel arrangements and sizes applied to the goods-traffic engine. Among the combinations, including the 0-4-2 and the 2-4-0, the first bogie 4-2-0 locomotive had already been exported to America. From the firm of Jones, Turner & Evans of Newton-le-Willows came the first of the batch of sixty-two. It was named the *Firefly*, giving a title to the class during March 1840, and set the seal on a most successful life-span for the group until overtaken by requirements for yet more power.

This was also the time of the 'gauge wars', the first battle raging over the spread of the broad gauge, with 'narrow gauge' exponents seen as the enemy. Trials were organised, including the Firefly class locomotive *Ixion* as the GWR representative. There was really in modern parlance 'no contest'. *Ixion* dominated the opposition in regard to speed, power, stability and handling. Although the battle was won hands-down, it must be said that the war was already lost as no one else wanted to 'think big' and standard gauge was spreading like wildfire over the rest of the country.

The Firefly class, it must be understood, were built at a time when there were no steam hammers, no micrometers, no milling machines, and shapers and planers were small in their infancy. There were no 'twist drills', only the carbon steel 'diamond-point' shape of flat drill made up and ground by the blacksmith. There were no grindstones made up of bonded abrasive, only stones cut from natural rock (what a job that must have been!), and there was no gas or electric welding, only the sparkling white heat of the blacksmith's fire. The Bessemer process was still two decades away, so there was no steel in large quantities, only small crucible amounts for tools. The material most used was thus wrought iron, formed to the required shapes and with holes hot punched by the blacksmith. Obviously there were no pneumatic or electric hand tools; drilling on site was by hand ratchet and drill post and arm and it was such a laborious job that it was avoided as much as possible. The lathe had developed into back-geared, sliding, surfacing and screw-cutting, but even uniform threads (Whitworth) were still in the future, so the makers used their own nuts and bolts. You lost a nut at your peril! Construction was mostly hard graft; hammer and chisel and manual work. The craftsmen who made the Firefly locos are to be admired.

The locomotives themselves, weighing around 24 tons each, had a wheelbase of 13 ft 2 in. – although this varied with some manufacturers, as did the cylinder dimensions. They had achieved speeds of around 60 mph by the mid-1840s, forming the main passenger motive power of the Great Western at this period. On 1 May 1844, on the opening of the Bristol & Exeter Railway, the Firefly class *Acteon*, with Gooch on the footplate, travelled from Paddington to Exeter and back in the day at an average speed of 40.11 mph. The journey distance and the speed were a world record at that time. The repair and rebuilding programme gave a Firefly an approximate thirty-year existence and an average mileage of 500,000 miles each. The oldest, *Ixion*, was thirty-eight years old when scrapped. Although inevitably being overtaken by even bigger and more powerful designs, the overall appearance of the class (as with the much later Churchward Stars) set the design format. The next step was the Great Western class, but that is another story.

In the meantime, *Firefly* lives on in the full-size working steam reproduction now operating successfully at Didcot. Thus the *Firefly* story has even now not really ended; so have a look at the progress when you next visit. Swindon's STEAM Museum now houses the patterns for the 7 ft driving wheels. The wheels are now steel castings and not formed, as in the original days, by the skill and muscle of the blacksmith. Modern technology may be a good thing – it just costs a lot more.

There was not, of course, a sudden ending to the sixty-two locomotives of the Firefly class and they continued working until around 1870, although rather quickly eclipsed by designs of more power. Some were converted to tank format as their importance declined; others were relegated to other than 'top link' duties. The tools and methods available for the construction of the Firefly class, and the real manual work of construction in the absence of equipment, we now take for granted. In those early years, the design of locomotives was also conditioned by what was actually available. For instance, if now we wish to check on a boiler pressure we look at a glass-faced dial with a pointer that immediately indicates against figures the pressure within. (We have again to thank a Frenchman, Bourdon, for this much later device.) On the *Firefly* and other engines of the period, the driver consulted a pointer running in the slot of a vertical Salter spring balance, securely attached to a lever pivoted across the top of the safety valve. This was either blowing or not blowing, giving very little indication on the balance, which was dependent on the feel and experience of the driver! It became standard practice in those early years to have two safety valves on a boiler, one locked and sealed to blow at above working pressure and sound practice, positioned out of the reach of the driver. Drivers had quickly realised that higher boiler pressures meant more power, so it became fairly common practice by some to fiddle with the adjusting screws on the spring balance to retard the blowing of the safety valve! After several 'fiddles' of this nature, the actual flow-off pressure of the boiler was anybody's guess. Too much screwing down and your worries were over very quickly!

A further problem coupled to boiler pressure was that of water level in the boiler. In

No. 3024, a broad gauge convertible 2-2-2, was one of eight locomotives built with 7 ft axles and wide cabs. The class only worked the broad gauge for about twelve months before being converted to the standard gauge. No. 3024 was then named *Storm King*. On the extreme right of the picture can be seen part of the 0-6-0 side tank locomotive *Saunders*, one of six of the Sir Watkin class built in Swindon in 1865–66. It was originally fitted with condensing gear for working goods trains on the Metropolitan Railway. This apparatus was removed after 1869 and in 1872 the engine was one of three sold to the South Devon Railway, who fitted an additional short saddle tank between dome and firebox. After the amalgamation of the SDR with the GWR in 1876, the locomotive passed into GWR stock and was fitted with a long saddle tank and numbered 2159. In that form it lasted until the end of the broad gauge and was withdrawn in May 1892.

the early years there were no water gauges and reliance was placed on three 'cocks', one above the other, somewhere on the side of the firebox. Great experience and care were required to use these to determine the water level above the firebox crown plate. Steam issuing from the top one was OK, steam from the middle one meant 'watch out', and steam from the bottom one yelled 'everybody out!' At best a jet of searing, boiling water shot out when the cocks were opened.

General boiler design with regard to the actual internals had by now been set in a pattern which would not really change for the life of the steam locomotive. The 'staying' pattern of firebox support (a mix of copper and iron stays), the use of copper for the inner box, and even the recommended size of boiler tubes; all were now almost 'standardised', although experiments of course continued. Experiments were still continuing and arguments raged on the best position to feed cold water into a hot boiler.

Actually getting the water into the boiler was another problem. The injector, a French invention by Giffard, would not be seen for almost another twenty years. The early locomotives had hand pumps, also fitted to the *Firefly*, which additionally had a pair of pumps worked from the crossheads. As boiler pressures became higher as design improved, the hand pump was no longer really effective to feed a boiler under working pressure, and as speeds increased, the crosshead pump gave more and more problems.

A major problem – one of several – was that unless there was movement of the locomotive the pump would obviously not pump. An engine retained in steam, for whatever purpose, had to have a length of track to move along in order to maintain water level. 'Steaming up' inside or outside the shed led to problems with keeping all locomotives apart to allow movement.

The incompressibility of water led to burst pumps and pipes when running at speed, particularly if water was not required for a short period as there was no way of stopping the pumping action, although the water pumped was being returned to the tanks. The same problem arose with eccentric driven pumps, both types suffering hydraulic damage. Brakes were virtually non-existent, the Firefly class being braked only on one side of the tender, which was worked by a hand-operated screw, with nothing at all on the locomotive!

From their introduction, and indeed for some years following, although quite rapidly overtaken by the Iron Duke class, the Firefly class carried the bulk of the Great Western passenger services.

These services were directed at those who, in the social structure of the time, could be classed as 'First Class passenger types'; at the other end of the scale, although later to form the majority, the 'Third Class' travellers were not really counted in the desirable passenger list! It took Parliament to decree in 1844 that third-class passengers were also clients of the railway, and as such were entitled not only to a seat (it had been standing room only), but also to a roof over their heads when they travelled. We appear to have gone full circle – we again stand – this time in dirty carriages! The cost of this still far from luxurious service was to be no more than 1*d* per mile. This, of course, was in the days of real money, when a penny was a penny.

This entitlement included one train a day as a 'stopper' at all stations on the line, and to forestall any shunting of the trains onto delaying sidings, a required speed of not less than 12 mph had to be guaranteed. Due to this new – or reinstated – passenger, the company was hard put to cope with its existing 'carriage' stock; indeed, the third-class passenger was referred to as the 'goods train' passenger, and accommodation had been provided, or so it had appeared, to suit such a description. Even so, the new design of third-class stock appeared without actual windows, the traveller looking for all the world like John Wayne and his contemporaries peeking over the bat-wing doors of a Western saloon. The engine driver and fireman were even worse off, and as previously mentioned, had absolutely no protection at all on the footplate except that which may be obtained from the haystack firebox of a Firefly class.

Although the fare-paying third-class passengers had now been recognised, further improvements to coaching stock would allow the third class small windows through which to view the passing countryside during daylight hours and a small oil lamp to view one another after dark. It was a further forty-five years before they would be allowed to set foot in the first-class 'holy of holies', the Flying Dutchman expresses.

By 1845 the Firefly class were doing a grand job. The pounding 7 ft singles were powering the Exeter expresses, a starting time allowance of five hours for the 194 miles soon reduced to four and a half hours; the world speed record of the period was firmly in their grasp. With the broad gauge now reaching Gloucester, Oxford and Exeter, the break of gauge problems on meeting the narrow gauge track at Gloucester initiated the gauge wars and the inevitable commission of enquiry. We previously discussed how broad gauge power and potential easily won the day in any trials, but overall, the commissioners were against the wide gauge. The Gauge Act of 1846 in effect standardised the 4 ft 8½ in., and while reluctantly tolerating 7 ft ¼ in., that and all else was to be the exception to the rule.

Mentioned earlier was the fact that Gooch appeared to be a bit of a stick-in-the-mud when it came to the development of the design of broad gauge locomotives. He did, however, have some good ideas which he put into practice on the technical side. The *Firefly* had been made to some of the first 'templates', introduced to ensure a measure of standardisation, and on the carriage side he introduced a very special one in 1848. This became known as the dynamometer car and was equipped with some of the world's first instruments to determine the resistances and efficiency of the steam locomotive.

There are a number of photographs in existence of locomotives of various classes on the Test Plant, a later static arrangement in Swindon Works on which a locomotive could be run on rollers, the locomotive firmly anchored at both ends. Although the wheels and con rods were an 80 mph blur, the loco itself wasn't going anywhere! In the background to all this stood the dynamometer car, its instruments accurately recording the internal happenings in the steam chest and cylinders, etc. In the early years before the static plant, the Gooch car would be hooked up to the locomotive and set off along the track with Gooch and some of his instruments on the buffer beam, the car with other recording gear rattling along at the rear. In the latter years of steam, as an apprentice, I remember seeing the locomotives with their wooden shields at the front (more protection than in Gooch's day) off for a trial run with the car in tow (see Chapter 13).

Among the innovations of the *Firefly* period, one of the outstanding is the 'indicator' apparatus of Daniel Gooch. This arrangement of drum, pen and chart prepared a diagram of what was happening within the cylinder with regard to the effective (or otherwise) use of steam. With experience, the chart could be read like a tell-tale story of how the valve gear was handling the inlet and exhaust steam, where the 'cut-off' occurred, and the expansion of the steam from a designated portion of the stroke, what and when was the back pressure before full exhaust, etc. This apparatus was of particular use and interest when the three-position 'gab' gear (forward, backward or standstill only) was replaced by the variable expansion gear of Gooch and Stephenson. In this case, the various positions of the reversing lever for a known percentage of cut-off could be compared, giving a guide in more efficiency for valve gear component design, with modifications applied as appropriate (see Chapter 12).

While Stephenson, Gooch and Walschaert gear gave a variable expansion to the steam controllable *outside* the steam chest, there were several attempts at such variable control *inside* the chest. The expansive power and qualities of steam had become known quite early in the steam engine saga, but controlling it was a different matter. Quite a number of designers favoured some combination of double valves, one valve usually working on the back of a main valve. A triple valve was patented in 1842, and in some designs there was also an adjustable valve seat! All of course led to friction, and a short life – both physically and in application – resulted.

Daniel Gooch was not immune to such dabbling and introduced a double valve, one cylindrical and one flat, joined by a link. While the arrangement worked, it made such a clatter that it was removed. There was also the fear of the damage that could be wrought in the cylinder if the link came adrift and disappeared into one of the steam ports. With steam controlled by variable setting arrangements, there were naturally always demands for more power. A problem with locomotives, and remember that in the early days the moving parts were not balanced, was that of rocking and rolling – long before the Beatles – along the tracks. Mention of two names earlier in this book may be recalled where I

A superb photograph of Rover class renewal 4-2-2 *Tartar*. This locomotive was rebuilt in 1876. There were twenty-four of these Gooch-designed singles; although classed as 'renewals', twenty were completely new in 1873. This picture shows the engine in working condition, complete with flaking paint on the boiler casing.

engaged in a little speculation on a combined design of locomotive to the principles of Crampton and Sturrock (see chapters 10 and 11).

Crampton, having left the Great Western to become a designer in his own right, developed a most difficult design not accepted extensively in Britain, but finding application in France and on the Continent. He found that the further he moved the large driving wheels back, the less vibration and movement were felt. His ultimate designs included a most distinctive layout, with outside cylinders halfway back along the engine and the main driving wheels positioned with the axle actually behind the firebox with big outside eccentrics and valve gear. These locomotives had good adhesion, stability and power.

Archie Sturrock, brought from Dundee by Daniel Gooch, had also departed from the Great Western to return home to the north, where he became superintendent of the Great Northern Railway. While the Gooch designs for broad gauge stagnated, the fertile mind of Sturrock, now back with narrow gauge, continued to look to the future and search for more power. During 1863 the development took the form of a 0-6-0 locomotive with a powered 0-6-0 tender, the tender having its own cylinders and valve gear, making in effect a 0-6-6-0 with twelve driving wheels. A portion of the exhaust steam was used to heat the water in the tender and any surplus exhaust escaped through a pipe at the back of the tender tank. It was one of the most powerful combinations of the day.

Something we shall probably never know – did Crampton and Sturrock leave the Great Western in the normal course of their own development, or did they leave feeling stifled by Daniel Gooch? They were both certainly forward-thinkers and outstanding engineers. Incidentally, during the 1920s and 30s, when the Mallet type locomotives had become established and the articulated Garretts were in use, the Virginian Railway developed what they termed a 'triplex' locomotive – shades of Sturrock! It had three sets of cylinders, one under the cab and tender, weighed 480 tons, was over 100 ft long and on trial on a comparatively flat track pulled 250 loaded wagons measuring 18,000 tons and 1.6 miles in length.

As I said before, how sad that the potential of 'broad gauge' was never realised.

27
LOCOMOTIVES JUST GET BIGGER – CLASSIFICATION OF WHEEL ARRANGEMENTS

The first 4-6-0 built by David Jones – Highland Railway, Lochgorm Works, Inverness, 1894.

As the requirements, size and power increased after a long spell of 4-4-0 combinations, the first British 4-6-0 was built in 1894 for the Highland Railway by David Jones at the Lochgorm Works in Inverness. These were quickly followed by two by William Dean of the Great Western in 1896. From then on they quickly found favour with many companies, but the locomotive designs continued to get even bigger; in America there seemed to be no limit and some smaller versions went into some rather bizarre formats, usually to serve a special service.

British & American	WHEEL ARRANGEMENT TYPES			German	
	US Name	French	New	Old
0-4-0	4-Wheel Switcher	0-2-0	B	2/2 Coupled
0-6-6	6 Wheel Switcher	0-3-0	C	3/3 Coupled
0-8-0	8 Wheel Switcher	0-4-0	D	4/4 Coupled
0-10-0	10 Wheel Switcher	0-5-0	E	5/5 Coupled
0-12-0	12 Wheel Switcher	0-6-0	F	6/6 Coupled
0-4-2		0-2-1	B1	2/3 Coupled
0-6-2		0-3-1	C1	3/4 Coupled
0-8-2		0-4-1	D1	4/5 Coupled
2-4-0		1-2-0	1B	2/3 Coupled
2-6-0	Mogul	1-3-0	1C	3/4 Coupled
2-8-0	Consolidation	1-4-0	1D	4/5 Coupled
2-10-0	Decapod	1-5-0	1E	5/6 Coupled
2-12-0	Centipede	1-6-0	1F	6/7 Coupled
0-4-4	'Forney'	0-2-2	B2	2/4 Coupled
0-6-4	4 Coupled	0-3-2	C2	3/5 Coupled
0-8-4	6 Coupled	0-4-2	D2	4/6 Coupled
2-4-2	Columbia	1-2-1	1B1	2/4 Coupled
2-6-2	Prairie	1-3-1	1C1	3/5 Coupled
2-8-2	Mikado	1-4-1	1D1	4/6 Coupled
2-10-2	Santa Fé	1-5-1	1E1	5/7 Coupled
2-4-4		1-2-2	1B2	2/5 Coupled
2-6-4		1-3-2	1C2	3/6 Coupled
2-8-4		1-4-2	1D2	4/7 Coupled
4-4-0	American	2-2-0	2B	2/4 Coupled
4-6-0	10 Wheel	2-3-0	2C	3/5 Coupled
4-8-0	12 Wheel	2-4-0	2D	4/6 Coupled
4-10-0	Mastodon	2-5-0	2E	5/7 Coupled
4-4-2	Atlantic	2-2-1	2B1	2/5 Coupled
4-6-2	Pacific	2-3-1	2C1	3/6 Coupled
4-8-2	Mountain	2-4-1	2D1	4/7 Coupled
4-4-4		2-2-2	2B2	2/6 Coupled
4-6-4	Baltic	2-3-2	2C2	3/7 Coupled
0-4-4-0	Mallet	0-2-2-0	BB	2.3/2 Coupled
0-6-6-0	Mallet	0-3-3-0	CC	2.3/3 Coupled
0-8-8-0	Mallet	0-4-4-0	DD	2.4/4 Coupled
2-4-4-0	Mallet	1-2-2-0	1BB	
2-6-6-0	Mallet	1-3-3-0	1CC	
2-8-8-0	Mallet	1-4-4-0	1DD	
2-4-4-2	Mallet	1-2-2-1	1BB1	
2-6-6-2	Mallet	1-3-3-1	1CC1	
2-8-8-2	Mallet	1-4-4-1	1DD1	
2-8-8-4	Yellowstone		1DD2	
2-10-10-2	Mallet	1-2-5-1	1EE1	
4-4-6-2	Mallet	2-2-3-1	2BC1	

BIG – BIGGER – BIGGEST!

In the aftermath of the First World War, the 'Boom or Bust' of the 1920s – the shortages, strikes, economic downturn and short-time working – the locomotive designers blossomed, coming up with exceptional concepts and designs. Some were quite unique, opening a new trend for the 1930s, all soon to be squashed again by the shadow of the Second World War, getting blacker through the decade. The same thing happened to a much lesser degree after the second conflict and can really be ignored. For example, the introduction in Britain of 'Nationalisation' and the 'Standard' range of locomotives (only really duplicating what the now 'Big 4' companies had already developed over the opening years of the century), using the 'best design' features of all and sundry. Rather a waste of time and money considering their short lifespan. However, to the 1930s –

(a) The *Mallet*, 2-6-6-4, illustrated, had been built to a principle established half a century before. The one shown had 26 in. diameter cylinders, four high-pressure in place of the previous compound arrangement (now 250 lbs/sq. in.) with a 30 in. stroke; wheels 5 ft 10 in. diameter; the loco complete 120 ft long. (The frames of this locomotive are illustrated in the 'Frame' notes of this book.) The locomotive weighed 500 tons.

4-8-0 four-cylinder triple-expansion locomotive No. 1403, *L F Loree*, of Delaware & Hudson Railway.

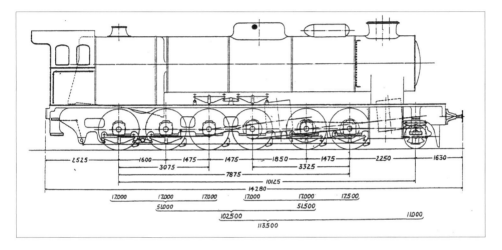

Six-cylinder compound 2-6-6-0 locomotive.

(b) At this period some companies had already tried 'compounding' and had abandoned it, but during the early 1930s the American Delaware & Hudson Railroad developed a triple-expansion 4-8-0 with a boiler pressure of 500 lbs/sq. in. It was also different from the run-of-the-mill locos in that it had a water tube boiler. It had four cylinders – one 20 in. diameter, one 27½, and two low-pressure cylinders of 33 in. diameter. Rotary cam poppet valves controlled the steam. The stroke was 32 in.

(c) The French at this period were noted for loco design, and had rebuilt a 2-10-0 compound expansion with four cylinders into the design illustrated, a 2-6-6-0 with a strange arrangement of six cylinders with a two-and-four combination; the four being under the smoke box driving, outside the leading pair of wheels, the inside pair the second pair of driving wheels, and the high-pressure pair the trailing six coupled wheels. This design was for hauling heavy freight trains. Weight 113 tons.

(d) A further French design, built by Schneider & Co. for high-speed express trains. Non-condensing Schneider-Westinghouse impulse turbines are the power source. Transmission by double reduction gearing and shaft drive. The turbines may be controlled individually. Designed for a top speed of about 87 mph, the loco weighs 122 tons. Wheel arrangement 4-6-4.

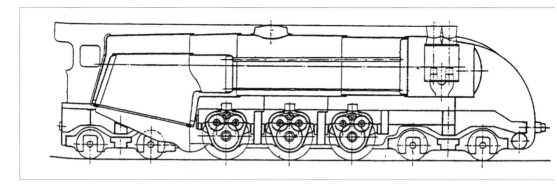

4-6-4 turbine locomotive by Schneider.

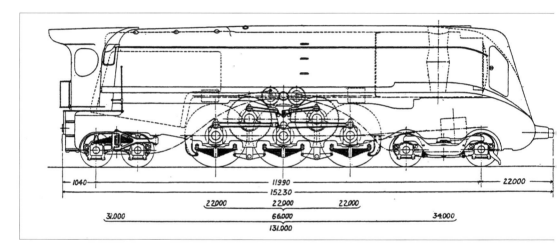

4-6-4 triple-expansion, non-condensing locomotive.

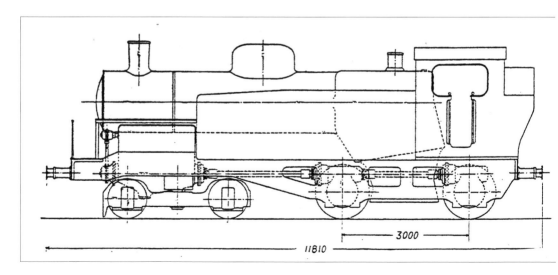

4-4-0 twelve-cylinder tank locomotive by Dabeg.

(e) Following the same wheel arrangement, 4-6-4, this design also follows the same basic shape as the turbine loco at 'D' but is a non-condensing triple-expansion six-cylinder engine with a complicated system of con rods and 'jack shafts' driving the wheels. The high-pressure cylinder is small, 11½ by 16 in. stroke, steam is supplied by a conventional boiler with Belpaire firebox, steel inner box, a combustion chamber, and a primary and secondary superheat system. Coal fired, the working pressure is 355 lbs/sq. in. The low-pressure cylinder is 26¾ in. diameter and stroke. Although streamlined, the driving mechanism will be exposed and accessible.

(f) The French State railways had a conventional-looking 4-4-0 locomotive which was anything but conventional! This was a design by Dabeg, with an engine unit that sounds like an aero engine. A twelve-cylinder 'V' design. The cylinders were 7⅞ by 11⅟₁₆ in. stroke. (Author's note: The funny sizes are due to conversion from the equally funny French measurement, metric!) The steel crank case also forms part of the loco frame. The valve gear works one valve per cylinder, the exhaust occurring when the piston reaches the end of its stroke and exposes an orifice. Shaft drive through gearboxes to 4 ft 1¼ in. diameter wheels.

(g) The 4-6-0 illustrated was an experimental modification to an ordinary four-cylinder compound with 6 ft 6¾ in. diameter. While the mechanism of cylinders and valves has not been changed, a completely new steam generation system has been introduced by the installation of a 'Velox'-type boiler. This exceptionally complicated system will not here be described, but the requirement of ancillaries for the system, to generate steam, will be noted from the detailed description and illustration. Steam would be supplied at 285 lbs/sq. in. pressure, fired by oil. The driver's cab was at the front, the tender combined into a streamlined outline. Normal speed was to be about 75 mph.

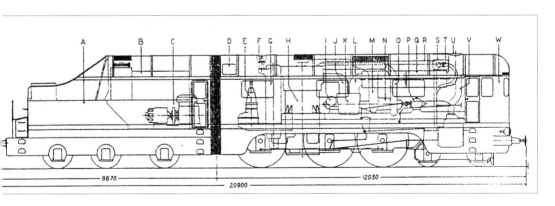

4-6-0 locomotive with Velox boiler, PLM Railway. 'A' water reservoir; 'B' oil fuel reservoir; 'C' motor-generator set for starting, etc.; 'D' feed water heater; 'E' pumps; 'F' safety valves; 'G' separator; 'H' combustion chamber; 'I' stand-by steam turbine; 'J' conduit for exhaust gases; 'K' exhaust gas turbine; 'L' conduit for exhaust gases from gas turbine to economiser; 'M' air entry duct; 'N' blower for compressing air for combustion chamber of boiler; 'O' conduit for air from blower to combustion chamber; 'P' electric starting motor; 'Q' economiser; 'R' steam pipe from boiler to regulator; 'S' regulator; 'T' steam pipes from regulator to engine cylinders; 'U' chimney; 'V' exhaust steam pipe; 'W' driver's cab.

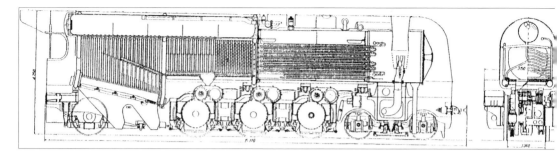

4-6-2 water-tube boiler locomotive with eighteen cylinders, for the Northern Railway of France, by the Swiss Locomotive Works.

(h) An anticipated 80 mph was expected from the locomotive built by Swiss Locomotive & Machine for the Northern Railway of France. This was a Pacific 4-6-2, fully streamlined, covering a completely different internal structure, an eighteen-cylinder engine and water tube boiler. An incredible boiler pressure of 853 lbs/sq. in., normal coal-burning grate! Driving wheels about 5 ft diameter. Six cylinders to each driving axle, each 6 in. bore by 10 in. stroke. Steam by rotary cam poppet valves.

(i) The French were not the only ones with unusual designs. The American Baltimore & Ohio completed, at their Mount Clare Works, a 4-4-4-4, wheels 6 ft 4 in. diameter, with 18 by 26½ in. stroke cylinders. An Emmerson Water Tube firebox fronts an ordinary fire tube boiler barrel. There was yet another example of highly skilled pattern-making and casting. The frame and cylinders were cast as one, in steel and 60 ft long! The first of its type cast with cylinders in 1936. A mechanical stoker takes some of the hard work from the crew, and the loco weighed 193 tons. There was a giant tender, 55 ft long, twelve wheels, 20 tons of coal and 18,000 gallons of water! 65,000 lbs tractive effort; 117 ft long.

(j) Among the big locomotives we must include the *Garrett*, a three-section design. This locomotive was in a class of its own, spreading across the world. The design strangely resembles somewhat one of Brunel's designs illustrated earlier in these notes, often classified as one of his 'freaks' because builders attempted to follow his specification. The weight distribution was wrong and the loco had a job to pull itself, let alone a train. This was *Hurricane*, built by R. & W. Hawthorn of Newcastle. Boiler in the centre, tender at the rear, driving mechanism (including a 10 ft diameter driving wheel) at the front. The firm of Beyer Peacock made the first *Garrett*, a special order specified as a compound with a 0-4-4-0 wheel arrangement for the 2 ft gauge of the Tasmanian government; two low-pressure cylinders at the front and two high-pressure for the back. Others with different wheel arrangements were built for many countries, the 2-6-2 plus 2-6-2 being the most ordered.

(k) The biggest (and probably longest) ever! Two of the most bizarre locomotives ever designed must be those detailed following, one for the Belgian National Railways and one for Russia. Built in 1932 to the *Franco* articulated design in the works of Atéliers Métallargique at Tubize, the Belgian loco was tried out on the Luxembourg line.

(k1) This locomotive design basically resembled a monster *Garrett* loco, as it is in three separate units, joined together with the boiler in the centre unit. The three sections each

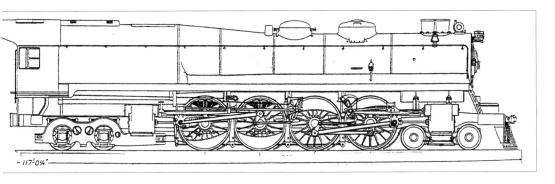

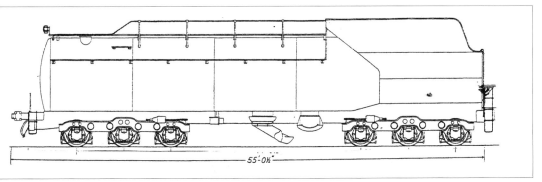

Four-cylinder 4-4-4-4 type locomotive, *George H Emerson*, Baltimore & Ohio Railroad.

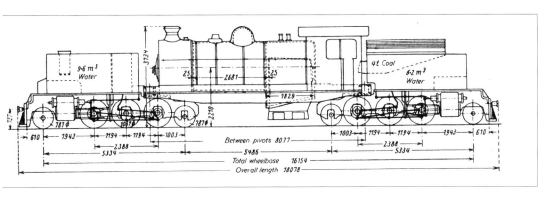

Garrett design.

have their own set of cylinders and coupled wheels so there the *Garrett* look disappears, as the central unit (and this resembles a Fairlie with a boiler fired in the centre and facing both ways!) is coupled to the end units by ducts. The firing covers two separate combustion chambers, as the firebox is split with a diagonal partition so it requires a fireman each side. Use must have been fairly restricted, although in spite of the overall length they could negotiate a 130-yard curve.

(k2) The other loco follows the same general format but has a different wheel arrangement. It appears that the Second World War held up any further development of such steps from

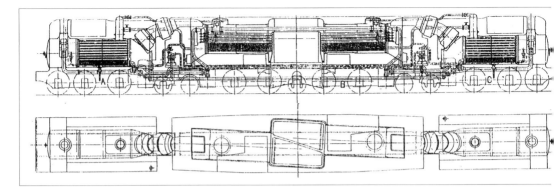

K1. General arrangement of the three-unit *Franco* locomotive, tried on the Schaerbeck-Luxemburg line of the Belgian National Railways. Built by the Atéliers Métallurgique at Tubize. 6-2 plus 2-4-2-4-2 plus 2-6 type!

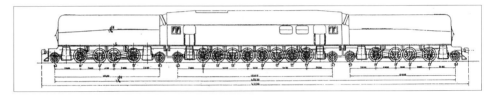

K2. Three-unit compound freight locomotive, 2-4-4-2 plus 2-8-8-2 plus 2-4-4-2 type. Designed for the Russian railway.

A Sturrock's steam tender locomotive, GNR, 1863.

tradition, and the aftermath was not conducive to such expenditure of an experimental or pioneering nature, plus with the sudden and swift demise of official steam, the 'pioneering spirit' was channelled into gas turbine, electric and diesel-electric locomotives.

(l) Archibald Sturrock's unique attempt, the earliest of the lot, and really years before its time.

28
THE AMERICAN DREAM — BIGGEST IS BEST UP TO THE 2-10-10-2

The illustrations which accompany this chapter were obtained in a job lot envelope from a bric-a-brac shop along with a number of others that, when sorted, fell into an outline of the general story of American loco design.

The classic characteristic appearance of the early locomotives will be familiar to all from the many films made that included travelling on a train. But as they got bigger – more wheels, more weight, more power – they changed into generally, again, a recognisable look which spread through the Americas and up into Canada.

Some designs became so big and unwieldy that they had a 'one-off' very short life; others were of very strange designs but seemed to be quite effective anyway. American designers appeared to have an aversion to inside cylinders, preferring that everything that could be hung outside certainly was. The early British influence of inside cylinders was rapidly ignored.

An American erecting shop.

John Bull, a British-built pioneer for the Camden & Amboy Railroad, 1831.

The first locomotive built by Robert Stephenson in 1835, for the Bangor & Milford Railway, Maine.

Pioneer, the first locomotive in Chicago, 1848.

Montezuma (2-4-0), the first locomotive to traverse the Rocky Mountains of Colorado, 3 July 1871. Its weight was 25,000 lbs, and of this amount 20,000 lbs were imposed upon the 40 in. driving wheels. The overall length was 30 ft, and cylinders 9 by 16 in.

The first mogul (2-6-0). Although this type was first exploited by the British builders, Robert Stephenson, it did not meet with success until 1867, in which year it was reintroduced by the Baldwin Locomotive Works.

Eight-wheeled 'American' locomotive.

Ten-wheeled freight locomotive.

The experimental 4-4-2 locomotive built for the Philadelphia-Atlantic Service. Built by Baldwins to the order of the Philadelphia & Reading Railway, with the view of exceeding the speed obtained from the American type. This object was attained and the type developed into the world-famous Atlantic type.

El Gubernador, the first locomotive to be fitted with ten coupled driving wheels.

4-8-2.

4-8-4.

This triple-compound locomotive (2-8-8-8-2 type) has twenty-four driving wheels of 63 in. diameter, and weighed 864,000 lbs fully loaded.

4-6-6-2.

A Union Pacific 4-8-8-4 'Big Boy', No. 4000.

4-4-4-4.

4-6-6-4.

Mallet (2-10-10-2).

A Fairlie wood-burner of 1873.

An early Camelback design.

A late Camelback design.

There were other designs that travelled 'across the pond', finding favour on some rail
roads, such as the Fairlie for the Denver & Rio Grande in 1871. One very strange-looking
locomotive design became known as a Camelback with the cab, solely for the driver, over
the middle of the boiler and the fireman on his own, in some designs completely in the
open front of the tender. When inferior fuel was all that was available, a design often
included a huge 'Wootton' firebox, or if anthracite was available, a narrow box was the
option. There were many different wheel arrangements, and some were conditioned by
using the Wootton firebox which was designed to use the non-commercial residual gritty
dust from the anthracite. Considerable fuel savings were made by using this rubbish in
a firebox designed for the purpose. The Camelbacks had a long life from about 1877 to
the 1940s.

29

LIFTING AND MOVING LOCOMOTIVES IN THE MAIN WORKSHOPS

The construction or repair of steam locomotives entails, during the procedures, lifting or moving the resulting structure, which gets heavier as repair or construction reaches completion.

In the workshops of the main railway companies there was a choice of layout for the erecting shop, the site of construction and major repairs. This was often conditioned by the construction of the Works itself, fitting into an available area. In a fairly restricted site such as on an already spreading industrialised area, saving space was at a premium, the workshop becoming one in which locomotives were worked on 'nose to tail'. In a less restricted area such as the greenfield site of Swindon Works, although the ground was 'built-up' to a uniform level, the larger erecting shop had bays across the shop, separated by a large area along which ran a 'traversing table'. Here there were two workshops: the 'B' shop for small locomotives and tenders, and the 'A' shop complex for the larger types.

As well as the traversing tables with which both shops were equipped, overhead cranage was essential; this applied to the nose-to-tail shops as well, but lifting was a different procedure in both. The overhead cranes at Swindon that ran sideways along the length of each line of repair bays had two carriages of lifting gear, each with an auxiliary hoist for lifting the heavy but smaller items, but both carriages came into play when a complete or almost complete locomotive had to be moved. Chains on each hoist, one to each end of the locomotive, and moving up or down the bay was easy as the repair or construction progressed to completion, involving fitting or attending to other items or procedures in a particular area of the bay. Incidentally, each bay – with the exception of the couple of bays in the new work area – had a full-length pit underneath the locomotive for construction within the confines of the frame and under the boiler, such as all the 'inside' valve gear, brake rods and gear, etc., the pit covered over for initial work on the frame.

One interesting job was 'wheeling' the locomotive. The axle boxes having been fitted to the axle journals on the end of the bay rails, the wheels would be pushed into position under a suspended frame, the frame often with the boiler in place. Men from the gang would be positioned in the pit to make sure the axle box was guided up into the 'horns' as the loco was lowered by the crane. If the box tilted or jammed, a call to the crane-man meant to lift up and reposition the box.

A hand-operated traversing table – Swindon Engine House.

Steam-powered traversing tables – B1 shop, the loco bays.

The tender bays – B1 shop, Swindon Works.

A nose-to-tail erecting shop – a 'two crane' job.

The 'across the shop' layout photos show the lifting chains, back and front.

On the traversing table; all in the days of the Great Western – AE erecting shop, Swindon.

Once the wheels were under, the 'rolling chassis' could be pulled by a winch on the traversing table onto the table for transfer across the bay or out of the main doors at the end of the table road.

Although the overhead cranes were electrically driven, a crane in the older part of the shop was hydraulic. The early traversing tables were originally steam-driven, a self-contained boiler and engine as part of the table structure, but in later years were all electrically driven.

30
LIFTING AND MOVING LOCOMOTIVES OUTSIDE THE MAIN WORKSHOPS

It was found that it was not always convenient to send a locomotive to a main works for a job which did not really require major 'shopping', so at selected depots a 'lifting shop' was introduced. Again cranage was required, so a serviceable 'sheer legs' device was installed for limited lifting requirements. Although an overhead arrangement, it could not be traversed and really followed on from the very early days when it was the only form of lifting assistance in the workshop.

Hoists constructed of wood were in use from the earliest period and although the structure changed to steel girder construction, the basic shape did not change. The lifting mechanism in the early years was the universal 'pulley block', hand-operated by a chain, but the girder versions were soon powered by electricity once it became available. The hoist could be inside or outside the lifting shop, the 'hand' version operated by geared hand-wheel from the earliest days.

A wood-structure, outdoor 'sheer legs', c. 1860.

The lifting shop was equipped with basic machine tools, often removed from a main works on updating: a lathe; milling machine; grind stones, rough and tool-sharpening; sometimes a shaping machine; and radial and pedestal drilling machines. There would also be work benches, vices, hand tools and a Blacksmith fire, anvil and tools.

This page: The lifting shop. It has a covered-in top, which would have protected the pulley block from the weather.

Sheer legs.

The hoist at the Great Western Society's workshop at Didcot is still in regular use. Note the pulley block and swinging jib attached to the main structure; a very useful later addition.

LIFTING OTHER THAN IN THE MAIN WORKSHOPS

Not an ideal lift!

A larger lifting shop with an overhead travelling crane. The crane movement was short but better than a static sheer legs.

The travelling steam crane – used throughout all railway systems for any outdoor lifting operations.

31
THE SWINDON WORKSHOPS
THROUGH THE YEARS

GENERAL VIEWS

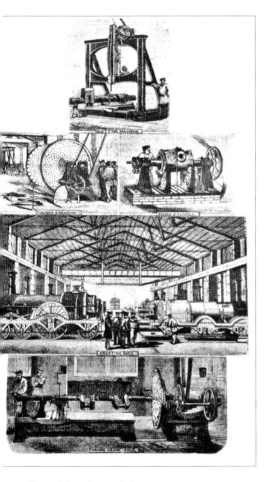

Above left: The workshops, 1842.

Above right: Sketches of contents, 1850s.

There are a number of publications on the market which show the works in what turned out to be the last stages of development before closure. Photographs of the erecting shops showing a mix of GWR and the later 'standard' locomotives, then mostly standard locomotives, and finally the shop filled with diesel locomotives. Then the most depressing photograph of the lot, the shop empty and awaiting demolition!

The following few photographs are reminders of how some shops looked in the years long before the author became an apprentice and that, at the time this was written, was sixty-six years ago!

B2 shop, Swindon Works, *c.* 1900.

Fitting and machine shop, *c.* 1920/30.

General period machine tools, *c.* 1920. Top left: Muir's facing and screwing lathe, with adjustable headstock. Top right: Pittler vertical turret lathe. Bottom left: Gordon & Oliver turret lathe, with vertical forming tool slide. Bottom right: Ward & Co's hexagon lathe.

The 'R' shop, Swindon Works – general machine and fitting shop, *c.* 1920.

Above: 'P' shop, Swindon Works – cylinder and general boring and fitting.

Left: Swindon Works pattern shop. Note the cylinder pattern.

Swindon Works, top to bottom: the steam hammer forge, the 'F' shop (Smiths') and the 'G' shop.

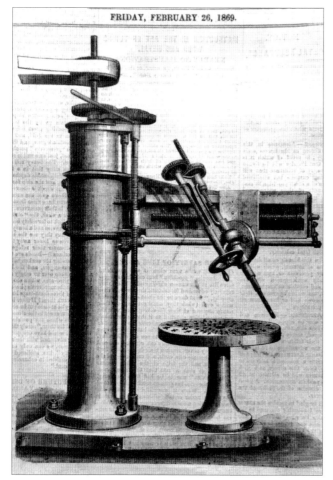

Above: Swindon Works – blacksmiths' shop. Like a foundry! They don't change much over the years.

Left: Improved radial drilling machine.

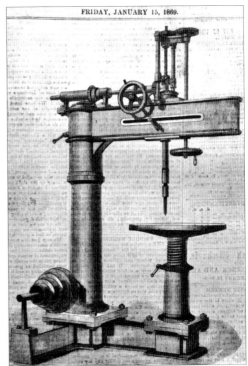

FRIDAY, JANUARY 15, 1869.

This page: Whitworth's drilling machine, *c.* 1850.

Improved radial press for drilling fixed work.

Pneumatic hammers – smiths' shop, 1940s.

The rolling mill – putting a white-hot steel billet through the rolls.

Repairs in the erecting shop – face-grinding the axle box horn blocks.

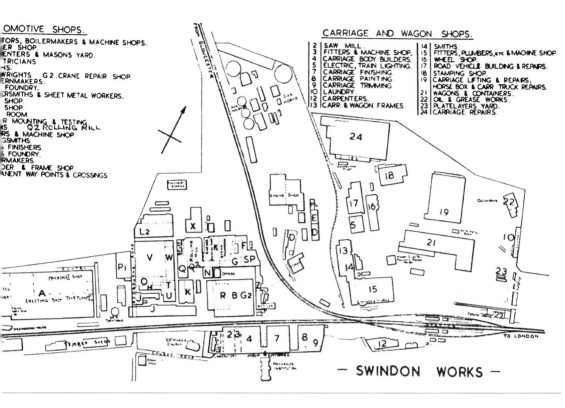

Swindon Works in the Great Western steam years.

32

WORKSHOP STAFF – TIME RECORDING AND PAYMENT METHODS

In the 'steam' years the employees in the industry, as in all others, were strictly controlled regarding adherence to working hours, and this was of paramount importance if employment was to be continued. 'Flexible working' was unheard of and lateness was not tolerated.

Many industries as well as the railways had developed systems based on the employees taking a metal 'check' or 'tally' off a numbered board on starting a shift, and returning it when the shift finished. There were various designs for the metal checks, some in different metals to show a different use. Shapes were also of several designs, each for a specific use of location. These, taking the case of Swindon Works, thus recorded the comings and goings of a workforce of many thousands, each workshop maintaining a register of all employed within.

The shift timings, again taking Swindon Works, was controlled by timed blasts on the factory steam 'hooter' or siren. Three blasts at five-minute intervals to start the shift and one blast to finish. If the individual had not removed his check when the last starting blast

An example of working-hours strictness!

faded away, the cover on the board, containing all the checks on individual numbered hooks, was slammed down and the individual was 'late'.

A few minutes late and the unfortunate was recorded in the time book and would lose a quarter of an hour's pay; over a quarter to half an hour and the loss would be half an hour's pay; more than that and on his check hook would be a shiny aluminium disc with the words: 'See Foreman before starting.' This was to be avoided at all costs, as the foreman could send the worker home for the complete shift. Too many recurring lateness episodes and the employee would receive a small form with name, shop and check number, and the legend, 'From [date] your services are no longer required.'

With the check system there were a number of checks for different recorded information. '¼' or '½' for lost pay, 'OS' if the check could not be removed as the employee was working somewhere 'Out of Station' away from the Works. 'N' signified the worker was on 'Night' shift work. 'CTO' showed the worker was working temporarily off the Works premises and was allowed to book in at the 'Central Time Office'. 'MT' indicated the employee had mislaid or lost his check, and 'Missing Ticket' was recorded.

'CHECKS' & 'CHEQUES'

A workshop 'pay table'.

Left: A 'Pay In' tin, full size.

Below: Examples of 'checks' and 'cheques'.

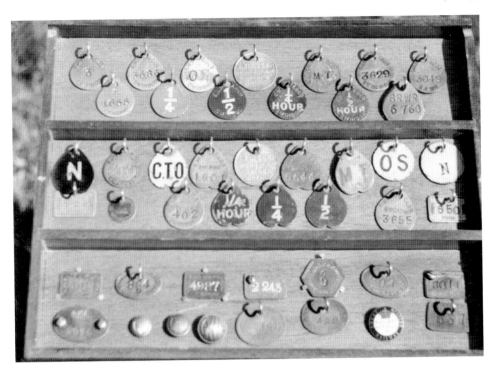

Above: The author's collection of various 'time recording' checks.

Right: A workshop check board, showing the sliding shutter.

Above: A selection of 'checks' or 'cheques' used to collect wages on 'pay day', exchanged for a 'pay tin'.

Left: A small tin, 1⅝ in. diameter by 1¼ in. deep, containing wages used during the author's apprenticeship.

There was one shift when the brass 'clocking-on' check was not used. On pay day, a different check hung on the hook, although the number was that of the operator. The check was of copper and was distinctive in that, apart from its different shape, it was marked 'pay cheque' (note spelling). The payment of wages at Swindon Works in those days was a unique happening, in that such a system would be impossible today.

First there was the method of collecting the money from the bank. Every Thursday morning, as regularly as the seasons, a large, four-wheeled iron-bound black box was hitched behind a factory 'runabout' vehicle at the main 'tunnel' entrance to the Works and proceeded by the same route at the same time to the bank, a journey of about three quarters of a mile to the town centre. Sitting on seats on the box were two pay officials in the style reminiscent of an early John Wayne film, sitting quite high up and with no protection whatsoever from inclement weather. The documentation would be duly presented and the money, in *cash*, was loaded into the box, which was then locked, and the procession reversed its route and returned to the Works. Entering again by the main entrance, the box was towed to the wages office, unlocked and the bags of cash and notes transferred to the waiting lines of desks at which sat the pay clerks, seconded for the job, ready to make up the individual amounts for every operator. The amount of total cash was many thousands of pounds.

Reading from a detailed wage bill per 'shop', the clerks selected cash and notes to the correct amounts, and with a deft folding action – achieved after much practice – a 'screw' of change, wrapped in possibly a ten-shilling or one-pound note, along with a slip of paper indicating the amount to be received, was placed swiftly into a small tin (see image 281). Earlier, coin was contained in the tin – who knows, maybe a guinea on occasions! When individually numbered tins were completed they were put into a larger, flat-black tin box with the shop designation painted on the lid – L2 Shop, V1 Shop, A(M) Shop, etc. – some of the larger shops having a number of such tins.

Meanwhile, preparations in the shops entailed the erection of a special narrow counter, with a metal 'chute' on top (see image 280) at a convenient point on the shop floor. At a predetermined time, a shop labourer would depart from the shop pushing his sack truck, and would meet up with a pair of designated pay clerks just outside the pay office. He would then load the flat tins for his shop onto the truck and the trio, usually including a young lady, would return to the shop, the labourer pushing possibly several thousand pounds on his truck.

Through the dark alleys of the Works, across storage yards and beside lines of wagons the trio would walk, and in all the time the system was in use, I know of no recorded incident of even attempted robbery on either collection of the money in cash from the bank, or from the transporting of the tins to the shops! Truly unique and an indication of the period; it could not happen now!

On arrival at the shop, and this was happening all over the Works, the tins were positioned on the shelf behind the narrow counter, the pay bill checked and the presence of the shop foreman awaited before any payments could be made. The assembled workforce had meanwhile sorted themselves out in check number order and a general buzz of chatter filled the shop. The approach of the foreman signalled silence, and with a glance of his watch and nod of the head, payment started. Consulting the pay bill, the clerk called a number. Almost simultaneously the man stepped forward, placed his copper pay cheque on the brass slide of the counter, and was handed his numbered tin and the 'cheque' was scooped into a special round tin container below the slide (see image 280).

The operator opened his tin in front of the foreman, checked its contents against the payslip, a small strip of paper indicating the amount to receive, and folded it in with the money. He then dropped the tin with lid replaced into a basket positioned for the purpose. The system was an accepted routine later, continuing with transparent envelopes when the amount of cash etc. became too awkward for the tin, but the copper 'cheque' remained in use.

There were very few mistakes with the amount of money in the tins. The payment process ran very smoothly and rapidly, the shop empty and the clerks folding up their pay bill as the hooter blew for the end of the shift. The clerks returned to the Pay Office; the foreman departed for home and the 'checky' folded the pay table and returned it to its storage spot to await the same procedure next week.

Similar procedures were in operation throughout the Great Western system for 'booking on' and for payment (and perhaps on other railways as well). At Swindon there were a number of different designs of 'pay cheque', stretching on into the days of British Rail and Nationalisation, and generally all were of copper with the exception of 'Stores' pay cheques, which were an aluminium alloy. Images 282 and 283 show the variations to be found in the 'checks' or 'cheques' of a system which reflected a much less hurried and, dare we say, much more honest age, when the sights and sounds of steam were everyday occurrences and a thriving industry kept the locos running.

The mighty 'A' shop complex of Swindon Works has now long gone. The last-minute rush to take your check off the hook or slap down the copper cheque on pay day are events of memory. Only the metal checks remain to remind us of what has gone.

33
THE END OF A STEAM LOCOMOTIVE WORKS

This is the fate which overtook many of the world's steam loco workshops, with the Great Western's Swindon as an example.

At the beginning:

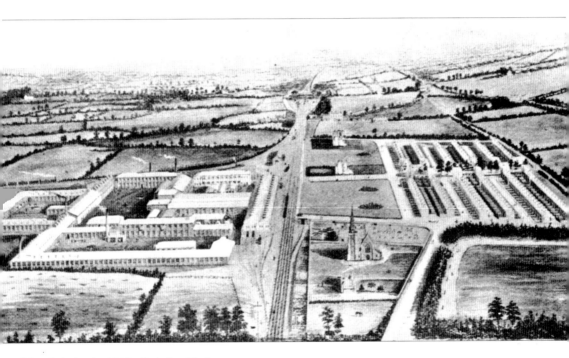

New Swindon in 1846 – Swindon Works.

And at the end:

Demolition of 'A' shop complex, covering 11.5 acres – all under one roof!

Middle and bottom: The end at Swindon Loco Works, *c.* 1990 – the A(E) shop complex.